GW00992303

The Supernatural Voice

A History of High Male Singing

The Supernatural Voice

A History of High Male Singing

Simon Ravens

THE BOYDELL PRESS

First published 2014
The Boydell Press, Woodbridge

ISBN 978 1 84383 962 0

The Boydell Press is an imprint of Boydell & Brewer Ltd
PO Box 9, Woodbridge, Suffolk IP12 3DF, UK
and of Boydell & Brewer Inc.
668 Mount Hope Ave, Rochester, NY 14620–2731, USA
website: www.boydellandbrewer.com

A catalogue record for this book is available from the British Library

The publisher has no responsibility for the continued existence
or accuracy of URLs for external or third-party internet websites
referred to in this book, and does not guarantee that any content on
such websites is, or will remain, accurate or appropriate.

This publication is printed on acid-free paper

Designed and typeset in Adobe Warnock Pro
by David Roberts, Pershore, Worcestershire

Contents

Illustrations

Figures

Music examples

Table

A Declaration of Disinterest

WHETHER the subject is a political party, the gay-rights movement, or your local football team, open any book on a minority interest and, chances are, it will have been written by someone sympathetic to the cause. The obvious problem with this is that the voices of interest groups are, by definition, unlikely to prove disinterested commentators.

It should be no surprise, then, that much writing on the subject of the falsettist has been the work of men who, at one level or another, have sung this way themselves, and who are inclined towards establishing the position of their own voice-type in history. By the same token, it is probably no coincidence that criticism of such writing has been the work of people who, if they sing at all, are not falsettists. The stance of a writer is rarely stated explicitly, but his position may well become known to us later, requiring that we reprocess what we have read. This always strikes me as an unnecessary irritation, which could easily be removed by an honest declaration of interest. Such as this: I am not a falsettist or a counter-tenor.[1]

I am, in fact, an indifferent baritone. I am also director of a choir which, when we sing a piece by Tallis, will do so without a falsettist on any line. Does this place me in the anti-falsettist, anti-counter-tenor camp? No. I have also directed performances and recordings with falsettists and – perhaps most significantly – I think the sound those singers make is glorious. If I have no 'interest', then, I will need to say why I had the interest to write a book on falsetto singing and its vocal relations. Before that, though, I should say why I think the topic will intrigue anyone who loves early music (by which, of course, I mean any music composed up to and including yesterday).

Throughout the twentieth century, the drive of performing earlier music was towards a dreamlike destination of 'authentic performance practice'. Occasionally, wishing to convince ourselves that we might have arrived there, we looked around at the realities of our performances, and tried to marry these to the details on our musicological maps. As humans often do in these situations, we noticed what fitted, and shrugged off what didn't fit – as a trick of perspective, perhaps, or a fault on the map. One such musical feature was the falsetto counter-tenor, which since the Second World War had become a ubiquitous part of the early music terrain – first in Britain and then elsewhere. Promisingly enough, there were falsettists and counter-tenors clearly evident on our historical charts, but it often took creative and selective justifications to match the realities of the present with the theories of the past. And worse, as our musicological charting of the past became

---

[1] If there is any confusion about these terms, one of the main purposes of this book is to remove it.

more detailed, the discrepancies only seemed to grow between our *now* and their *then*. This book is full of such discrepancies and some of these, I freely admit, may prove shocking to readers. For instance, I shall argue that whilst on their alto lines Tallis, Purcell and S. S. Wesley would not have recognised our modern counter-tenor, on their soprano lines Palestrina and Bach probably would. And I will suggest that Adolphe Nourrit (a favourite tenor of Rossini) and Mick Jagger (of the Rolling Stones), used falsetto more freely than any singer John Dowland knew.

Today, a more realistic alignment of present and past musical practices is taking hold. In the ways we play, sing and (most fundamentally) hear, increasingly we accept that we can never fit ourselves perfectly into the past. Today's average counter-tenor is no more likely to glide effortlessly through a Bach soprano aria than, without stooping, he could walk through a medieval door frame. Nor should accepting such realities be any kind of bar to the way we make music. The purpose of this book is not to lay down limits, but to offer information on the past which creative minds can use to help plot their own honest positions in – and routes through – the musical present.

As for my own fascination with the subject, this began at university, where I had the good fortune to be taught by David Wulstan, then director of the Clerkes of Oxenford. In his introductory lecture to students, Professor Wulstan laid down a challenge: 'When I teach you something as fact, it is your duty to try and disprove me.' Thirty years on, the irony of this remark is not lost on me, since his theories come under critical scrutiny in this book. I remain, though, hugely indebted to him. Back then, it was not so much Wulstan's words as the sound of his choir that led me towards early music and, in due course, inspired me to be a choral director. Shortly afterwards, however, I read his theory on the English counter-tenor voice with the kind of dubious eye he had encouraged and, sure enough, found good cause to question what I saw. Not that, then and there, I could provide a convincing answer of my own. It was not until years later, having come across the separate researches of a laryngologist and a professor of economics, that I could begin to unpick what I saw as the main flaw in Wulstan's theory. Indeed, it has often been non-musical perspectives which have given the most revealing insights into musically murky topics: various fascinating histories – of human height, genetics, perceptions of gender, national stereotyping, and etymology – have significantly shaped my understanding of high male singing in Western music. To reflect the trans-historical importance of these issues for the topic as a whole, I have devoted small 'extempore' chapters to each, and interspersed my chronological survey with them.

One of the paradoxes of this book, it strikes me, is that more of its words are devoted to the high male voice in England than anywhere else. This is not because falsetto singing has a longer history in England than elsewhere – I shall argue that quite the reverse is true. But since the modern counter-tenor revival and the voice's supposed history in Western music have leant towards England, it is perhaps inevitable that this one country assumes a disproportionate weight in the subject's historiography. Mine, though, is certainly not a parochial interest. From my own starting point of the Tudor counter-tenor, a growing curiosity has led me backwards and forwards chronologically, and outwards geographically.

Historically informed musicians often use the analogy of picture restoration for their rediscoveries of a particular work. In the case of a history such as this, I would liken the process to re-examining a huge, Bayeux-Tapestry-like narrative tableau. Looking at any aspect of it under the microscope, it soon becomes apparent that the history of the falsetto voice and the counter-tenor part is not a single yarn made of one or even two fibres, but something much more complex. As we move on from period to period, and country to country, we find the falsetto and counter-tenor threads mixed with others. Sometimes these other historical threads are different vocal types – soprano, castrato, contralto, alto, *haute-contre* and tenor. And frequently, other musical and non-musical strands are woven into the fabric. On a larger scale, in reinterpreting the individual panels which these threads produce, I have often been guided by the expertise of other specialists. Inevitably, many parts of the tableau have become difficult to recognise from the way that tradition has encouraged us to see them. As for biggest picture, when I stand back and look at the whole of this less-familiar history of high male singing, the narrative it offers seems to me complex but coherent. Doubtless future students of the topic will uncover further details which will again alter the way we see the picture: it is (I remind myself) their duty. So be it. For the time being, what I have sought to do in this book is look in a disinterested way at what I see, and then make it appear as fascinating as I think it is.

Simon Ravens, Ilkley, 2014

Unless otherwise noted, pitch in this book is assumed to be modern concert pitch ($a' = 440$). Specific pitch levels are classified according to the Helmholtz system of pitch notation:

C   c   c'   c"   c'''

Acknowledgements

F IRST and foremost my thanks are due to Andrew Parrott, not just for encouraging me to write on a topic I know he wanted to address himself, but also for later spending many hours scrutinising my text. Even when he did not agree with the conclusions I arrived at, the way he questioned my route to them was, for me at least, always a hugely positive experience. I invariably drove away from Andrew and Emily's house feeling that my mind and heart had been well exercised.

To Andra Patterson at the National Library of New Zealand and the British Library, who for quarter of a century has cheerfully dealt with my information requests, I express my continued appreciation.

To the singers of first the Tudor Consort, and later Musica Contexta, I offer my thanks that for many years they have unwittingly acted as guinea pigs for my ongoing experiments in realising historical vocal scoring. To our listeners, I can only offer the hope that they were unaware of any such experiments.

I am grateful to Michael Middeke of Boydell & Brewer, not just for his own expertise and guidance, but for finding two (anonymous, although they may find their names below) readers: without their input the failings of this book would be much, much greater. For their assistance at various stages of the editing and production process, I am also grateful to Megan Milan, Rosie Pearce, Marianne Fisher and David Roberts.

I am particularly grateful to Dr Roger Bowers, Peter Giles and Professor David Wulstan, who were helpful with specific information about their own researches, even though they probably knew that I was unlikely to be endorsing their conclusions. In an age when the email inbox of every academic is being filled with requests far more pressing than mine, I am also grateful, and touched, that the following took the trouble to reply so fully to my queries: Ian Aitkenhead, Professor Martin Ashley, Professor Patrick Barbier, Professor Sally Brodermann, Professor Donald Burrows, Professor John Butt, Professor Giles Constable, Dr Brian Crosby, Mark Deller, Dr John Dereix, Dr Stefan Drees, Professor Matthias Echternach, Professor Martha Feldman, Professor Mary Frandsen, Peter Garland CB, Christian Gaumy, Professor Giuseppe Gerbino, Dr Vera Goldman, Hugh Griffith, Dominic Gwynn, Professor Corinna Herr, Professor Arnold Jacobshagen, Professor Heather Josselyn-Cranson, Professor Jeffrey Kurtzman, Professor Bruce C. MacIntyre, Professor Timothy McGee, Professor Angel Medina, Dr Eckhard Neubauer, Professor Michael Noone, Jonathan Ravens, Dr Owen Rees, Clara Sanabras, Dr George Dimitri Sawa, Professor Thomas Schmidt, Professor Thomas Seedorf, Professor Richard Sherr, Professor Amnon Shiloah, Dr Katharine Sykes, Dr Erik van Dongen, Dr Laura Weber Wallace, Professor Richard Wistreich, Professor Craig Wright.

Sadly, I can never repay Sally Dawson for her crucial encouragement when, before she died, she asked me to 'write that book'. Finally to my wife, Caroline, I owe the greatest debt: she made writing the book not only possible, but hugely enjoyable.

CHAPTER 1

The Discovery of Alfred Deller

Tradition is just cosiness and laziness.
Gustav Mahler[1]

T HERE are perhaps more likely places for a new musical species to be
propagated than the choir vestry of an English provincial cathedral.
For centuries these vestries, hidden away in the fabric of the country's
great churches, have tended and nourished tradition. Rarely have they
functioned as hothouses for breeding musical novelties. Yet in one such
room, during the Second World War, two musicians planted the seed of
a vocal phenomenon that was to flourish rapidly, bearing magnificent
musical fruit in our own time.

The choir vestry in question was that of Canterbury Cathedral, and
the two musicians who met there on that afternoon in 1943 were Michael
Tippett and Alfred Deller. Tippett, then thirty-nine and fresh from the
notoriety of his new oratorio *A Child of our Time*, had travelled down
from London to hear a short choral piece of his, which the cathedral choir
had commissioned. He did so at the invitation of the cathedral's precentor,
Canon J. W. Poole. But Poole had another agenda for Tippett's visit, and
that was to have him listen to the voice of Deller, an alto lay-clerk at the
cathedral. Tippett, as a rather unworldly man whose ethical conscience
had recently landed him in prison for conscientious objection, hardly
fitted the standard mould of a musical impresario. In the barren musical
scene of wartime England, though, this was a role Tippett effectively found
himself playing, because as Director of Music at Morley College in London
he was responsible for staging a series of concerts. Naturally enough, these
innovative concerts reflected his particular interests, not just in modern
music, but also in the music of the English seventeenth century.

With the benefit of hindsight, it is easy enough to prepare ourselves for
the context in which Tippett sat down to hear Alfred Deller sing for the
first time. We, after all, are familiar with the sound of a modern counter-
tenor. Tippett, we should remember, had no such preparation. What, if
anything, did he expect? Certainly not what he heard. Deller sang Purcell's
'Music for a while', and as Tippett later recollected, 'In those moments the
centuries rolled back. For I recognised absolutely that this was the voice
for which Purcell had written.'[2] Almost immediately afterwards Tippett

---

[1] 'Was ihr Theaterleute Tradition nennt, das ist Bequemlichkeit und
Schlamperei.': Anecdote of Mahler speaking to the Vienna Opera Orchestra,
1904.

[2] Michael Tippett, 'Alfred Deller', *Early Music* 8(1) (1980), p. 43.

invited Deller to sing at a Morley College concert, and subsequently in a London performance of Purcell's *Song for St Cecilia's Day*. For an alto in a provincial cathedral choir this was a significant breakthrough. Yet Tippett's invitation made it plain that the transformation of Deller's career was to be total: he was not to remain an 'alto'. 'When you sing for me', Tippett said to Deller, 'I shall give you the English classical name for your voice, which is countertenor.'[3] Not only did Deller agree to this, but he also began to describe himself as a counter-tenor in subsequent solo performances. Such was the influence of Deller's singing that within a matter of years every self-respecting male alto was using the term.

The reasons Tippett chose to redefine Deller's voice with a virtually obsolete musical term are fascinating. Although Tippett himself was not a musicologist, he may have known the most recent study of Purcell, in which case he would have read that 'the male alto (or counter-tenor) is a real voice and a traditionally English one [...] [and] was a very popular solo voice in Purcell's day.'[4] But Tippett's 'absolute' realisation – that Deller's was the counter-tenor voice for which Purcell had written – was probably based less on historical theory than on the practical dictates of his own experience as a performer. Attempting to realise these parts, commonly ascending an octave above middle C, Tippett was faced with music that was literally untenable – at least for his male singers. His only options were the unsatisfactory compromises of tenors, who had to fake the high-lying passages in a falsetto voice they were unaccustomed to using, or contraltos, who struggled with the bottom end of the range. The latter option, in particular, raised not just practical but aesthetic problems for Tippett. When he settled for a contralto on a counter-tenor part Tippett was faced with the fruity, rich sound of a low voice, rather than the high voice Purcell irrefutably had in mind. Bound up with the aesthetic consideration of vocal timbre was the question of gender. There may have been little in the texts or contexts of Purcell's counter-tenor solos to make them exclusively male, but there was precisely nothing to lend them to a female singer. Tippett obviously sensed this when he assumed that in Deller's voice he had at last found the true Purcellian counter-tenor. Betraying his own Modernist leanings, Tippett wrote of the counter-tenor voice that 'to my ears it has a peculiarly musical sound because almost no emotional irrelevancies distract us from the absolutely pure musical quality of the production.'[5]

At the time he discovered Deller, Tippett had no experience of historically informed Baroque singing. Nineteenth-century singing technique, with its steady vibrato, may have been apt for an Elgar oratorio, but in a Purcellian

---

[3] Michael and Mollie Hardwick, *Alfred Deller: A Singularity of Voice* (London, 1980), p. 46.

[4] Arthur Keith Holland, *Henry Purcell: The English Musical Tradition* (London, 1932), pp. 124–5.

[5] Hardwick and Hardwick, *Alfred Deller*, Foreword.

ode it could communicate little except 'emotional irrelevancies'. It might be tempting to ask whether Tippett would have been drawn quite so strongly to Deller's voice had he been familiar with the pure style of today's specialist Baroque tenors and contraltos, but however diverting it might be, such speculation is fruitless. Ultimately, the only view from which we are really justified in seeing Tippett's redefinition and championing of Deller's voice is his own, and in that context it seems not just reasonable but obvious. Without belittling the attraction to Tippett of Deller's artistry, we need to note the purely practical appeal his voice held. At modern pitch, Deller's voice seemed to fit these Purcellian parts like a glove. Moreover, the sound of a singing voice which was not a mere extension of a speaking voice seemed, to Tippett, peculiarly well suited to words which were more objective than subjective. Yet to appreciate the rationale for Tippett's definition is not necessarily to endorse it.

The flowering of the modern counter-tenor voice, which sprang directly from this meeting, has become one of the vocal glories of our own age. For a number of years, though, it rested largely on Deller's shoulders. Deller's rise to fame coincided with the great revival of early music, and because of his background – he was not educated as a musician or linguist – it was inevitable that English music formed the core of his repertory. And so it was that, before long, English music from Dunstable to Purcell had become virtually synonymous with the sound of Deller's style of singing. At the same time that Deller's voice was coming to public attention Nevill Coghill, modernising Chaucer's 'Miller's Tale', came to the couplet:

> And pleyen songes on a smal rubible
> Therto he song som tyme a loud quynyble;[6]

'Rubible' (also known as a rebec) and 'quynyble' (in this context a descant sung at the interval of a fifth) obviously needed translating. This Coghill did with the following:

> He played a two-stringed fiddle, did it proud,
> And sang a high falsetto, rather loud;[7]

Although strictly speaking it bore no relation to the original, few would have questioned Coghill's second line back in the 1950s. It seemed to fit with an aural construct of Olde England which Deller's voice was beginning to establish. Actually, embellishments such as Coghill's subtly added veracity to the new musical edifice – at the same time diverting attention from the unstable premises on which the whole was built. Yet the link between England of past times and the falsetto voice only grew. It is now

---

[6] Geoffrey Chaucer, 'The Miller's Tale', in *Works of Geoffrey Chaucer*, ed. F. N. Robinson, 2nd edn (Oxford, 1957), p. 49, lines 144–5.

[7] Geoffrey Chaucer, *The Canterbury Tales*, ed. and trans. Nevill Coghill (London, 1951), p. 108.

further reaching, and its effects more insidious, than we might perhaps realise. Today, when men in tights appear on a screen in front of us, we can safely guess what soundtrack will accompany them. Other than a rather strangulated counter-tenor, what voice could have introduced us to the comedy of the medieval *Blackadder*?

Since early counter-tenor parts were known to have been first sung by adult males, and since on paper their range often suited the voices of Deller and his ilk, there seemed little need for further verification that the two were indeed synonymous. Still, the movement of enthusiasts and emulators which formed itself around Deller sought to establish a musicological history for the voice. Without the benefit of time travel (which would have made this book and many others happily redundant) they cast back into the murk of musical history, and duly came across apparent references to singing in falsetto (a term we will unpick in Chapter 2). Often these references were ambiguous, and tended to crop up in unlikely places or curious contexts, but from the twelfth to the nineteenth centuries contemporary reports at least appeared to confirm that falsetto singing had been known before the present day.

So the falsettist had a history. But was that history the same as the counter-tenor's? And how English was it? None of us should claim to be wholly free of confirmation bias – the psychological trait of favouring evidence which supports an existing belief – but it is probably fair to say that this tendency was particularly strong in Deller's admirers, who gathered up any crumbs of evidence which supported Tippett's 'realisation'. More dispassionate observers saw things differently. As far back as the 1960s a strong case was being advanced to suggest that two of Purcell's favoured counter-tenors, John Freeman and John Pate, had in fact been (in our terminology) tenors.[8] And if Purcell's counter-tenors were not falsettists, how about Byrd's, Handel's, or those from British choirs of other centuries? Or those from other countries: precisely what kind of voices did Palestrina, or Rameau, or Bach have in mind for their alto parts? No sooner had Deller and his followers appropriated each of these lines as the preserve of the falsettist than the evidence of historical pitch, contemporary observations, and even the changing nature of human physiology, began to suggest otherwise.

Thankfully for the falsettist, though, this slow sifting of historical evidence has often merely moved him to another part in the score, or perhaps to another country. So, whilst Palestrina probably never heard a falsettist sing one of his alto lines, perhaps this was a voice he heard as a soprano. Similarly, although Lully in France may not have recognised the sound of Deller and his fellows, perhaps Monteverdi in Italy would.

In this sense, any attempt to define the 'true' counter-tenor as a single

---

[8] Olive Baldwin and Thelma Wilson, 'Alfred Deller, John Freeman, and Mr. Pate', *Music and Letters* 50(1) (1969), pp. 103–10.

historical entity is always likely to be futile. Imagine the ridicule he would be subjected to if an economic historian, observing the value of the American dollar today, argued that this value should be applied to the dollar (or indeed thaler, or daler) of every country, and for all time. Yet this is precisely the kind of lazy empiricism which has often been applied to the counter-tenor – as if the term constituted a single, simple currency. Much ink has been spilt in trying to conform our modern understanding of the counter-tenor with various historical occurrences of the term – even when old and new meanings appear flatly to contradict each other. A true history of the chimeric counter-tenor is far more complex and fascinating, I would argue, than a chimeric history of the 'true' counter-tenor. So if, by picking up this book, you are looking for a simple definition of what the counter-tenor *is*, you will be disappointed. Anyone with a CD player to hand can have defined for themselves precisely what a counter-tenor *is* today. No, what interests me is what the counter-tenor *was*, or rather *has been*, and how this history has resulted in a modern phenomenon.

Already I have likened the totality of this history to a multi-panelled tapestry. If this analogy holds true, then when Tippett first defined Deller as a counter-tenor, the latest panel in the tableau of high male singing was created. In the decades since then, the earlier panels have been restored and revealed. If the overall picture which this book now presents is not always one that Tippett and Deller would easily recognise, it undeniably bears the stamp of their genius.

An Inartistic Trick:
Physiology and Terminology

As the term implies, falsetto is a false voice. I consider falsetto to be merely an illegitimate way of getting an effect which, at best, is only vulgar; good voices never have occasion to adopt such an inartistic trick.

Sims Reeves[1]

I think Sims Reeves was the greatest singer I ever heard, but when he wrote or spoke, like Jean de Reszke, he often attested nonsense.

Charles Lunn[2]

To hear the falsetto voice at its most natural, take a seat in the stand of an average sports match on a Saturday afternoon and wait for the home team to score. At that moment, high above the usual throaty cheers, around you in the crowd you will hear some men whooping with delight. What you are hearing may not be singing, nor is it a thing of beauty, but it *is* falsetto. The irony of this scenario is that even in the most macho and uninhibited of environments can be found a naturally produced voice which, at various times in the last eight hundred years, has been deemed both effeminate and false.[3]

The excited sports fan offers one example of falsetto being used naturally. Perhaps a more telling one, from a singing perspective, is the response many men show if they find themselves alone in a cavernous space. Particularly if the space is dark – a cave, for instance – the temptation will be to probe the acoustic with a loud falsetto hoot. A high-frequency sound will produce a more significant reverberation in a large resonant space, be it a cave or a cathedral.

Paradoxical though it may be, the fact is that falsetto is a natural phenomenon, and one which almost every adult male can create. In what way, then, is it 'false'? Most obviously, if a speaking tone is our 'true' voice then this other tone, which both feels and sounds quite different, is by implication 'false'. Before the invention of the stroboscope, physicians speculated with impunity on the mechanics of this difference. So Maffei, writing in Naples in the mid-sixteenth century, could reasonably compare the tracheas of a cow and a man, and conclude that the velocity of air

---

[1] Sims Reeves, *On the Art of Singing* (London, 1901), pp. 5–6.

[2] Cf. J. Louis Orton, *Voice Culture Made Easy* (London, 1900), p. 8.

[3] It is in this context (and this context alone) that the author's own falsetto capacity is regularly exercised, on the touchline of Wharfedale RUFC.

moving in their throats was the crucial factor in determining the pitch of their voices: so, he went on, 'if a person in his own way wants to fake it with the voice called falsetto, he can do so by making the movement of the air faster.'[4] Advances in medical science during the next three centuries did little to further an understanding of the physiological nature of falsetto, other than offering an enlarged vocabulary for the various elements supposedly involved. Confirming that a little learning is a dangerous thing, vocal pedagogues seized on this terminology to create their own quasi-scientific theories. In their disputations, terms such as 'naso-pharyngeal voice', 'frontal-sinus tone', 'velum position' and 'cranial resonation' were – and still are – bandied about in an attempt to illuminate various aspects of voice production.

The stroboscope and laryngoscope should have rendered these terms, and the opinions behind them, largely redundant. Since the 1930s, when scientists first observed the workings of the vocal cords through a stroboscope, the essential difference between the common speaking (henceforth 'modal') and falsetto voice-types has been largely undisputed. This difference lies in the amount and type of vocal cord involvement. In falsetto, only the edges of the vocal folds enter into vibration, while the main body of each fold is more or less relaxed. In modal voice production, the wavelike motion involves the whole vocal cord, with the glottis opening at the bottom first and then at the top.

When viewed through a stroboscope, in our modal voice the vocal folds are seen to make contact with each other completely during each vibration, closing the gap between them fully, if just for a very short time. This closure cuts off the escaping air. When the air pressure in the trachea rises as a result, the folds are blown apart, while the vocal processes of the arytenoid cartilages (the pair of tissue-masses on the sides of the larynx, to which the vocal cords are attached) remain held together. This closure creates an oval shaped gap between the folds, and some air escapes, lowering the pressure inside the trachea. Rhythmic repetition of this movement, a certain number of times a second, creates a pitched note.[5]

In falsetto, however, when the vocal folds are blown open, in untrained falsetto singers a permanent oval orifice is left in the middle between

---

[4] 'Che se volesse alcuno à suo modo fingerlo [...] e per mancamento di soprano fingesse la voce, chiamata falsetto, potria con fare il movimento dell'aere piu veloce, à posta sua farlo.': Giovanni Camillo Maffei, *La lettera sul canto ... libri primo* (Naples, 1562), p. 26; online at <http://www.maurouberti.it/vocalita/maffei/lettera.html> [accessed 4 April 2014]. Translation from Carol MacClintock, *Readings in the History of Music in Performance* (Bloomington, IN, 1979), p. 42.

[5] For an illustration of the larynx during modal and falsetto singing, readers are referred to Reinaldo Kazuo Yazaki's YouTube video, 'Singing tone-by-tone during stroboscopy, using different registers', 25 April 2013 <http://www.youtube.com/watch?v=6u-CHgm_vOo> [accessed 4 April 2014].

the edges of the two folds through which a certain volume of air escapes continuously as long as phonation continues. In some skilled falsettists, meanwhile, the mucous membrane of the vocal folds contact with each other completely during each vibration cycle, and these appear to be the only parts vibrating. Also, the arytenoid cartilages are held firmly together in this vocal register. The length or size of the oval orifice between the folds can vary, but it is known to get bigger as the pressure of air pushed out is increased.[6]

Our understanding of the physiology of vocal production continues to grow. In particular, the research led by Matthias Echternach (an otolaryngologist and tenor), offers tantalising hints that certain physiological issues which he has identified could be the focus of work by future student singers. These singers may, as a result, be able to facilitate smoother register changes. Echternach's MRI-based studies (on not just the larynx, but the whole of the vocal tract) have revealed many physiological differences in falsetto singing – between different voice-types, trained and un-trained singers, and ascending and descending register changes.[7] Despite its obvious potential, quite how this knowledge can be translated to the practical education of singers remains to be seen. Unlike the teaching of an instrument, where the workings of both the tool and the toolsmith are plainly in view, the hidden workings of the voice have traditionally been taught with a heavy reliance on imagery and analogy, and a move from the language of baked-potatoes-at-the-back-of-the-throat to physiological analysis is unlikely to happen overnight.

The scientific clarity with which this difference between 'falsetto' and 'modal' voices can be observed and recognised is hardly matched by our terminological vagueness for the types themselves. In this sense, it is unfortunate that the recent renaissance of the falsettist has coincided with an age of acute linguistic sensitivity. Nowadays it is unfashionable to describe a group of people by using a potentially pejorative term such as 'false'. By the same token, the term 'normal' to describe our fundamental, or common speaking voice is unacceptable to many, since it implies *ab*normality on the part of any other voice. It is easy enough to avoid 'normal' by using 'modal' – the meaning of which in this context is purely statistical, simply recognising that it is the most commonly used voice. So in this book 'modal' will now lose its inverted commas, and do service for the sung equivalent of our common speaking tone. Yet what of 'falsetto'? Even if we wish to, can we avoid this term? People have certainly tried. Most obviously, in our own time 'counter-tenor', 'alto' and 'haute-contre' have been used to refer

[6] Stanley Sadie (ed.), *The New Grove Dictionary of Music & Musicians* (London, 1980), *s.v.* 'Falsetto'.

[7] Matthias Echternach and Bernhard Richter, 'Falsett: stimmwissenschaftliche Untersuchungen', in *Der Countertenor: die männliche Falsettstimme vom Mittelalter zur Gegenwart* (Mainz, 2012), pp. 55–64.

to various falsetto singers. As modern definitions these terms are perfectly reasonable, since the falsettist tends now to sing parts with precisely those names. With a historical survey such as this book, however, the problem is that before our own time these terms defined not necessarily the falsettist, but what we would think of as the tenor voice. (And historically the tenor voice was, in turn, more akin to our modern baritone voice.) 'Alto', of course, simply means 'high', but because today it also denotes a falsettist, this modern reading is commonly misapplied. When a medieval document refers to 'J. de alto Bosco' it is not offering a reference to an early counter-tenor, but simply telling us who he was – literally someone who came from a place where there was a high wood.[8] And when Shostakovich described the Police Inspector in *The Nose* as a 'tenor altino' he was writing for a high tenor and not a 'tenor falsettist', as the term has been translated.[9] Similar confusion attaches to the term 'sopranist', or 'soprano': literally 'one [who sang] above', this term was used to describe falsettists in past times, but now generally refers to a high female voice. 'Head voice' has been used to describe falsetto (with modal voice being 'chest voice' in this terminology). This way lies confusion, though, since other writers have used 'head voice' to define a light tone in high modal voice. Wayne Koestenbaum proposes 'undisguised register break' to replace falsetto.[10] Wordiness aside, the obvious problem with this new term is that historically singers have more often striven for precisely the opposite – to disguise the break between their registers. Short of creating yet another new term, then, we are left with 'falsetto'.

'Falsetto' certainly has historical pedigree. The word has its roots in the Latin word 'falso', meaning 'false'. The first known writer to use the word false ('falsis vocibus') to describe womanly ('femineo') singing by men was Bernard of Clairvaux, in the twelfth century.[11] The phrase 'in falso' first appears in the rubrics for the Feast of Fools at Sens, in northern France, in the thirteenth century.[12] (There are, however, other possible interpretations of these references, which we will discuss in due course.) The actual word 'falsetto' entered common usage in the sixteenth century, and since the eighteenth century has taken its place in musical dictionaries and reference works. Like many other Italian musical terms, it has entered English usage unaltered. Because fundamentally it refers to a physiological

[8] Cf. Peter Giles, *The History and Technique of the Counter-Tenor* (Aldershot, 1994), p. 27.

[9] Richard Taruskin, *Oxford History of Western Music* (New York, 2004), vol. 4, p. 782.

[10] Cf. Diana Fuss (ed.), *Inside/Out: Lesbian Theories, Gay Theories* (New York, 1991), p. 221.

[11] Cf. Joseph Canivez (ed.), *Statuta Capitulorum Generalium Ordinis Cisterciensis* (Louvain, 1933–41), vol. 1, p. 30.

[12] Henri Villetard (ed.), *Office de Pierre de Corbeil ...* (Paris, 1907), vol. 4, p. 78.

capacity and not a musical part, as a definable term 'falsetto' has proved relatively unsusceptible to the vagaries of taste and pitch. (Although the influential nineteenth-century pedagogue Garcia was part of a – thankfully short-lived – movement which wanted to define the falsetto as being the intermediate tone *between* the modal and our falsetto – which he termed 'head voice'.) Even today, although a singer might describe himself as a counter-tenor, if asked about his vocal production he is also likely to acknowledge that he sings primarily 'in falsetto'. In this sense, with a long and largely consistent meaning, 'falsetto' is an ideal term for a musical history – whatever misgivings people might currently have about the word's implications. So, for the remainder of this book it too can drop those self-conscious inverted commas.

This, then, is what we mean by the falsetto as opposed to the modal voice. These are, demonstrably, two distinct registers. Yet there is, by implication, a border between them, and as with most property disputes, the conflicting claims of vocal sages have centered on this small area. Does this grey area constitute a 'third' register, and if so should it be referred to as (to take a selection of terms) 'voix mixte', 'head voice', 'voce di mezzo petto', 'feigned' or 'covered'? This book will try to steer clear of judging these claims of registers, not so much because there are so many of them, but ironically, because there are not enough. In dismissing a particular five-register theory, one twentieth-century English singing teacher noted that 'one may say with equal truth that for every note and every degree of force pertaining to the note, there is a mechanism suitable to it alone.'[13] Our confusion in terminology for the registers of the human voice is further fuelled by a failure to grasp one of the simplest and most self-evident truths: we are all individual. Every human being is different, and by implication so is every voice.

If we acknowledge this, then we can either create as many vocal types as there are voices, and as many registers as there are notes, or we can simply rely on the evident distinctions of modal and falsetto, and leave the middle ground as an area of interested observation. This book will adopt the latter option. As David Wulstan has written, 'the fact that the two types of singer produce sounds of rather different quality cannot justify the use of two separate words unless a further range of terms, such as 'throttle-tenor' and 'bull-bass', are to be called into use to describe differences in voices other than the alto.'[14] Yet aside from the vocal appellations for the falsettist which we have already met, one can find elaborate conjunctions such as 'light tenor altino' and 'tenor contralto' doing recent service for techniques which

---

[13] William Shakespeare, *Plain Words on Singing* (London, 1924), p. 38: cf. James Stark, *Bel Canto* (Toronto, 2003), p. 81.

[14] G. M. Ardran and David Wulstan, 'The Alto or Countertenor Voice', *Music and Letters* 48(1) (1967), pp. 17–22, at p. 19.

are fundamentally similar. One study of vocal terminology found nearly a hundred appellations scattered amongst the writings of vocal pedagogues.[15]

Inevitably, singers will move between their modal and falsetto registers at slightly varying pitches, and will manage this change differently. The sounds they create will certainly be different. But does this make them separate vocal species? Is there, for instance, a difference between the 'male alto' and the 'counter-tenor', as is often suggested? One interesting radiographic experiment aimed to establish whether there was actually any such practical difference. Having observed examples of these two vocal 'types' (presumably self-termed) singing the same note in both modal and falsetto voices, the resulting pictures showed that there was no difference between the 'alto' and 'counter-tenor' techniques.[16] As one of the authors later observed, the perceived differences between such singers simply rests 'on the difference between the good and bad vocal management of a predominantly head voice [falsetto] technique'.[17] This similarity in technique appears to contradict the earlier distinction observed between 'untrained' and 'skilled' falsettists, but not necessarily. If both the 'alto' and 'counter-tenor' singers were 'skilled', we would expect their observable techniques be similar. What is certain is that, from the point of view of research aimed at establishing empirical results, 'alto' and 'counter-tenor' are hopelessly subjective terms. Arguably, 'untrained' and 'skilled' are little better.

Finally, before we embark on the history of high male singing, one important distinction needs addressing: each man who sings has the capacity to sing in falsetto, and (however occasionally) most will use it. This does not make all of us falsettists. In this book, the term 'falsettist' is reserved for the singer who uses falsetto to the virtual exclusion of his modal voice. This distinction may appear a semantic nicety, but as we shall see, there have been many historical eras when it was considered the norm for every trained singer to utilise both modal and falsetto registers as a matter of course. We will encounter many singers who were famed for their falsetto, but who cannot accurately be described as falsettists.

So, as we move from our own time backwards in history, we need to keep a careful eye on the etymology of the terms we find and use. Historically, counter-tenor and alto, as well as tenor and soprano, are variables. Modal and falsetto – natural emissions both – are constants.

---

[15] M. Mörner, F. Fransson and G. Fant, 'Voice register terminology and standard pitch', *Speech Transmission Laboratory Quarterly Progress and Status Report (STL-QPSR)*, 4(4) (1963), pp. 17–23, at pp. 20–1.

[16] Ardran and Wulstan, 'The Alto or Countertenor Voice', p. 21.

[17] David Wulstan, *Tudor Music* (London, 1985), p. 223.

CHAPTER 2

The Ancient World to the Middle Ages

L IKE the famous tunnel at Colditz which began at the top of a chapel's clock tower, the history of the falsetto voice in Western music begins in the most improbable of places. As a specific, identifiable style of singing, falsetto may have first surfaced in fifteenth-century Europe. But to find out why this happened then and there, we first have to trace a course back many centuries, and many thousands of miles away. We also have to begin with another type of voice altogether.

The Eunuch in the Ancient and Early Christian Worlds

T HE castrato plays a significant role in the early history of falsetto chiefly because wherever the castrato voice has been cultivated, a more general appreciation of high male singing – in all its guises – seems to have been fostered. It can be no coincidence that during the early Renaissance one nation, Spain, almost simultaneously introduced both the castrato and falsetto voices to the rest of Europe. But there is another, more practical reason why one cannot discuss the falsettist without first introducing the castrato. Particularly in the Renaissance church, which appreciated the castrato voice aesthetically but disapproved of it socially, complicit records hid the true nature of the castrati by describing them as falsettists. This was possible because the two shared the same territory, singing the same part at the top of the choral texture. Since one was commonly disguised as the other, evidently they also shared something of the same vocal quality. At a seminal moment in the history of both voices, then, the castrato and the falsettist became virtually synonymous. Yet one has a much longer observable history than the other.

Eunuchs – castrated men – were a feature of many ancient Eastern and Near-Eastern societies, from China along the vague route of the Silk Road to the Mediterranean. There is evidence that eunuchs had existed in very early societies, created by accident or isolated acts of punishment. But the practice became historically significant when it became methodical. Dating from around 2100 BCE, surviving cuneiform tablets from the city of Lagash, in modern-day Iraq, give the earliest written evidence of the systematic castration of men.[1] From the relatively liberal standpoint of modern Western society, we might ask how a barbaric practice such as mass castration could ever have become an accepted practice. The rationale behind it is particularly problematic for us to understand now because, whilst our most

---

[1] Kazuya Maekawa, 'Female Weavers and their Children in Lagash: Presargonic and Ur III', *Acta Sumerologica* 2 (1980), pp. 81–125.

recent experience of eunuchs is with the extinct vocal species of the castrati, early Eastern societies were led to castrate men for reasons altogether more prosaic. Noting that animals became docile when castrated, slave-owners began to castrate their captives. This duly increased their trading value, meaning that the existence of eunuchs became geographically diffuse. Not that eunuchs in the ancient world were confined to the lowest rungs of society. Since a eunuch could never create a dynasty, rulers felt safe to have them as intimates at court (the word 'eunuch', of Greek origin, literally means 'keeper of the bed'). Amongst slaves, the advancement that eunuchs could therefore achieve meant that castration was not necessarily regarded as undesirable. Indeed, castration was sometimes self-imposed, particularly as an act of religious devotion.

Whether as courtier, slave, or religious celibate, the eunuch was evidently commonplace. Yet it did not go unnoticed that the act of castration, if carried out before puberty, could significantly affect a man's voice in adulthood. The treble range of the boy was preserved, but to this were added the power of developed lungs and an adult sensibility. As Gary Taylor says, 'the eunuch choir was an unanticipated useful by-product of an operation that had, for centuries, been manufacturing sexual guardians.'[2] In the margins of the eunuch's early history there are tantalising hints of them singing. In particular, dating from around 2600–2500 BCE there survives an alabaster statue of Urnanshe, a singer at the Mari court in Syria (Fig. 1). Even to historians familiar with ancient Mesopotamia's social conventions, decoding this figure is not easy. Julia M. Asher-Greve suggests that while Urnanshe's name and skirt are 'masculine markers', the statue 'also exhibits features primarily coded as feminine, such as an effeminate face and bulging breasts'.[3] Although this predates any documentary evidence for systematic castration, Asher-Greve suggests that Urnanshe may have been a eunuch.

Plaque figurines from Mesopotamia that date to 2000–1750 BCE also offer intriguing depictions of androgynous musical performers which, it has been suggested, are eunuchs (Fig. 2).[4] Dating from around the eleventh century BCE, similar depictions exist in modern-day Israel. From the instruments they hold, it is clear that these performers play, but do they also sing? For suggestive evidence of this we have to turn to biblical texts describing similar scenes.[5] The Old Testament, incidentally, is ambivalent

[2] Gary Taylor, *Castration: An Abbreviated History of Western Manhood* (New York, 2000), pp. 38–9.

[3] Julia M. Asher-Greve, 'The Essential Body: Mesopotamian Conceptions of the Gendered Body', in *Gender and the Body in the Ancient Mediterranean*, ed. Maria Wyke (Oxford, 1998), pp. 8–37, at p. 8.

[4] T. W. Burgh, ' "Who's the man?" – Sex and Gender in Iron Age Musical Performance', *Near Eastern Archaeology* 67(3) (September 2004), pp. 128–36, at p. 131.

[5] For example, Judges 5:1–31; Numbers 21:17–18; 2 Chronicles 23:12–13.

Fig. 1 Seated statuette of Urnanshe

Fig. 2 Seventh-century relief showing musicians with instruments,
from the Palace of Ashurbanipal, Syria

regarding castration. In Deuteronomy 23:1 castration is outlawed: 'He that is wounded in the stones, or hath his privy member cut off, shall not enter into the congregation of the Lord.' In the New Testament, on the other hand, Matthew 19:12 has Jesus appear to accept the practice:

> For there are some eunuchs, which were so born from their mother's womb: and there are some eunuchs, which were made eunuchs of men: and there be eunuchs, which have made themselves eunuchs for the kingdom of heaven's sake. He that is able to receive it, let him receive it.

One of the earliest descriptions of the castrato voice comes from the fourth century BCE, when Aristotle (or at least a follower of his) noted the peculiar vocal characteristics of the eunuch: 'Why do the unfruitful, such as children, women, those who are now old and eunuchs, make high sounds with their voice but men deep ones?'[6] Al-jahiz, writing in Baghdad in the early ninth century CE, also noted that the peculiarity of eunuch voices was recognisable by everyone.[7] From at least the early fifth century, when Socrates of Constantinople referred to Briso (the leader of the Empress Eudoxia's cantors) as being a eunuch, castrati were prominent in the music of the Eastern church.[8] This practice lasted many centuries. In the late twelfth century Theodore Balsamon, Orthodox Patriarch of Antioch, tells us that all church cantors were by then castrati: 'in the past the class of singers consisted not only of eunuchs, as is the case today, but also those not of that kind.'[9] Balsamon also makes a tantalising comment on singers: 'Likewise note that the warblings of singers and theatrical melodies are utterly forbidden.'[10] The word translated here as 'warbling' is 'minurisma', which in classical times was used of both an eagle and a nightingale. This, together with Balsamon's earlier comment, suggests that it was eunuch singers which he had in mind here, though he does not specify them. (It may be timely to sound a cautionary note on the nature of prohibitions,

---

[6] 'Dia ti hoi agonoi, hoion paides, gunaikes, kai hoi ēdē gerontes kai hoi eunouchoi, oxu phthengontai, hoi de andres baru?': Aristotle, *Problema/Problems*, ed. and trans. W. S. Hett, Aristotle in Twenty-Three Volumes 15 (London, 1970), p. 263. Translation by Hugh Griffith.

[7] Cf. Taylor, *Castration*, p. 38.

[8] Socrates Scolasticus, *Historia ecclesiastica*, bk VI, chap. 8: cf. *The Ecclesiastical History of Socrates Scholasticus*, ed. and trans. Rev. A. C. Zenos (New York, 1891). Available online through <http://www.documentacatholicaomnia.eu/> [accessed 23 April 2014].

[9] 'To palaion ouk ap' eunouchōn monon to tōn psaltōn tagma sunistato, kathōs ginetai sēmeron, alla kai apo mē toioutōn.': *Patrologiae cursus completus, series graeca* 137, ed. J.-P. Migne (Paris, c. 1857), p. 532. Translation by Hugh Griffith.

[10] 'Hōsautōs sēmeiōsai hoti kai ta tōn psaltōn minurismata kai ta thumelika melōdēmata pantē kekōluntai.': *Patrologiae cursus completus, series graeca* 137, ed. Migne, p. 1361. Translation by Hugh Griffith.

since this is the first of many we will meet. Depending on their agendas, commentators have often tended to seize on prohibitions as either flat denials of particular practices, or proof of their currency. Logic suggests a more equivocal answer. Self-evidently, since a prohibition is always made by someone in authority, it tells us that a practice was not officially accepted. Yet it is equally obvious that no practical authority will waste time making an abstract prohibition.) Balsamon, then, is probably telling us here that castrati had a tendency towards ostentatious singing, but that this was kept in check by the church authorities.

Interesting though this Near-Eastern history is, it becomes relevant to Western music only when the citations occur as part of cross-cultural contacts. How, then, did the vocal practices of the Muslim world tie in with those of the West? One obvious link was through the Crusades. In 1147, for instance, during the Second Crusade, the French historian Odo of Deuil described an ecumenical mass in Constantinople:

> These clergy certainly differed from our own as to words and order of service, but they made a favourable impression because of their sweet chanting; for the mingling of voice, the robust with the graceful, to wit the eunuch's with the manly (for many of them were eunuchs), softened the hearts of the Franks.[11]

From Constantinople castrati evidently travelled north and east. Russian sources record that castrati, including a Greek eunuch named Manuil (or Manuel), arrived at Smolensk in 1137 and taught church song there.[12] Following the sack of Constantinople by the Crusaders in 1204, the castrato was largely to disappear from the Orthodox church, never to reappear.

There is circumstantial evidence that the redundant castrati of Constantinople were exiled to Sicily, where King Roger II was establishing Byzantine forms of ceremonial.[13] Albeit tentatively, those looking for the origins of the Renaissance castrato tradition in Italy have traced a possible link here: since southern Italy was held by the House of Aragon during the Renaissance, it may be that the 'Spanish' castrati who first appeared in the Sistine Chapel actually came from the heel of Italy, and represent the continuation of this Byzantine practice.[14] Although it tells us nothing

---

[11] 'Illi quidem a nostris clericis verborum et organi genere dissidebant, sed suavi modulatione placebant; voces enim mixtae, robustior cum gracili, eunucha videlicet cum virili (erant enim eunichi multi illorum), Francorum animos demulcebant.': Odo de Deogilo, *De profectione Ludovici VII in orientem*, ed. and trans. Virginia Gingerick Berry (New York, 1948), pp. 68–9.

[12] Peter Charles Remondino, *History of Circumcision from the Earliest Times to the Present* (Philadelphia, 1891), p. 94.

[13] Neil K. Moran, 'Byzantine Castrati', *Journal of the Plainsong and Medieval Music Society* 11 (2002), pp. 99–112, at pp. 110–11.

[14] Moran, 'Byzantine Castrati', p. 112.

specifically about musical practices, we might note in passing a well-known reference that implies a link between Italy and castrated men. Chaucer's Pardoner, we are told in the General Prologue to the *Canterbury Tales*, was 'streight comen fro the court of Rome'.

> A voys he hadde as small as hath a goot.
> No berd hadde he, ne nevere sholde have;
> As smothe it was as it were late shave.
> I trowe he were a gelding or a mare.[15]

This is not the last time we will find a northern European associating the eunuch with Mediterranean lands.

Ziryab and Medieval Iberia

THERE may have been occasional links through the Crusaders, and with the traders of the Italian peninsula, but in the medieval period the most likely confluence of Eastern and Western vocal practices was in Spain. The Moorish invasion of the Iberian peninsula, which began in the eighth century, brought with it a trade which made the capital of the caliphate, Córdoba, the richest city in Europe. The cultural influence of the Moors, who settled in great numbers in the peninsula, was no less significant. In particular the arrival at the Moslem court of Córdoba by the singer, lutenist, composer and polymath Ziryab (789–857) was seminal.[16] Ziryab, literally meaning 'blackbird', was the nickname given to Abu al-Hasan. The earliest historical source of Ziryab's history claims that he had been trained as a musician in Baghdad, from whence he travelled through Northern Africa to Spain. At the court of 'Abd al-Rahman in Córdoba, Ziryab won immediate acclaim for his innovative performing style, accompanying himself on an oud of his own making (which revolutionised the design of an instrument that was to become the lute). He also established a school of music in Córdoba, which was influential in disseminating Eastern practices in Iberia. Although Ziryab was a freed slave, as the father of ten children it should be stressed he was certainly not a eunuch. Neither can we say with any certainty that he sang in falsetto, although there is, as we shall see, suggestive evidence that he might have done.

---

[15] Geoffrey Chaucer, *General Prologue*, in *Works of Geoffrey Chaucer*, ed. Robinson, p. 23, lines 688–91.

[16] The chief sources (often contradictory) of Ziryab's biographical details are the *Al-Muqtabas* by the Andalusian historian Ibn Hayyan (987–1076), and a later treatise *Mut'at as-asthma' fi 'ilm al'sama*, by Ahmad al-Tīfāshī (1184–1253): cf. Julian Ribera, *Music in Ancient Arabia and Spain* (London, 1929), pp. 100–7; Amnon Shiloah, 'Muslim and Jewish Musical Traditions of the Middle Ages', in *Music as Concept and Practice in the Late Middle Ages*, ed. Reinhard Strohm and Bonnie J. Blackburn (Oxford: Oxford University Press, 2001), pp. 1–15, at pp. 1–5.

Despite these disclaimers, the existing history of the earliest European castrati gives a prominent place to Ziryab. According to the French music historian Christian Gaumy, whose research centred on the cathedral archives of Córdoba and Seville, Ziryab had young Muslim boys castrated to preserve their singing voices.[17] In *The World of the Castrati* another French writer, Patrick Barbier, continued this lineage into the twelfth century, noting the 'amazing voices' of castrati singers in the Spanish Mozarabic church.[18] Sadly, neither author cites specific sources for these statements, and current authorities on the Muslim chroniclers and early Arabic performance practice can find no supportive evidence for them.[19] However, it is difficult to dismiss Gaumy and Barbier's claims. With our earlier observations of castrato singing in the Near East, not only have we confirmed the beginning of the line which Gaumy and Barbier claim to trace, but in due course we will identify an end to the line – the arrival of Spanish falsettists and castrati in Rome during the Renaissance. In other words, we stand like speleologists who have put dye in the water at the top of a cave system, and have duly seen dye flow out at the bottom: there is evidence of a link, but the passage itself remains hidden.

As far as the singing style of Ziryab and his contemporaries is concerned, the most likely cause of confusion lies in the translation of Arabic terms. In particular the words 'khuns' and 'mukhannath' are open to interpretation – at least as they relate to singing. Medieval dictionaries defining the 'khuns', speak of qualities of softness, tenderness, languor, delicacy and effeminacy. Men exhibiting these qualities were known as 'mukhannathun'. According to the tenth-century *Book of Songs*, Ziryab's own teacher in Baghdad, Ishaq al-mawsili, introduced the 'khuns' into his singing;[20] and Ibn Hayyan tells us that one of Ziryab's sons, Muhammad, was a *mukhannath*. Male singing in any form was something of a novelty in the Muslim world, since in the early history of Islam most singers were female, the *qiyān*. But in eighth-century Mecca the *qiyān* began to pass on their art to male singers such as al-Gharid, a *mukhannath* who was known for his heart-rending

[17] Christian Gaumy, 'Le Chant des castrats', *Opera International*, December 1984, pp. 26–9, at p. 26. My assistant, John Dereix, had a lengthy phone conversation with the elderly M. Gaumy. This conversation left us in no doubt that M. Gaumy's research and discoveries were genuine; sadly, it did not bring us any closer to the precise bibliographical sources of his findings.

[18] Patrick Barbier, *The World of the Castrati* (London, 1998), p. 8. Professor Barbier, in a personal correspondence with me, acknowledged that his source for this information was secondary and not primary, although he could not recall what that source was.

[19] I am particularly grateful to Dr. Eckhard Neubauer and Dr. George Dimitri Sawa for their assistance in unraveling this topic.

[20] Abu al-Faraj al-Isfahani, *Kitab al-Aghani* (Cairo: Egyptian National Archive, 1927), vol. 5, pp. 326–7.

elegies.[21] Did the 'effeminacy' of the *mukhannath* reflect their vocal attributes? Or did it refer only to their general nature? Like the eunuchs of the harem, the *mukhannath* were seen as being a trans-gender group, and as musicians, singing in falsetto would be an obvious reference back to the female *qiyān*.[22] So the evidence that the *mukhannath* sang in falsetto is suggestive, if inconclusive. But how could modern scholars have confused the *mukhannath* with eunuch singers? There do appear to be some grounds for confusion: in one recorded instance a *mukhannath* who was not a eunuch was punished and castrated because of his *khuns* qualities.[23] On the other hand, the chroniclers frequently use an explicit term for eunuch – *khasí* – when referring to servants, and yet never use this when referring to singers.[24] Until this area has been fully researched by historians of early Iberian music, we may have to content ourselves with these tantalising suggestions of falsetto and castrato singers in Muslim Spain.

'Falsis vocibus' in the Medieval Church

S PAIN is typically seen as being peripheral to developments in the history of medieval music. Compositionally this might be true, but in terms of theory and performance practice Spain's influence was seminal. From Spain, the work of Arab theorists was translated into Latin and disseminated northwards, as were Arabic instruments. Vocally, Spain's influence took longer to infiltrate other parts of Europe. Certainly in the Renaissance the falsettists and castrati of Spain were to make their presence clearly felt, but in the meantime all we have are occasional clues that Spanish voices had a particular reputation outside the peninsula.

Take, for instance, the writings of Aelred of Rievaulx, a twelfth-century Cistercian who was abbot of a monastery in northern England. In seeking to restore the Rule of St Benedict, the Cistercians committed themselves to a life of simple austerity, and Aelred's words reflect this ethic. Instrumental participation, polyphonic elaboration and the vanity of singers are all subjected to Aelred's withering blast. Of the way the voice is used, he writes:

[21] Everett K. Rowson, 'The Effeminates of Early Medina', *Journal of the American Oriental Society*, 111(4) (1991), pp. 671–93, at p. 685.

[22] Cf. Gary David Comstock and Susan E. Henking (eds.), *Que(e)ryng Religion: A Critical Anthology* (New York, 1996), p. 82.

[23] Cf. Edward William Lane, *Arabic–English Lexicon* (London, 1865), vol. 2, pp. 814–15.

[24] George Dimitri Sawa, *Music Performance Practice in the Early Abbasid Era, 130–320 ah/750–932 ad* (Toronto, 1989), pp. 119–20.

> Sometimes, and I write it with shame, it is forced into the whinnying
> of a horse, and sometimes it lays aside its manly power, and puts on
> the sharpened graces of the female voice.[25]

As part of his duties as an abbot, Aelred travelled to Rome in 1142. We
have no way of knowing what he heard there, but he was in no doubt about
where these 'female' vocal practices had their origin:

> Compared to that mode of singing which the Holy Ghost instituted
> through His own organs, the most holy Fathers Augustine and
> Ambrose, and especially Gregory, it may be, then, that someone [...]
> prefers these Spanish ditties [...].[26]

Is there a hint here of an equine version of cynocephaly – that curious
medieval phenomenon whereby members of one region believed that in
others there existed men with the heads of dogs? To be sure, a notable
feature of early vocal commentators (whom we shall frequently encounter
in the pages that follow) is their willingness to attribute unusual vocal styles
to singers of distant parts.

Before we go further, we need to ask whether Aelred is actually referring
to falsetto singing here. Likening this style of singing to the 'femineae vocis'
might suggest that he is, since the analogy of womanly singing with the
falsetto voice is one which has persisted (intermittently) to our own day. But,
bearing in mind the chauvinism of many early clerics, it is always possible
that the feminine characteristic he has in mind is weakness, and not high
pitch. Others, as we shall soon see, leave us with a similar question mark.
And yet, whether Aelred's comment is founded in myth or knowledge, and
whether it is about weakness or falsetto, we can at least note that as a centre
of unusual musical practices – which included effeminate singing – the
reputation of Spain was evidently widespread.

Aelred's disparaging reference to exotic singing is interesting, because it
is part of a small but significant body of similar observations from twelfth-
century clerics, most of whom were connected with the Cistercian order
during its formative years. These need discussing, because in the ongoing
battle to establish or discount the place of the falsettist in northern Europe
during the Middle Ages and onwards into the Renaissance, the unwitting
words of these clerics have been dragged into both front lines. On the
one hand, these clerical edicts have been used to conclude that 'it is clear

[25] 'Aliquando, quod pudet dicere, in equinos hinnitus cogitur, aliquando virili
vigore deposito in femineae vocis gracilitates acuitur.': Aelred of Rievaulx,
Speculum caritatis, bk 2, chap. 23. Translation from Robert Hayburn, *Papal
Legislation on Sacred Music* (Collegeville, MN, 1979), p. 19.

[26] '[...] modo cantandi, quem Spiritus sanctus per sanctissimos Patres quasi
per organa sua, Augustinum uidelicet, Ambrosium, maximeque Gregorium,
instituit: hiberas, ut dicitur, naenias [...]': Aelred of Rievaulx, *Speculum caritatis*,
bk 2, chap. 23. Translation from Hayburn, *Papal Legislation*, p. 19.

that something akin to the modern countertenor voice was well known in the Middle Ages'?[27] On the other, critics of this argument have suggested that the edicts tell us nothing so specific, and that it is 'more reasonable to consider [...] tenor and bass' to have been the norm.[28] The battle is perhaps an unnecessary one, since at its heart lies an either–or fallacy. The question 'was the kind of modern falsettist we know also known to medieval ears?' invites a simple 'yes' or 'no' answer – and yet reality is rarely quite so neat. Responses to such false dichotomies – as easy to mark as they are to offer – are beloved by academics and journalists alike, but however tempting they might be, 'yes or no' answers to such complex questions are simplifications. It will be one of the aims of this history not to be seduced by their easy charms; as we shall see, there may be truth in both arguments.

Let us look at the words of the most influential of the early Cistercians, Bernard of Clairvaux:

> It befits men to sing with a virile voice, and not in a womanish, ringing manner, or as it is said in the vernacular, with false voices, as if imitating the lasciviousness of minstrels. And therefore we have stipulated that a medium is to be used in the chant, not only so that it should exude seriousness, but also so that devotion may be conserved.[29]

Since they were influential figures in the same institution, it is not surprising that Aelred and Bernard are similarly 'on-message' with the Cistercian ethic. (Actually, Aelred's text was probably written at the request of Bernard.) In particular, the same key image of 'womanly' singing occurs, although as with Aelred, Bernard's 'femineo' could simply be a euphemism for 'weak'. But if his meaning was 'weak', why would it be allied with the word 'tinnulis' – commonly translated as 'ringing'? Different bells ring in different ways, of course, and it could be that for Bernard 'tinnulis' here meant something closer to 'tinkling'. But as Bernard's writings make clear elsewhere, to a Cistercian monk, surely the primary reference to a bell would have been as a resonant summons. In the first century BCE the Roman poet Catullus had used the expression 'voce carmina tinnula' in the context of singing at a wedding celebration, and it seems likely that later medieval writers such

---

[27] Roger Bowers, 'The Performing Pitch of English 15th-Century Church Polyphony', *Early Music* 8(1) (1980), pp. 21–8.

[28] Christopher Page and Andrew Parrott, 'False voices', *Early Music* 9(1) (1981), pp. 71–5.

[29] 'Viros decet virili voce cantare, et non more femineo tinnulis, vel ut vulgo dicitur falsis vocibus veluti histrionicam imitari lasciviam. Et ideo constituimus mediocritatem servari in cantu, ut gravitatem redoleat, et devotion conservetur.': Bernard of Clairvaux, 'Statuta Ordinis Cisterciensis, 1134', chap. 123, in *Statuta Capitulorum Generalium Ordinis Cisterciensis*, ed. Josef Canivez (Louvain, 1933), vol. 1, p. 30. Translation from Page and Parrott, 'False voices', p. 71.

as Bernard persisted with this meaning – of resonant or ringing voices. As for the word 'mediocritatem', David Chadd suggests that it 'relates to the Cistercian ideal of a mean between excessive jollity and lugubriousness'.[30] But, bearing in mind the sentence which precedes it, and the following words 'et ideo', 'mediocritatem' here seemingly refers to a moderation in all things – including pitch. Lending weight to this reading is another Cistercian text, the *Instituta patrum*, which requires psalms to be sung 'with an even voice, at a steady tempo that is not excessively drawn out, but at a moderate pitch'. And sure enough, the *Instituta* (at least part of which may have been written by Bernard himself) proceeds to lambast 'feminine, and all false singing', which 'we prohibit from our choirs'.[31]

Even more baffling words occur in the rule of the Gilbertians, a monastic community for both sexes closely allied to the Cistercians. Gilbert of Sempringham (who also knew Aelred) was founder of the order, and wrote: 'The use of organum and descant, falsetto and *pipeth*, at the Divine Office we prohibit to all [of our members] of both sexes.'[32] Two words here raise obvious questions. Firstly, there is the rogue word 'pipeth', which is not Latin at all, and despite its odd grammar, would appear to be English. Dr Katharine Sykes, who has transcribed the Gilbertine *Institutiones* from their sole manuscript source, says that English usages appear elsewhere in the manuscript as glosses to help explain more secular issues.[33] Such English glosses sometimes wave the warning flag 'ut vulgo', telling us that we are using the vernacular, but they do not always. In this context, the English word 'pipeth' (from the Latin 'pipare', meaning to chirp or peep) could be suggestive of a hooting falsetto, or of weak, flutey singing (it is no more likely, incidentally, to refer to actual pipe-playing, than 'organum' is to refer to the playing of an organ). Secondly, there is the word 'fausetum'. In modern musical and Latin dictionaries – even in Niermeyer's Medieval

[30] David Chadd, 'Liturgy and Liturgical Music', in *Cistercian Art and Architecture in the British Isles*, ed. C. Norton and D. Park (Cambridge, 1986), pp. 299–314, at p. 305.

[31] 'Fœmineas, omnemque vocum falsitatem, iactantiam seu novitatem detestemur, et prohibeamus in Choris nostris.': Anon., *Instituta patrum de modo psallendi sive cantandi*, available online at <http://www.chmtl.indiana.edu/tml/13th/ PATPSAL_TEXT.html> [accessed 4 April 2014].

[32] 'Organum tamen & decentum, fausetum & pipeth, omnino in divino ofiicio omnibus nostris utriusque sexus prohibermus.': Gilbert of Sempringham, 'Regulae Ordinis Sempringensis sive Gilbertinorum Canonicorum', in *Lucæ Holstenii [...] Codex regularum monasticarum et canonicarum: quas ss. patres monachis, canonicis & virginibus sanctimonialibus servandas præscripserunt* (Augsburg, 1759; repr. Graz. 1957), vol. 2, pp. 467–536: cf. Page and Parrott, 'False voices', p. 71.

[33] Personal correspondence with the author. Cf. Katherine Sykes, *Inventing Sempringham: Gilbert of Sempringham and the Origins of the Role of the Master*, Vita Regularis 46 (Munster, 2011).

Latin Dictionary – 'fausetum' is simply equated with 'falsetto'. And the modern French word for falsetto is indeed 'fausset', sounding conveniently similar to French 'faux', meaning 'false'. Yet the Latin 'fauces' means throat (hence the modern meaning of 'faucet' as 'tap'). Could the words 'fausetum' and 'falsetum' therefore have meanings different from our own understanding of 'falsetto'?

Christopher Page has noticed that a late fourteenth-century treatise on organ pipes contains an instruction beginning:

> If you wish to have a *falsetum*, or semitone – which is the same thing – between C and D [...][34]

In this context, 'falsetum' means a semitone, or literally a 'false-tone'. Could this – chromatic inflections – be Gilbert's meaning? Before we are drawn downwards into a semantic spiral, we should perhaps take a step back, and note a broader point made by Joseph Dyer: 'the term *falsa musica* is used as a grab bag to cover everything from careless singing or music copying to quite specific elements of notation, mainly those involving chromatic inflections.'[35] Although 'falsis vocibus' and 'falsetum' appear narrower in meaning than 'falsa musica', even in a single instance they could still have referred to a plurality of 'offences'. We might also note that musical terminology (even in our own time) is notoriously ambiguous. Words such as 'tone' and 'key' have various meanings to us, depending on context. In the same way, just because an organ builder took 'falsetum' to mean a semitone does not mean that two centuries earlier Gilbert could not have used the same word to mean falsetto singing. At the very least, this riddle reminds us of the yawning gap between Gilbert of Sempringham's intended readers and ourselves. Those intended readers were members of the Gilbertine order – an order which included women, whose falsetto voice is barely perceptible as such. Does this indicate that Gilbert could not have meant falsetto with his 'fausetum'? Not necessarily: in a memorandum on practices in the work-place today, we would not expect every individual to be guilty, even potentially, of each listed prohibition. Moreover, although Gilbert states that this dictat is for both sexes, it actually appears in a section addressed to the male canons only. Ultimately, we probably have to accept that for us, Gilbert's original meaning will remain elusive.

Perhaps the most remarkable Cistercian comment on high male singing comes from a dialogue between a Cistercian author (anonymous, but perhaps Idung of Prüfening) and an imaginary member of the less austere Cluniac order. This was transcribed in the early eighteenth century from a manuscript at the now-ruined Cistercian monastery of Morimond in northern France.

---

[34] 'Falsetum sive semitonium, quod idem est, si habere volueris inter C fa ut primum naturalem et D sol R [...]': Page and Parrott, 'False voices', p. 71.

[35] Joseph Dyer, 'A Thirteenth-Century Choirmaster: The *Scientia Artis Musicae* of Elias Salomon', *The Musical Quarterly*, 66(1) (1980), pp. 83–111, at p. 91.

CISTERCIAN: Those ringing and castrated [evirate] voices, which you have termed 'slender' [graciles], and which are usually sharpened by a drink made from liquorice and choice ectuaries – what are they but delights to the ear forbidden by the Rule?

CLUNIAC: Where does the rule forbid them?

CISTERCIAN: Where it orders that we read and chant 'with humility and dignity'. St Ambrose in his book *De Officiis ministrorum* also forbids them in the following words: 'Let the voice be full with manliness and not sounding like a woman's.' Contrary to the respected canonical decrees, you make use of such voices in new and frolicsome songs on your new and unauthorised feast days.[36]

Since the Latin original of this text introduces a number of new terms, it is worth taking a moment to examine them. 'Evirate' is literally translated as 'unmanned' (the initial 'e' being an abbreviated 'ex', and 'vir' meaning 'man'). Perhaps confusingly, 'graciles' ('slender') is not related to 'graceful', which has a different etymological stem. Taken at face value, then, this text could suggest that castrated singers were known in Benedictine monasteries by the twelfth century. The lavish Cluniac order, which comprised nearly a thousand houses, was largely responsible for integrating Spanish wealth and culture into the European mainstream; in this context, the presence of castrati seems plausible. Is it possible that castrati were a feature of the more opulent medieval churches – including some monasteries? Perhaps so – as we shall see when this history reaches the Renaissance, until the mid-sixteenth century a veil was drawn over the presence of castrati singers in the church. If such singers were largely hidden from the world in their own time, we should hardly be surprised if we cannot positively reveal their identity now.

Yet before we accept castrati to have been a feature of the Cluniac order, we need to raise some significant caveats. Idung had a strong anti-Cluny agenda, and his use of 'evirate' could be a colourful way of describing effeminate singing. In truth, without having conducted a medical examination of the singers in question, if Idung's meaning was that castrati sang at Cluny, at best he could only have been reporting hearsay. If castrati were his target, there is certainly something curious in his remark that their

---

[36] 'CISTERCIENSIS: Illae tennulae et evirate voces, quas vos graciles vocatis, et fucco liquericii et sumtuosis electuariis acuere soletis, quid sunt, nisi oblectamenta aurium, contra regulae interdictum? CLONIACENSIS: Ubi interdicit illas regula? CISTERCIENCIS: Ubi praecipit legere et cantare cum humilitate et gravitate, et sanctus Ambrosius interdicit eas in libro de Officiis his verbis: Vox ipsa plena succi virilis, nihil femineum sonnet. Talibus vocibus cum novis et usurpatis festis vestries utimini contra veneranda canonum decreta.': Idung of Prüfening, 'Dialogus inter Cluniacensem et Cisterciensem monachum', in *Thesaurus novus anecdotorum*, ed. Edmond Martène and Ursin Durand, (Paris, 1717), vol. 5, p. 1586.

voices were 'improved' by a particular drink: actual castrati, whose voices were formed by a physiological condition, would not be reliant on a dietary supplement to sing high. Perhaps this suggests that Idung used the word 'evirate' to mean 'effeminate', rather than literally 'unmanned'. In any event, we need to note that however suggestive of falsetto we might find their words, neither Iddung nor Ambrose directly equates feminine singing with high pitch. Here, in translation, are Ambrose's words:

> 84. The voice itself should be not weak, not feeble, making no womanish sounds, the sort of voice that many men are accustomed to imitate by way of showing seriousness, but maintaining a certain manner and pattern and manly strength. For this is the way to adhere to excellence in our life, by assigning to each sex and person the things that belong to it. This is the best arrangement of our actions, this is the adornment that suits everything we do. But just as I do not approve a sound of the voice or a bodily gesture which is effeminate and feeble, so too I do not approve the coarse and rustic. Let us imitate nature: its likeness is a rule of instruction and a pattern of goodness.[37]

Nowhere here does Ambrose actually refer to men singing at the *pitch* of women (as this passage has sometimes been translated). Ambrose, and Idung after him, perceived females as sounding weak, and it is this characteristic which they objected to in monastic singing. It is possible that the authors also sought to criticise falsetto, or in Idung's case even castrated voices, but the evidence for this is less secure.

Falsetto in Early Polyphony

ANOTHER twelfth-century cleric to criticise monastic singing was John of Salisbury. His life and thought share much in common with the men discussed above, though the likely musical target of his ire was, on balance, more polyphony than chant. John may have known Bernard of Clairvaux and his ideology, but as Bishop of Chartres the reality of his experience was more worldly than the Cistercians. For all that, at first glance his words have a familiar ring:

---

[37] '84. Vox ipsa non remissa, non fracta, nihil femineum sonans, qualem multi gravitatis specie simulare consueverunt, sed formam quandam et regulam ac sucum virilem reservans. Hoc est enim pulchritudinem vivendi tenere, convenientia cuique sexui et personae reddere. Hic ordo gestorum optimus, hic ornatus ad omnem actionem adcommodus. Sed ut molliculum et infractum aut vocis sonum aut gestum corporis non probo, ita neque agrestem ac rusticum. Naturam imitemur; eius effigies formula disciplinae, formula honestatis est.': Ambrose, *De Officiis Ministrorum, libri III ...*, ed. Johann Georg Krabinger (Tubing, 1857), 19:84, p. 61. Translation by Hugh Griffith, for a forthcoming publication by Andrew Parrott.

It pollutes the very practice of devotion that in the sight of God [...] by the debauchery of their wanton voices, by their self-display, by their womanish manner of making little notes and their chopping up of phrases, they try to remove all manly firmness from the dazed little minds of their listeners. When you have heard the effeminate melodies of those *praecinentium et succinentium, concinentium et decinentium, intercinentium et occinentium,* you would think it was the singing of Sirens, not humans [...] That facility, if such it is, of going up high or down low, that dividing up or multiplying of short notes, that repetition of phrases and endless reinforcing of individual sections, all so mingle the high notes, even the very highest [acutissima], with low and ultra-low notes that the ears almost lose their power to judge. The mind is lulled by the attraction of all this sweetness and has not the strength to assess the merits of the sounds it hears. When they go beyond due measure, these things will more readily arouse itching in the genitals than devotion in the mind.[38]

Much of John's text could be referring to facets of singing other than falsetto. One word, however, is difficult to bypass: 'acutissima' – 'the very highest'. The very highest notes a man can sing must have been produced with falsetto. Does this mean that John was describing falsettists? Before we can try to answer this question, we need to think of the context of his words. Elsewhere in this passage, John's mention of harmony reminds us that, more emphatically than Aelred and Gilbert, his subject is not just chant, but polyphony. Written in the middle of the twelfth century, just after he returned from Paris, John's quarry was probably the daring new music he had heard there. Known as 'organum', this music has a special place in this history of music because it is the first polyphony to be associated with specific musicians – Albertus, Leonin and Perotin. We should be careful,

---

[38] 'Ipsum quoque cultum religionis incestat quod ante conspectum Domini [...] lascivientis vocis luxu, quadam ostentatione sui, muliebribus modis notularum articulorumque caesuris, stupentes animulas emollire nituntur. Cum praecinentium et succinentium, concinentium et decinentium, intercinentium et occinentium praemolles modulationes audieris, Sirenarum concentus credas esse non hominum [...] Ea siquidem est ascendendi descendendique facilitas, ea sectio vel geminatio notularum, ea replicatio articulorum singulorumque consolidatio, sic acuta vel acutissima gravibus et subgravibus temperantur ut auribus sui iudicii fere subtrahatur auctoritas [...] Cum haec quidem modum excesserint, lumborum pruriginem quam devotionem mentis poterunt citius excitare.' John of Salisbury, *Ioannis Saresberiensis episcopi Carnotensis Policratici,* ed. Clemens C. I. Webb (New York, 1979), vol. 1, pp. 41–2. Translation by Hugh Griffith, for Parrott's forthcoming publication. Hugh Griffith comments: 'I have not translated the words above in italics. These are six different compounds of the basic verb 'cano', piled up one after another to create a rhetorical effect of absurdity and excess, but I doubt if anyone now knows exactly what each one is meant to convey.'

Ex. 1 Perotin, *Sederunt*, conclusion

though, not to think of these men as 'composers' in our sense. Evidence suggests that Parisian organum was primarily an oral (and aural) art – improvised and memorised by soloists – which these men artfully edited into cogent works. As it appears on the page, organum does not easily suggest a role for falsettists. It is true that some early works of two-part organum, roughly contemporary with John's time in Paris, have a *discantus* part which is higher than the long notes of the chant; these higher parts could have been sung by a falsettist, although there is no particular reason for thinking that they were. Indeed, the way that organum developed suggests that there was no falsettist tradition at Notre Dame. In later pieces such as the great four-part *Sederunt* attributed to Perotin, the ranges of the various criss-crossing parts in the polyphony are virtually identical (see Ex. 1), implying the same vocal types on all parts.

More than this, the chant which underscores and then continues on from the polyphonic music shares this same range – and according to the rubrics of the liturgy this chant would have been sung by all the clerics present: 'In a true sense this full clergy was the choir of Notre Dame.'[39] So, if we want to believe that any one of the polyphonists was a falsettist, not only do we have to believe that they all were, but also that all the rest of the Notre Dame clergy – from the Bishop of Paris downwards – were falsettists too (unless they joined in with the chant an octave lower). Realistically, then, we need to look beyond the written record of the music to find what prompted

[39] Craig Wright, *Music and Ceremony at Notre Dame of Paris, 500–1550* (Cambridge, 1989), p. 318.

John's reference to 'acutissima' notes. At this point it is salutary to note that the *Magnus Liber*, which is the primary source of Notre Dame organum, is physically *minimus* (see Fig. 3): its tiny size, and the way its contents are arranged, tell us that it could never have been used as a practical performing resource. This, in turn, reminds us that the performance practice of organum was one of improvisation and memorisation. Doubtless there were moments in performance when individual singers displayed, extempore, the tantalising ornaments mentioned by other theorists – ornaments such as the *longa florata, floricatio vocis* and *flos harmonicis*. If John of Salisbury was referring to falsetto singing, it is at such moments that he probably heard it.

In considering the implications of all these Benedictine, Cistercian and Gilbertine texts, not just context, but historical perspective is vital. With the inevitable telescoping that modern writers often use in viewing early history, dots of evidence – in reality separated by much space and time – are joined together. In this way, all of the clerics' texts cited here have been used to help validate the role of the falsetto singing from as much as three centuries later.[40] The anachronisms of such arguments have been highlighted, but often by fighting fire with fire – witness the use, above, of a fourteenth-century organ treatise to elucidate a twelfth-century liturgical edict. We should surely allow that practices would have become established some time before they were documented. And it is true that there can be no hard and fast rules about how far back – or how widely – we can project written evidence: a matter of years, probably, and decades, possibly. But centuries?

Taken individually, the ambiguities of these twelfth-century descriptions can be dissected to infer that their authors are describing practices other than falsetto. Taken together, though, the consistent thread – of womanly singing by men – would seem to suggest that falsetto of some sort is being described. This obvious interpretation is countered most notably by Andrew Parrott, who argues that terms such as 'in falso' and 'falsetum' actually refer to a wider range of musical practices which clerics considered inappropriate: falsetto (as we understand the term) could of course be one such practice, but so could chromaticism or improvisation. Further, Parrott argues that 'muliebribus' and 'femineo' were used by the clerics as euphemisms for sounds they considered lascivious or weak: again, this could include falsetto, but it could also refer to soft or self-conscious singing. It is certainly true that medieval churchmen and academics regularly used women as a byword for undesirable and corrupting influences, and not just with reference to vocal matters. And whatever the subject of these cloistered references to women, we might note that they were made from a stance of almost total ignorance: we might even wonder whether, as an adult, Bernard of Clairvaux had ever heard a women actually sing.

---

[40] Bowers, 'The Performing Pitch of English 15th-Century Church Polyphony'.

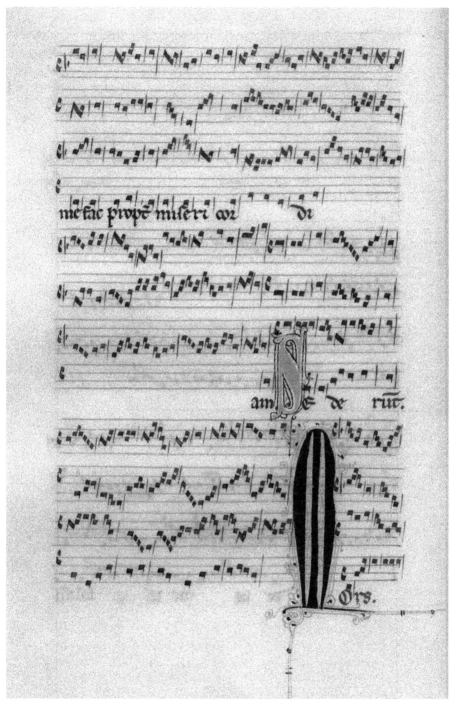

Fig. 3 *Magnus Liber* (I-Fl MS Pluteus 29.1, fol. 7v). The music is shown at actual size, though the wide borders have been cropped; the full page size is approx. 232 × 157 mm – almost exactly the page size of this book. At the bottom can be seen the polyphonic excerpt quoted in Ex. 1.

Perhaps inevitably, given the sporadic evidence and yawning gap in time between the Middle Ages and now, neither argument is wholly provable. When we look closer, though, both arguments allow at least for the possibility of falsetto singing, albeit to radically different degrees. Yet even if we accept the seemingly obvious reading, that falsetto alone is being described, quite what are we accepting? Are we accepting that modern counter-tenors would have been familiar voices to twelfth-century ears? And if we do not accept that the clerics are specifically describing falsetto, are we concluding that only the likes of our tenor and bass voices were the norm? Perhaps the truth lies somewhere other than in these stark alternatives: perhaps *falsetto* (as an occasional method of production) is being solely or partly referred to, though *falsettists* (as a specific vocal type) are not.

At this point we perhaps need to remind ourselves that, whether in chant or polyphony, there was no fixed pitch. With this borne in mind, another possibility presents itself. Without the reference point of a particular note equating to a particular frequency, singers could only gauge the pitch they sang at by what felt 'right' for any single piece. Yet what was right for one singer was not necessarily right for all. Imagine that one week a cantor with a lowish voice intones a particular piece in the middle of his own range. Although some may have to grumble through the lower passages, everyone present can sing the highest notes. The next time the piece is sung, perhaps a cantor with a naturally high voice intones. Again, he chooses a comfortable pitch in his own voice, but in its upper reaches the chant is now too high for the low-voiced singers. Other than reach these notes by 'belting' in the style of a modern show singer, the only viable option for those singers, at this high pitch, is to switch into falsetto for the parts above their comfortable modal range. In doing so, some of these singers may have realised that they had a natural facility for falsetto. With this discovery, they may have been more than happy to indulge themselves in using falsetto whenever the chance arose. In polyphony improvised by soloists, the opportunity for such indulgences would have been great. For those who disapproved, the easiest way to guard against such falsetto singing was to insist on a medium pitch, rather than a high one. With his 'mediocritatem servari in cantu', this may be what Bernard of Clairvaux is stipulating. The significance of variable pitch, though, goes well beyond this. Although lip-service is often paid to variable pitch in early vocal music, the actual implications are worth considering. Fundamentally, if we remove the notion of an empirical pitch standard, our modern notions of vocal types cease to hold much meaning at all. What is a tenor? Or a bass? Nowadays, someone who claims to be a professional tenor or a bass knows what range will be contractually required of him. In the Middle Ages, depending on the day, or the city, or the pitch chosen by the cantor, the singer who comfortably sang a tenor line in Paris last month may, in Rheims today, prefer the prospect of the line above or below. In the Renaissance (when any kind of fixed pitch was still rare) the paucity of vocal classifications for individual singers, or the way in which one singer can appear in records as, say, both tenor and alto, suddenly makes sense.

Returning to our disapproving clerics, it is also important to bear in mind the wider context of these French and English sources. Firstly, they date from the period of the Crusades. For all the sordid *realpolitik* of these campaigns, their nominal motivation meant that they took with them members of the church hierarchy. Men like Odo of Deuil returned with experience of the religious cultures of the Middle East and Iberia. Descriptions of falsetto, then, may represent not so much a strong reality in Christian Europe, as a perceived influence – or even threat – from the Muslim world. John of Salisbury writes elsewhere that 'He who [...] prostitutes the voice to his own desires [...] is revelling with Babylonian strains in a foreign land.'[41] This carries with it more than a whiff of foreign influence. Doubtless some clerics returned keen to experiment with the exotic vocal styles and sonorities they had heard. But to what extent did these practices become established practice in Western Christendom? Do the words of a handful of clerics form a body of supportive evidence? This brings us to the second, and most significant point about the context of our four twelfth-century sources: they are all prohibitions.

Perhaps there is one apparent exception to this – a rubric in an early thirteenth-century source from Beauvais Cathedral. This states that all antiphons on a particular feast day are to be intoned from behind the high altar 'cum falsetto'. This is not a prohibition, true, but when seen in context it surely underlines the pejorative way in which falsetto was typically viewed by the medieval authorities.[42] On the one hand, it seems likely that this usage of 'falsetto' tallies with our own: of the other modern interpretations of 'falsis vocibus' we have discussed, soft-singing from behind the altar could not have been inaudible, and it is difficult to see what role chromaticism or extremes of tempo could have in a simple chant intonation. On the other hand, this 'falsetto' was most certainly not a common practice. The feast day in question was the Feast of Fools, just after Christmas, at which horseplay was the chief ingredient. The horseplay was literal, since the feast included the 'Prose of the Ass', in which a donkey was processed through the church. During mass (celebrated by a boy bishop elected for the day) obscene songs were sung and dances performed, cakes and sausages eaten at the altar, and cards and dice played upon it. It was in this context that the authorities at Beauvais permitted falsetto. The argument that falsetto had a place in the daily round of the medieval church is hardly bolstered

---

[41] 'Qui autem voluptatis aut vanitatis affectus exprimit, qui vocix gratiam prostituit concupiscentiis suis, qui leniciniorum clientulam musicam facit, ignorat quidem canticum Domini, modis Babiloniis festivus in terra aliena.' John of Salisbury, *Frivolities of Courtiers and Footprints of Philosophers [...] the Policraticus of John of Salisbury*, ed. Joseph B. Pike (Minneapolis, 1938), p. 33.

[42] Cf. Wulf Arlt (ed.), *Ein Festoffizuium des Mittelalters aus Beauvais in seiner liturgischen uned musikalischen Bedeutung* (Cologne, 1970), vol. 2, p. 7.

by this kind of reference. The truth is that not a single benign observation (let alone a positive endorsement) of falsetto has yet come to light from northern Europe during the medieval period.

Falsetto and the Medieval Theorists

PERHAPS the closest we come to approval for falsetto comes in a treatise by Jerome of Moravia, who lived in Paris during the latter part of the thirteenth century. Jerome's *Tractatus de musica* is in large part an overview of earlier authors on music, yet it contains original observations on contemporary performance practice. These observations include the following:

> Therefore, in order that ecclesiastical chant may be sung in such an ordered and proper way at the same time by two people or even more, five things are necessary for the singers [...]
>
> The third is, that they should not join unlike voices in chant of this sort, since speaking in common parlance (though this does not agree with the facts of nature) some voices come from the chest, some from the throat and some from the head itself. We call chest voices those that form the notes in the chest; throat voices in the throat; and head voices in the head. Chest voices are strong on deep notes, throat voices on high notes, and head voices on very high notes. Generally, coarse and low voices come from the chest; delicate and very high voices come from the head; while those midway between the two come from the throat. None of these, therefore, should be joined in chant with another [kind], but chest voice with chest voice, throat with throat, and head with head.
>
> But since all voices find their strength from the chest, for this reason it is necessary fourthly that the chant should never be begun so high, especially by those who have head voices, that they do not establish in the chest at least one note which is lower than the others as a foundation for their voice; and they should always begin neither too low, which is to growl, nor too high, which is to shout, but in the middle, which is to sing, in such a way that the chant is not subject to the voice but the voice to the chant. Otherwise sounds of beauty cannot be made.[43]

---

[43] 'Ut igitur tam ordinate simul et debite a duobus vel etiam a pluribus cantetur cantus ecclesiasticus, quinque sunt cantantibus necessaria. ¶ 'Tertium est, ut voces dissimiles in tali cantu non misceant, cum non naturaliter, sed vulgariter loquendo, quedam voces sint pectoris, quedam gutturis, quedam vero sint ipsius capitis. Voces dicimus pectoris que formant notas in pectore; gutturis que in gutture; capitis autem que formant notas in capite. Voces pectoris valent in gravibus; gutturis in acutis; capitis autem in superacutis. Nam communiter voces grosse et basse sunt pectoris; voces subtiles et altissime sunt capitis;

Ex. 2 Ranges and registers, as given by Marchetto of Padua

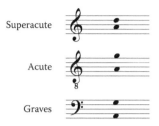

Superacute

Acute

Graves

This passage has been interpreted in a number of different ways. Although it has been assumed by some commentators that Jerome is referring to monophonic chant, this hardly tallies with his stated reason for these rules – namely that by following them 'two people or even more' can sing together: since chant was routinely sung by entire church communities, such small numbers (and their evident need for rules) suggest that Jerome was referring to polyphony of some kind. Even so, what are we to make of Jerome's 'head' voice? On the one hand, 'formant notas in capite' and 'voces subtiles et altissime' are more suggestive of falsetto than modal singing. On the other, Jerome does not use terms such as 'falsa' and 'femineo' which, as we have seen, were commonly used by others at the time. Jerome's avoidance of pejorative language may even indicate a tacit acceptance of this high male singing.

One interesting commentary on vocal registers which might shed some light on Jerome's meaning comes from a northern Italian choirmaster and composer, Marchetto of Padua. Though written around 1317, about fifty years after Jerome's *Tractatus*, Marchetto's theoretical treatise *Lucidarium* nevertheless identifies the same three vocal registers as Jerome (see Ex. 2). So far, so unremarkable. Where Marchetto's text goes further, though, is that he links these registers to notes of the medieval gamut.[44] Presumably Marchetto had in mind here specific pitches – most likely those of an organ he was familiar with, in Padua, Cesena or Verona. Sadly, we have no way

voces vero inter has medie sunt ipsius gutturis. Nulla igitur ex his alteri ligatur in cantu, sed vox pectoris pectorali, gutturis gutturali, capitis autem capitali.
¶ 'Quoniam autem omnes voces vigorem consequuntur ex pectore, ideo quarto necessarium est ut nunquam adeo cantus alte incipiatur, precipue ab habentibus voces capitis, quin ad minus unam notam ceteris bassiorem pro fundamento sue vocis statuant in pectore, et nec nimis basse, quod est ululare, nec nimis alte, quod est clamare, sed mediocriter quod est cantare, ita scilicet ut non cantus voci, sed vox cantui ducetur, semper incipiant. Alias pulchre note formari non possunt.' Jerome of Moravia, *Tractatus de musica*, chap. 25, available online at <http://www.chmtl.indiana.edu/tml/13th/IERTDM2_TEXT.html> [accessed 23 April 2014]. Translation by Hugh Griffith.
[44] Marchetto of Padua, *Lucidarium of Marchetto of Padua: A Critical Edition, Translation, and Commentary*, ed. Jan W. Herlinger (Chicago, 1985), pp. 540–1.

of knowing what Marchetto's assumed pitch was. Even if we did know, the fact that Marchetto provides a one-size-fits-all vocal range suggests that he was only giving a rough average, or an example, of what he had perceived amongst his singers. Nonetheless, the one thing which does stand out is that the range he outlines – two and a half octaves – is larger than the working modal ranges of most male singers. His range for the head voice, which is smaller than the other ranges, would indeed appear to be falsetto.

Writing around the same time as Jerome, Roger Bacon, a Franciscan friar and philosopher then working in Paris, provides evidence that various aspects of exotic singing continued to be practised – despite ongoing clerical disapproval:

> But in our time there has gradually spread through the Church bad practice in the chant, which has declined from the gravity and uprightness of old and lost its gentle and natural goodness through sinking into shameless effeminacy. This is evident in the passion for new harmonies, the dangerous devising of new proses, and an unseemly delight in multiple melodies. The same thing is shown above all by the voices debasing in falsetto the manly and holy harmony, immoderate as boys and licentious as women, almost throughout the entire Church.[45]

By now the subject (harmonised music) and indeed the location (Paris) are familiar. There is a significant change in emphasis, though, from the clerical prohibitions of previous century. Put simply, this is not a prohibition, but a lament. The musicians, one senses, are gaining the upper hand. Bacon refers to the 'universal prevalence' of practices including falsetto, but as he is only known to have had personal association with Paris and Oxford, we can hardly apply this too literally. Indeed, the lack of corroborating evidence from elsewhere in Europe speaks with a silent eloquence. Hugh Griffith points out that instead of 'voces in falseto', one source gives 'voces insulsae' – literally 'unsalted' (i.e. insipid) voices. Even if this is not the correct reading but a corruption of Bacon's original, it may imply that the scribe was not familiar with the phrase 'in falseto' and did not understand what it meant.

By the end of the Middle Ages, falsetto seems to be gaining something of a toe-hold in Europe. This, though, is still a world away from meaning that falsettists, as we know them, were well known. Viewed in isolation, the documentary evidence is simply too thin and too ambiguous to support

---

[45] 'Sed jam per ecclesiam paulatim crevit abusus cantus, qui a gravitate et virtute antiqua cecidit, et in mollitiem inverecundam lapsus, mansuetam et naturalem probitatem amisit; quod novarum harmoniarum curiositas, et prosarum lubrica adinventio multipliciumque cantilenarum inepta voluptas manifestat. Et super omnia voces in falseto harmoniam virilem et sacram falsificantes, pueriliter effusae, muliebriter dissolutae fere per totam ecclesiam comprobant illud idem.' Roger Bacon, *Opera quaedam hactenus inedita*, ed. J. S. Brewer (London, 1859), p. 297. Translation by Hugh Griffith, for Parrott's forthcoming publication.

this view. Those wishing to make a case for the widespread existence of the falsettist in the age of early polyphony, then, are left pointing to evidence within the music. Such internal evidence is to be treated with caution even in later music, but in the case of unaccompanied polyphony, which was sung without reference to a fixed pitch, we should be particularly wary. When we first open a medieval manuscript, seeing the term 'contratenor' beside a vocal line might initially suggest that we are looking at music written for an early equivalent of our own counter-tenor, but one thing which all modern commentators agree on is that this is not so. In early polyphony 'contratenor' simply tells us that this is literally a part written to counter the tenor (plainsong) line. Appellations, then, are of no help. And what of the actual music? Sadly, the notion that 'much information relating to the manner in which church polyphony was performed is encapsulated within the musical notes themselves' is wishful thinking, since this 'information' can be interpreted to support entirely different propositions.[46] Promisingly, we know that almost all medieval polyphony was composed for groups of adult males, and with this knowledge we might hope that the overall compass of the parts would indicate the voice types originally used. Put at its simplest, if medieval polyphony had an overall compass wider than that which basses and tenors could cover, it would suggest that falsettists (or castrati) must also have been involved. However, in reality the narrow total ranges mean that at a higher pitch any piece of polyphony written before the time of Dufay can be comfortably sung by a group of what we would term falsettists, tenors and baritones or, pitched lower, by tenors, baritones and basses. The Parisian organum of Leonin and Perotin typically has a range of one and a half octaves. Even a work as sonically mould-breaking as Machaut's mid-fourteenth-century *Messe de Nostre Dame* has a total range of only two octaves – a compass which a combination of tenors and basses can manage with ease.

So far, this discussion of the early falsetto voice in Europe has centred on practices within the church. There is an inevitability about this, since the church was the fulcrum of literate musical developments in the Middle Ages. Although there is no specific evidence, it is possible that troubadours and *Minnesänger* used falsetto, since the rules which governed musical performance in church did not necessarily apply in the secular world. At least in theory, Paul's dictat that 'women should remain silent in the churches', and the medieval church's related disapproval of womanly singing cited above, had no bearing on how one might sing a *chanson*.[47] Yet in practice, the musical worlds of church and chamber were very closely related. The thirteenth-century motet, for instance, was a secular form,

---

[46] Roger Bowers, 'To Chorus from Quartet', in *English Choral Practice, 1400–1650*, ed. John Morehen (Cambridge, 1995), p. 2.

[47] 1 Corinthians 14:33.

despite its often-religious texts; yet, as the Parisian theorist Johannes de Grocheio makes clear, the motet was the preserve of the intellectual elite: in other words, individuals from the University of Paris who, in turn, were the voices and ears of Notre Dame organum.[48] This, together with the similar ranges of sacred and secular polyphony, suggests that in the church and chamber, vocal practice was similar. There is an argument (the strength of which seems to diminish with time) that instruments had an occasional and limited role to play in medieval secular polyphony. There is no evidence, though, that the falsetto voice, as a specific type, had a role to play.

So, whilst occasional falsetto might have been known to the medieval ear, the case for the falsettist as a recognisable feature of the musical landscape of northern Europe during the medieval period remains unproven – at best possible rather than probable. If the falsettist does indeed have such a shaky provenance we might ask why the voice should have become, in our own time, associated with medieval music. Partly, this was the result of a series of understandable (but ultimately erroneous) deductions. When Tippett unveiled Deller's voice to the wider public in the mid-1940s, he quite correctly presented it not as a discovery, but as a rediscovery. The unspoken logic of this was that if the falsetto voice was not new, and not really something of the immediate past, then it must be old. So far so logical. But how old? Tippett himself believed it to date back at least to the seventeenth century, but to others the fact that this voice had come to light in a medieval building and institution was obviously suggestive of an earlier existence. At the same time, the falsetto voice seemed to slot into existing knowledge of how sacred medieval polyphony was first performed – without boys or women. So, when the Deller Consort came to record Machaut's *Messe de Nostre Dame*, they did so (along with instruments) with Deller's falsetto but no basses. Of course, the Deller Consort was synonymous not just with the whole gamut of early music, but with Deller's own voice. In theory, an alternative scoring of high tenors and basses presented itself to groups at this time, but the combination of heavy, vibrato-laden voices with a lower pitch made the results aurally indigestible. Despite dubious evidence for their usage, the reedy sounds of early instruments offered one way out of this sonic morass. And since these sounded so different from modern instruments, why not compliment the sound with a voice which itself sounded different from modern voices?

Perhaps this is a case of the right premise but the wrong conclusion. Certainly, for those wanting to rediscover the medieval sound-world, a willingness to embrace vocal styles other than our own is a healthy starting position. How, for instance, can we begin to equate any modern vocal technique with the requirements which the ninth-century St Gall monk Notker makes of singers? Particular letters placed above notes in chant

---

[48] Johannes de Grocheio, *De Musica*, discussed in Richard Taruskin, *Oxford History of Western Music* (New York, 2004), vol. 1, pp. 207–8.

books, he says, variously indicate that they should be 'performed with a harsh or percussive attack' ('fragore seu frendore feriatur, flagitat'), 'gargled gradually in the throat' ('gutture gradatim garruletur'), or sung 'with straight or forthright vibratoless [tone]' ('Rectitudinem vel rasuram non abolitionis, sed crispationis rogitat'). Other adjectives Notker uses to describe certain desired sounds include 'ringing', 'sibilant', 'aspirate', 'seizing or grasping', 'light', and 'heavy'. Nor is Notker unique. Although they differ in many details, theorists throughout the Middle Ages are similar in their demand for a flexible voice which can deliver music which is not so much notes with ornaments, as one perpetual ornament. To Notker's list we might add terms, mentioned by other theorists, which appear to describe rapid throat articulation (*bistropha* and *tristropha*), pulsing (*morula* and *tremula*), different speeds of vibrato (*flos harmonicus*), and sliding between non-diatonic pitches (*liquescunt*). In his appraisal of the medieval theorists' approach to singing, Timothy McGee concludes that, far from looking to our own present-day culture to find a suitably fluid and flexible sound image for the medieval voice, we would be better looking to the Eastern Mediterranean countries and India.[49] For the origins of medieval vocal style, then, the evidence of the theorists points in the same easterly direction as we looked in earlier to find the origins of high male singing.

Fluidity is perhaps the key word to understanding the early history of falsetto singing. Good singers – all good singers – were expected to possess a technique which utilised the full capacity of their vocal apparatus. This was not so much an aesthetic whim as a practical necessity. Whether music was performed from memory, improvised, or occasionally sung from a written source, it would always have been sung without a reference to a fixed pitch. And that, as we have seen, potentially requires of singers an ability to move outside their modal vocal ranges. Occasional falsetto, then, was an inevitability. Conservative clerics may not have liked falsetto, but as law-makers their role was largely reactive. The active role, vocally, was taken by the musicians themselves. Creative musicians, of whatever age, will respond to the impetus of a new sonority by exploring its potential. It was only a matter of time before the vocal gamut was expanded to accommodate falsetto as a specific timbre. A hundred miles north of Paris, the greatest musician of the early Renaissance was soon to do just that.

[49] Timothy J. McGee, *The Sound of Medieval Song: Ornamentation and Vocal Style According to the Treatises* (Oxford, 1998), p. 42.

A Famine in Tenors:
The Historically Developing Human Larynx

Physiologically, the human larynx has remained basically unchanged since man became a speaking and singing creature. Taking into consideration the influence upon it of racial types, this mechanism can be used as a reliable measuring device in the determination of basic vocal types and ranges.

Rebecca Stewart[1]

AMONGST all the variables of pitch, contexts and aesthetics, the one constant we might expect to find in a history of the falsetto voice is the instrument itself. The larynx, and human body that houses it, may differ from individual to individual, but the tendency has been to assume that it has not differed from age to age. Glance at the image of any male singer in history, and structurally they look similar to us. If so, then presumably their larynxes are also fundamentally similar.

A violinist would make no such assumptions about his own instrument. By way of illustration, when Corelli reputedly demanded of his pupils that they be able to sustain a *forte* for ten seconds with a single double-stopped down-bow he was, as any aspiring Baroque violinist knows, making a supreme challenge to their technique.[2] That such a demand should seem relatively unremarkable to the same player on a modern violin neatly underlines a truth which the early instrumental world has long taken for granted: namely, that to appreciate the peculiar demands made during any one period in the evolution of musical style, we must also look at the parallel evolution of instrumental technology.

Scholars of early vocal music, on the other hand, have been far less inclined to recognise such a parallel evolution. Although elements of early vocal style and technique have been examined in some depth, the possibility that the physiology of the voice itself has evolved, has been largely ignored. Further, one of the common touchstones of early vocal and choral performance practice has been its relationship to modern performing ensembles: a historical theory is generally thought to be rubber-stamped if it can also be shown to work as a modern practice. By making the understandable assumption that modern vocal types and ranges represent a historical constant, modern writers have created unnecessary problems for themselves. For instance, regarding the original performance practice

---

[1] Rebecca Stewart, 'Voice Types in Josquin's Music', *Proceedings of the Josquin Symposium* (Cologne, 1985), p. 99.

[2] Robert Bremner, *Compleat Tutor for the Violin* (London, *c.* 1760).

of a work by Dufay, his biographer David Fallows writes that 'probability favours the use of pitches that more or less correspond to modern pitch [...] but one could also accept the possibility of transposition downwards by a fourth.'[3] The tacit understanding here is that these two fairly specific pitches work best for modern falsettists and tenors, or modern tenors and basses, and so would have also worked best for Dufay's singers; conversely, the intermediate pitch levels do not work so well for modern performers, and so are not entertained as likely options for Dufay's ensemble. Yet if we remove vocal pitch ranges as historical constants, the likelihood that Dufay was faced with such stark alternatives is also removed. (In any case, we may note that without a fixed pitch, Dufay and his contemporaries could not have practically understood the concept of 'transposition' in this way.)

In fairness to scholars of early vocal practices, we might point out that they are at an obvious disadvantage to their colleagues researching instrumental practices: awareness of the violin's historical capabilities would not be quite so advanced had every early instrument been decaying for hundreds of years under six feet of soil. Neither would we so fully understand the violin – early or modern – if its mechanisms were hidden in the labyrinthine workings of a much larger instrument. In these respects, studies of earlier voices have been hindered. Yet a growing understanding of the relationship between the larynx and the human body, together with measurements of the historical human frame, suggest ways in which the pragmatic vocal demands made in past eras may not match those of our own time. Put at its simplest, a vocal line which the modern choir director would automatically think of as a falsetto part may, five hundred years ago, have proved a better fit for a modal voice.

In 1990 two British otolaryngologists observed two important relationships: first, that a relationship existed between laryngeal size and vocal pitch; second, that laryngeal size is, broadly speaking, related to height.[4] In practical terms – and it should be stressed that the study included exceptions to the trend – the conclusion of this research was that 'a strong correlation between the external laryngeal measurement and speaking fundamental frequency was found.' In other words, the taller the individual the larger the larynx, hence the longer the effective vocal cord length and the deeper the pitch of the voice. Variable factors such as tissue density can somewhat cloud the waters of this correlation, but the trend remains.

---

[3] David Fallows, 'Specific Information on the Ensembles for Composed Polyphony, 1400–1474', *Studies in the Performance of Late Medieval Music*, ed. Stanley Boorman (Cambridge, 1983), pp. 145–59, at p. 119.

[4] R. G. Williams and R. Eccles, 'A New Clinical Measure of External Laryngeal Size which Predicts the Fundamental Frequency of The larynx', *Acta Otolaryngologica* 110 (1990), pp. 141–8.

Table 1 Heights of tenors and basses in British opera choruses, 2000

Company	Tenors		Basses	
	No. of singers	*Average height (cm)*	*No. of singers*	*Average height (cm)*
ENO	12	177.4	12	181.2
Opera North	9	178.9	9	179.8
Royal Opera	12	177.8	10	178.3
Scottish Opera	9	173.8	8	182.6
WNO	11	176.7	9	176.4
All companies	53	177.0	48	179.6

When I included these findings in my first published work on pitch and voices in Tudor music, a reasonable doubt was raised: could we safely apply research on speaking pitch to the modal ranges of singers?[5] Were tenors really shorter than basses? I had, in fact, backed up the findings of the clinical trial by providing data from the Taverner Choir's 1986 television production of the Florentine Intermedi (for which I could access wardrobe measurements): in this production the ten tenors had an mean average height of 177 cm and the ten basses had an average of 179.8 cm. But, accepting that this sample group was too small to be statistically reliable, I undertook a survey of the tenors and basses in the choruses of all Britain's professional opera companies. One reason for choosing this sample group was a wish to avoid including the kind of singer who, though termed 'tenor', commonly sang the top of his part in falsetto: I had come across such singers in amateur and even cathedral choirs, but not on the professional operatic stage. Having set these criteria, this was the most complete population I could access in Britain. The other obvious advantage of this group was that each company's wardrobe department had reliable measurements for each singer. The results of my survey matched those of my earlier data from the Taverner Choir, and the clinical research on speaking voices: the mean average height of the basses was greater than that of the tenors (see Table 1).

From the heights of these 101 singers, on average the tenors were 2.6 cm shorter than the basses.[6] These averages included individuals who did not conform to the pattern: for instance, the chorus of the Royal Opera House at the time included a tenor measuring 190.5 cm (6′3″), and a bass who stood at 165.1 cm (5′5″). It is worth openly acknowledging anomalies such as these, because we can all call to mind individual singers who contradict

[5] Simon Ravens, '"A sweet shrill voice": The Countertenor and Vocal Scoring in Tudor England', *Early Music* 26(1) (1998), pp. 123–136; see also Trevor Selwood, 'Counterarguments', *Early Music* 27(2) (1999), pp. 349–50.

[6] Simon Ravens, 'Countertenor counterblast', *Early Music* 28(3) (2000), pp. 507–8. This, to my knowledge, was the last published evidence regarding this argument.

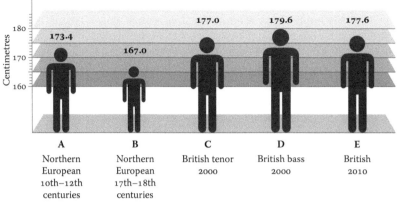

A	**B**	**C**	**D**	**E**
Northern European 10th–12th centuries	Northern European 17th–18th centuries	British tenor 2000	British bass 2000	British 2010

Sources
A, B Steckel, 'New Light on the "Dark Ages"', p. 216
C, D Ravens, 'Countertenor Counterblast'
E *Health, Social Care and Lifestyles* (Health and Social Care Information Centre, 2010)

Fig. 4 Historical heights of adult males

the stereotype of short tenors and tall basses; however, we should be careful not to fall into the trap of confusing anecdotal with statistical evidence. Of course, 'statistical evidence' can itself be a chimera – especially in a field where genetics, age, diet and – above all – human agency are all variables. Doubtless there will be subsequent research which refines our understanding of how singers' heights relate to the pitch of their modal voices, but in the meantime we can at least observe that a correlation seems to exist.

The significance of this correlation for early vocal music becomes clear when we take into account how much shorter human beings were in previous centuries. The science of calculating historical height is as fascinating as it is complex. From any time before the early nineteenth century, when records of military recruits begin to offer us decent written evidence, height can best be ascertained from skeletons. This evidence is obviously not as precise as a modern scientific sampling would offer. Nonetheless, in the fullest recent study, by Richard H. Steckel, a clear 'U' pattern emerges. In the early Middle Ages, and again in the early twentieth century, the typical northern European male stood at around 173.4 cm; between these dates, average male height is estimated to have sunk as low as 167 cm.[7] The growth in height has accelerated markedly since the Second World War, with the 2010 average for adult British males being estimated at 177.6 cm (see Fig. 4). The interaction of the reasons for changes in height – urbanisation, nutrition, war, disease from contact through increased trade, and climate – is fascinating, if ultimately unquantifiable.

[7] Richard H. Steckel, 'New Light on the "Dark Ages": The Remarkably Tall Stature of Northern European Men during the Medieval Era', *Social Science History* 28(2) (2004), pp. 211–28, at p. 216.

All of this implies that the average Renaissance singer (about 10 cm shorter than his modern counterpart) would have had a higher fundamental frequency, and therefore a higher modal singing voice. How much higher? This is impossible to quantify, but (and if any sentence in this book deserves emphasis it is this one) at least we can observe that if a little over 2.6 cm accounts for the difference between a modern tenor and bass, then 10 cm between the average modern and average Renaissance man suggests a very significant difference in the pitch of their modal voices.

Of course, to varying degrees this differential applies to singers of every century from the Middle Ages to our own time, and in the chapters that follow we will occasionally need to remind ourselves of this. There is a temptation, when we see a Purcellian counter-tenor line ascending above the range of a normal modern tenor (even allowing for our higher pitch) to assume that this part must have been written with the falsettist in mind: the much shorter stature and higher voice of the average seventeenth-century man warns us against such an easy assumption. Nor, incidentally, does the relationship between human height and vocal pitch have significance only for high male voices or 'early' music: those who have wondered why much mass-market vocal music from the nineteenth century – Romantic lieder and older hymn-tunes being obvious examples – sits uncomfortably high for today's average singer, will find their answer here.

Related to human height, there is at least one other variable we should consider. As well as environment (particularly nutrition), height is also connected to race. This is an issue as sensitive as it is complex, but the effect of racial flux on vocal types needs addressing. Race is not, in itself, a direct determinant of vocal pitch. Back in 1922 two German geneticists, Bernstein and Schläper, established that Sicily produces one bass to every four tenors, compared to a ratio of five basses to one tenor in Northern Europe.[8] This finding has been cited as evidence of race as a factor in vocal pitch. In fact, race only indicates certain physical characteristics (in our case height being the most salient), which in turn indicate vocal pitch.[9] Shorter races of men – be they Indonesian or Sicilian – will tend to produce higher-pitched voices. However semantic a quibble this may sound, it is significant because, assuming race to be the direct determining factor, commentators have used its apparent immutability to suggest that the vocal tendencies of specific peoples are similarly fixed. In any event race, like height, is not immutable – certainly not as much as it may have seemed in the culture of pre-war Germany. Population movements in the decades since then have diminished racial distinctions.

[8] F. Bernstein and P. Schläper, 'Uber die Tonlage der menschlichen Singstimme', *Sitzungsberichte der Preussichen Akademie der Wissenschaftern* (Berlin, 1922): cf. Wulstan, *Tudor Music*, p. 221.

[9] Robert T. Sataloff, 'Genetics of the Voice', *Journal of Voice* 9(1) (1995), pp. 16–19.

It is certainly true that in past times Scandinavian men have been taller (and therefore had deeper voices) than Mediterraneans. In the middle of the nineteenth century, the average Norwegian man was 169 cm, whilst the Italian was 161 cm. Yet today the figures are proportionally closer, with Norwegians averaging 180 cm compared to the Italians' 176 cm. In other words, in terms of height we see here an averaging-out, which in turn suggests that we now produce more middling voices – baritones and mezzo-sopranos. If we take another obvious characteristic, skin colour, and note how the acceleration in racial flux over the last half-century has produced a greater proportion of indeterminate shades, we can see how a similar movement towards the middle ground could be taking place vocally. The suggestion that we are now producing proportionally more baritones, and fewer tenors and basses, is certainly one borne out by many directors of modern amateur choirs, who lament the discrepancy between the distinct ranges in the score and the more homogenised ranges in front of them. Frederic Hodgson wrote in 1965 that 'The twentieth-century decline in singing is marked by the virtual disappearance of the basso-profundo and the deep contralto, and now there is said to be a famine in tenors.'[10] By implication, if in earlier periods there was a greater variety of vocal ranges available, this would explain why we might find high tenor and low bass parts (as we would regard them) in the same repertoire. Just because Monteverdi's singers were shorter on average, does not mean that he would not have known tall, deep basses.

In reviewing the evidence that historical and modern singers must have had very different capacities, it is interesting to speculate about why early musicians have been reluctant to accept (or attempt to rebut) this argument. As we have already noted, the same musical community has happily recognised the differences between modern and historic instruments. The obvious reason for our reluctance is that, whereas reconstructing and playing Corelli's violin is relatively straightforward, recreating the likely vocal instruments of Dufay's singers is quite beyond us. And, since most historically informed performers approach the music of the past in the hope of finding personal resonances, accepting this limitation (that we are, literally, unable to recreate the personal resonances of early singers) might act as a terminal buffer. Needless to say, this buffer only exists for those who believe that recreating an original performance is an achievable final destination; to those who happily and realistically accept the limitations of their approach, the musical compromises implied by these physical differences do no more than join a list of signals and points.

Ignoring the changing nature of the human voice will always skew our perspective of the forces earlier composers and directors had at their disposal. As we shall see, falsettists were very much part of the vocal pallet

---

[10] Frederic Hodgson, 'The Contemporary Alto', *The Musical Times* 106, no. 1466 (1965), pp. 293–4.

during the Renaissance in Europe. But with higher tenors more commonly available to sing their alto lines, Renaissance composers did not need the falsettist to produce filling on inner parts; rather, their need for the falsettist was to provide colour on the surface.

CHAPTER 3

Renaissance Europe

S O far, almost all of the documentary evidence we have seen regarding the falsetto voice has been written by non-musicians. We now come to a text which is very different, in that it was written by a singer and composer of the front rank. Though not without its own ambiguities, a careful reading of this document helps us to understand how falsetto might have been used at the start of the Renaissance.

Guillaume Dufay and 'submissa voce'

G UILLAUME Dufay was born in or around Cambrai, in northern France, at the end of the fourteenth century, and entered the choir of the town's cathedral in 1409. Ravaged by the French Revolution and two world wars, Cambrai today is an unexceptional northern-French town. But the Cambrai Dufay knew as a boy, and in his last years as a canon of the cathedral, was no mere provincial settlement. In the late Middle Ages it was a major centre in the cloth trade (the town gave its name to cambric) as well as the seat of an archdiocese of immense power. Cambrai's demise is encapsulated in the history of its gothic cathedral, once known as 'the wonder of the Low Countries', but secularised during the French Revolution and used as a stone quarry, finally collapsing in 1809. In its medieval heyday, though, Cambrai's fabulous wealth could compare with that of any European city, as could the lavishness of music heard in its cathedral. The Cambrai choir acted as a magnet for the best musicians in the Low Countries. And the best in the Low Countries were the best in Europe: as Adrian Coclico wrote later in the Renaissance, 'those seen in Belgium, Hainaut, and France [...] who have a singular gift in singing above those of other nations'.[1] Italy, and in particular the Papal Chapel, sought in turn to entice the pick of these musicians further south, and Dufay himself was duly lured there. After travels and work in Italy and Savoy – of which more soon – sometime around his fortieth year Dufay returned to Cambrai.

In finding a market for his talents abroad, Dufay was to prove a model for later Renaissance musicians. Predominantly these itinerant musicians were northerners – Josquin and Lassus were to tread similar paths to and from the south. But in the marginalia of Renaissance music one also finds

---

[1] '[...] in Belgicis, Hannoniensibus et Gallis, qui singulare quoddam donum in canendo prae alijs nationibus habent.': Adrian Petit Coclico, *Compendium musices descriptum ab Adrian Petit Coclico discipulo Josquini de Pres* (Nuremburg, 1552), fol. Hiijv. Translation from MacClintock, *Readings*, p. 31.

Belgians in Prague, Spaniards in Rome, and Swiss in Austria. The result of this was not just the diffusion of musical language, but (to a lesser extent) of performance styles too. By and large, England remained musically aloof during the Renaissance, and needs to be treated separately. At this seminal moment in the development of the falsetto voice, however, Continental Europe offers a more interrelated picture. To judge from the comments of travellers around mainland Europe, although each centre retained its own idiosyncrasies, few places remained wholly immune to new performance trends. Falsetto singing is a case in point. By the middle of the Renaissance, albeit having arrived by myriad routes, falsetto was known in many of the major churches and chapels of Europe. Tracing these routes backwards does not quite lead us to a eureka moment when falsetto became an accepted practice, but the evidence does at least point us to one area. Perhaps not surprisingly this is, give or take a hundred miles, the same place in which, at the end of the previous historical chapter, most observations of 'falsetto' were noted.

Cambrai, during Dufay's later years there, had about a dozen adult singers in its cathedral choir.[2] There were six choirboys too, who formed an independent group, positioned apart from the men in the cathedral. The boys occasionally sang polyphony with the men, but otherwise it was the men alone who sang the music of Dufay and his successors. The first record of an adult male 'superius' (soprano) at Cambrai dates from 1500, after which the presence of over fifty such singers at the cathedral has been identified.[3] But a well-documented instance from quarter of a century earlier has often been cited as evidence of falsetto singing at Cambrai. At Dufay's death-bed in 1474, along with a request for boys and three men to sing his antiphon *Ave regina caelorum*, the composer had requested in his will that the plainsong hymn *Magno salutis gaudio* was to be sung 'submissa voce' by eight clerics:

> Eight of those who are clerics of the church, in *submissa voce* will sing the hymn *Magno salutis gaudio* ... which hymn being finished, altar boys, with their master, and two clerics, will in like manner sing my motet *Ave regina caelorum*.[4]

---

[2] Craig Wright, 'Performance Practices at the Cathedral of Cambrai, 1475–1550', *The Musical Quarterly* 64(3) (1978), pp. 295–328.

[3] 'Duo vicarii quidam Jacobus Castellain tenorista alius superius Johannes de Boves hodie simul recipientur.': Bibliothèque Municipale, Cambrai, 1064, fol. 233 (5 Feb 1500). I am grateful to Professor Craig Wright for providing the original Latin text of this document.

[4] '[...] sint octo ex sociis ecclesie juxta Lecti meum qui, submissa voce cantent hympnum Magno salutit gaudio [...] quo hympno finito pueri altaris, una cum magistro eorum ei duobus ex sociis, inibi similiter presentes decantent motetum meum de Ave Regina Cælorum.': Franz Xaver Haberl, *Wilhelm du Fay* (Leipzig, 1885), p. 516.

What is the meaning of 'submissa voce'? The first thing we should note is that a medieval churchman would have been familiar with this term from liturgical rubrics – in which it was used to instruct clerics to intone certain passages quietly: in this context it was a descriptor of volume, not pitch. In their account of his will, though, Dufay's executors translate this into French as 'en fausset' – a term which, in turn, is today commonly translated into English as 'in falsetto'. But if we rely on the executors' translation, in its modern meaning, we are faced with the unlikely conclusion that all eight clerics sang the plainsong hymn in falsetto. And if this was the case, and there were so many adult sopranists present, why were boys alone required to sing – 'in like manner' – the top line in the four-part polyphonic piece? Boys singing in falsetto? We are also faced with the apparent riddle that *sub*missa singers such as these would generally sing the *sopra*no part in the cathedral. Something here does not quite add up. But perhaps there is a semantic route that leads us out of this maze. Bearing in mind the subdued context of the composer's death-bed, could 'submissa voce' not be read in its literal, liturgical meaning, as 'in a submissive (quiet) voice'? In this sense it, too, would refer to volume rather than pitch, in the same way that writers often used 'alta voce' to mean 'in a high (loud) voice'? Without mentioning these terms specifically, the contemporary German theorist Conrad von Zabern suggests a way in which singing 'under the voice' and falsetto could indeed have been synonymous. Von Zabern writes that a good singer of chant will sing loudly ('grossius') in his lower range, but quieter ('subtilius') as the voice ascends: the logical extension of this approach is that a male singer will end up moving into falsetto – albeit a quiet one.[5] Actually, if we imagine ourselves in the context of the clerics around Dufay's death-bed, and sing a melody as quietly as possible, we (at least men) will find our natural vocal production tending towards falsetto at a surprisingly low pitch. From all this we can hesitantly deduce that in 1474 'submissa voce' meant a vocal style which embraced something we might recognise as falsetto, but only as a by-product of a subdued mode of singing.

The scene at Dufay's death-bed, fraught with ambiguities as it is, carries with it one significant aid to our understanding: it deals with a specific piece of music, the range (if not the pitch) of which we can verify. (Few other descriptions of performances from this period refer so specifically to identifiable pieces of music. Indeed, we always run risks in assuming that early instances of 'falsetto' singing refer to written music at all. Right through until the Renaissance and beyond, a great deal of choral polyphony was sung 'super librum' – in other words, with each singer improvising on

---

[5] 'Grossius suce tubalius in acutis…et subtilius in acutis.': Conrad von Zabern, *De modo bene cantandi* (Mainz, c. 1473): cf. Karl-Werner Guempel, *Die Musiktrakte Conrads von Zabern* (Wiesbaden, 1956), p. 276.

a given piece of chant.[6] For such music, notions of stratified parts, ranges and vocal designations are anachronistic.) A glance at the music Dufay composed during his years at Cambrai, which typically has a range of around two and a half octaves, adds weight to the argument that he was familiar with men singing in falsetto (see Ex. 3). Whilst this range is not as extensive as the three-octave range typical of modern music composed for men and boys, it nevertheless marks a very significant increase in range from the music of Machaut and his generation. Unlike that repertoire, or indeed his own earlier work, Dufay's mature music cannot be sung by today's tenors and basses alone. In fact, its range is ideal for an ensemble of men's modal voices on the lower parts, with either falsettists or low boys' voices – or both – on the top part.

WERE it only Dufay's will, and its translation by his executors, which conflated 'submisse voce' and 'en fausset', we might be excused for attaching little significance to it. But the same terms are similarly used in another Cambrai document, this time dating from 1536:

> It is said to the master of the choirboys that he may make provision for some new boys and may teach the boys of the choir to sing in *submisse voce* or, as they say, in falsetto.[7]

From the original Latin, 'puerorum', 'submisse' and 'fousset' all pose questions of context and translation. 'Puerorum' could refer to boys of any age – including those whose voices were changing. Certainly if we think of the Cambrai boys singing like fledgling Anglican cathedral choristers today, then having them taught to sing 'falsetto' (in anything like our understanding of the term) would make no sense. If, on the other hand, their natural mode of singing was more akin to the modern 'Continental' choirboy tone, then any use of head voice (as we refer to the upper boy's voice) would have needed to be taught.[8] So, whilst it is not easy to see any particular virtue in boys being specifically taught to sing quietly, if this was part-and-parcel of developing a quieter head voice, it may have had the great advantage of encouraging the development of falsetto as the voice

---

[6] Johannes Tinctoris, *Liber de arte contrapuncti* (1477), 2/20, available online at <http://www.chmtl.indiana.edu/tml/15th/TINCPT2_TEXT.html> [accessed 25 April 2014]. Cf. Andrew Parrott, 'A Brief Anatomy of Choirs, c. 1470–1770', in *The Cambridge Companion to Choral Music*, ed. André de Quadros (Cambridge, 2012), pp.7–26, at p. 8.

[7] 'Dicatur magistro puerorum quod provideat habere aliquos novos pueros et faciat ipsos pueros chori submisse voce en fousset cantare.': Bibliothèque Municipale, Cambrai, 1070, fol. 182v. I am grateful to Professor Craig Wright for providing the original Latin text of this document.

[8] Anecdotally, George Malcolm, who in the 1960s was Director of Music at Westminster Cathedral (where the boys were famed for their 'Continental' tone), claimed that 'good singing is a form of shouting'.

Ex. 3 Guillaume Dufay, *Ave regina caelorum a 4*, conclusion

began to change. Extending the shelf-life of a boy's voice had the obvious advantage of increasing the musical experience on the soprano part, and this, in turn, offered composers the chance to increase the range and demands of their polyphonic music.

Although the above reading makes liberal use of the word 'if', the resulting scenario – of boys learning to use their head voices as they began to change – does seem to tally with evidence regarding the cathedral's sopranists. To judge from their numbers, far from being disparaged (as we have seen they were by earlier church authorities) male sopranists at Cambrai were evidently coveted and actively recruited. Who were these individuals? Although older singers were sometimes recruited, in large part the Cambrai sopranists were young men – 'juvenes'. (The fact that they were admitted as vicars and not choirboys, incidentally, tells us that these 'youths' were post-adolescent.) Yet the implication that the skill of falsetto singing was sometimes introduced before, or at least during, the changing of the boys' voice suggests that at Cambrai the singing of boys and falsettists was very much seen as a continuum. Certainly our own neat distinction between boys and adult falsettists does not hold true for Cambrai. And other documents, which tell us that sopranos were to be admitted 'as long as their voices shall last', reinforce the image of the typical Cambrai falsettist as being not so much an adult singer with a fully formed and dependable technique, as a choirboy's voice extended as far as possible into adulthood. At Cambrai it was evidently realised (as Deller and others were to realise five hundred years later) that some boys, even as their speaking voices broke, retained their capacity for singing in a high head voice.

However influential Dufay was, it would only perpetuate a romanticised 'great composer' myth to see him as operating in isolation. Not just his fellow musicians at Cambrai, but those active elsewhere in northern France, were seemingly party to this new vocal culture. Around 1470, at the lavish Burgundian court of Charles the Bold (with which Dufay had earlier been associated) there was a polyphonic repertoire with a two-and-a-half octave range, as well as an all-adult choir:

> Item: for singing chant of the book there shall be at least six high voices, three tenors, three contrabasses and two means [...][9]

What exactly is meant by 'chant of the book' ('chant du livre')? Does it mean the same as 'super librum' – improvised polyphony, or does it mean 'from the book' – written polyphony? Either way, the fact remains that at the Burgundian court there was a singing group similar to the adult choir Dufay had in Cambrai.[10]

The Sopranists of Renaissance Italy

A N isolated genius he was not, but we certainly get a sense of Dufay as a practically responsive and innovative composer when we compare the range of his later music with that he wrote during his earlier years in Italy and Savoy. Between 1428 and 1437, he served in the pope's own choir, the Cappella Pontificia. The mid-fifteenth century was a time of radical change for this institution. By 1480 the new Sistine Chapel had been built, and the Cappella Pontificia rebranded as the Cappella Sistina. During Dufay's

---

[9] 'Item pour le chant du livre y aura du moyns six haultes voix, troys teneurs, troys basses contres et deux moiens [...]': Fallows, 'Specific Information on the Ensembles, p. 119; Craig Wright, 'Dufay at Cambrai: Discoveries and Revisions', *Journal of the American Musicological Society* 28 (1975), pp. 175–229, at p. 179.

[10] Cf. Parrott, 'A Brief Anatomy of Choirs', p. 9.

time in Rome, though, the fundamental nature of this famous choir was becoming established. To judge from the archival records, after 1425 use of the term 'puer' suggests that boys were twice briefly experimented with as part of the chapel. But if we think of these 'boys' as being young trebles, we are probably wide of the mark, for 'puer' can also mean 'servant' and 'bachelor'. One of the 'boys', Bartholomeus Poignare, was seventeen when he entered the chapel for a period of eight years, which suggests that at least some of these singers may have been young men.[11] Whatever their precise nature, after 1441, when the term 'puer' disappears from the records, the choir seems to have become adult-only.[12]

Neither of these periods with younger men coincided with Dufay's tenure in Rome, which suggests that the music he wrote for the chapel was sung by men only. Firmly identifying works Dufay wrote specifically for the papal chapel has proved difficult, but the most likely contenders – works such as *Nuper rosarum flores* – typically have a range of around two octaves.[13] It is possible that the top line in this music was taken by men singing exclusively in falsetto, but there is no specific evidence for this. In truth, the whole concept of specialised voice-types remains somewhat anachronistic for this music, and if falsetto was used by singers it was more likely used as an adjunct to their modal voice. Even as late as 1500, a letter to the Duke of Mantua from an elderly 'contratenore' singer, Jachetto de Marvilla, suggests that if singers on lower parts used falsetto at all, it could hardly have been the staple of their technique: 'I have not lost any of my voice, except for the falsetto, which I never had anyway.'[14] Since Jachetto sang the contratenor part and refers to his lack of falsetto, it is worth stating a wider but fundamental point here: there is no evidence that the 'contratenor' part was sung by falsettists during the Renaissance. Tinctoris's remark that 'The Contratenor is he who sings contratenor' might strike us as comically uninformative but, however unwittingly, it perhaps conveys just how unremarkable were the part and its singers.[15]

[11] Reinhard Strohm, *The Rise of European Music, 1380–1500* (Cambridge, 1993), p. 163.

[12] Although an engraving of Mass in the chapel from 1578 by Etienne Dupérac, which seems more literal than figural, does appear to show boys singing in the choir loft.

[13] Perhaps confusingly, although this work was written for the dedication of the Cathedral in Florence, it was probably the Capella Sistina that performed it on that occasion.

[14] 'Io non ho persa ne la voce nel cantare salvo lo falxeto che non have may io cantorò fine ala morte per natura [...]': Lewis Lockwood, *Music in Renaissance Ferrara, 1400–1505* (Oxford, 1984), p. 185.

[15] 'Contratenorista est ille qui contratenorem canit.': Johannes Tinctoris, *Diffinitorium musicae*, ed. Edmond de Coussemaker (Paris, 1864–76; repr. Olms, 1963), p. 180. Also available online at <http://www.chmtl.indiana.edu/tml/15th/TINDIF_TEXT.html> [accessed 25 April 2014].

Although it was about to change, the papal chapel's repertoire during Dufay's time there was predominantly chant and *falsobordone* (a formula for improvising harmony around a given chant). This is perhaps the reason why the Sistine archives tell us nothing about the voices of the singers, giving us only their names. It is only towards the end of the fifteenth century, as the compass of Roman polyphony increased and parts become more stratified, that voice-types make an appearance in Vatican records. The first documentary evidence of adult male sopranos in Rome comes from the 1470s, when Pope Sixtus IV began engaging them (alongside boys) for the Cappella Giulia of St Peter's.[16] In these Vatican documents the singers are variously termed 'supra', 'supran', 'suprano' and 'soprano' – a neat etymological reminder that defining the role of these singers was work in progress. One of these men, Egidius Crispini, appears to have been employed by the Duke of Savoy about ten years previously, which confirms that he (at least) was a mature adult and not an adolescent waiting for his broken voice to settle.[17] A similar development was taking place in northern Italy: writing from Milan in January 1473, Duke Galeazzo Maria Sforza instructed Gaspar van Weerbecke to bring back from Flanders and Picardy '10 good sopranos, a high contratenor such as Bovis, a tenor such as Peroto and two *contrabassi*'.[18] (Although Spain was to become the chief provider of sopranists to Italian choirs later in the Renaissance, during the fifteenth century Flemish falsettists were in demand.) To judge from the overall vocal range of music known to have been sung by the Cappella Sistina at the end of the fifteenth century, it was around this time that adult sopranos also appeared in that institution.

The question is, who were these adult sopranos in Italian choirs – castrati, falsettists, or both? Taken at face value, the evidence points to their being falsettists, since castrati were not mentioned in Roman records until the 1560s. And perhaps they were. Yet we must be cautious here. Until Sixtus V sanctioned their use in a papal bull of 1589, castrati remained taboo within the church.[19] But taboo or not, there is good evidence that the first documented castrati in Rome were not the first in reality. Unpicking this history is far from straightforward. One of the first historians of the papal choir, Matteo Fornari, was aware of (and even cited) evidence pointing to the existence of castrati in the Vatican before they were officially sanctioned.

[16] Franz Xaver Haberl, 'Die romische Schola Cantorum und die papstlichen Kapellsanger bis zur Mitte des 16. Jarhunderts', *Baustein fur Musikgeschicte* 3 (1888), at p. 237.

[17] Marie-Therese Bouquet, 'La cappella musicale dei duchi di Savoia dal 1450 al 1500', *Rivista italiana di musicologia* 3 (1968), pp. 233–85, at p. 283.

[18] Cf. Stewart, 'Voice Types', p. 126.

[19] 'Cum pro nostro pastorali munere', 27 Sept 1589, in *Collectionis Bullarium, brevium, aliorumque diplomatum sacro sanctae Basilicae Vaticanae* (Rome, 1752), vol. 3, p. 172.

Perhaps Fornari was uneasy with admitting that Sixtus V was reacting to events, rather than prescribing policy. Either way, Fornari misled his mid-eighteenth century readers into believing that all the Cappella Sistina's sopranists were falsettists.[20] A singer masquerading under different names, but most likely the Spaniard Diego Vasquez, is described as 'eunuco' in the Sistine Diaries in mid-1588. Yet this singer was admitted (without reference to his vocal nature) a year earlier, along with another Spaniard known to have been a castrato.[21] Going back even further, as early as 1565 a letter from Cosimo de Medici in Florence asks his ambassador in Rome to procure a castrato from either the Cappella Sistina or Cappella Giulia. Similarly, six years later the Mantuan court secretary, charged with tracing the whereabouts of a castrato in Rome, reports back to his Duke that shortly after the singer's arrival in the city 'he entered the papal chapel'.[22] Castrati in Rome seem to have been an open secret. References from the 1550s to a 'Soprano maschio' in Rome, and 'cantoretti Francese' in Ferrara, are equivocal, but in both cases there is circumstantial evidence that these little-used terms denoted castrati. In the latter case, the singers in question may well include the 'castrato Francese' referred to in the same Mantuan archive. This, and other correspondence of Duke Guglielmo of Mantua, confirm that France, as well as Spain, was producing castrati towards the end of the Renaissance.

How far back did the practice of hiding the true identity of castrati reach? From the sixteenth century, when Vatican archives more consistently identify both vocal type and nationality, it appears that there were a significant number of Spaniards among the Roman sopranos. Indeed, throughout the Renaissance, Spain was to prove the chief exporter of castrati to Rome. As we have already seen, there are suggestions that in earlier centuries Spain produced castrati singers. With only pointillist evidence it is impossible to state categorically that Spain had an old tradition of castrati which moved seamlessly into the Renaissance. But from as early as 1506, in the archives at Burgos Cathedral, there is evidence pointing to the selection of singing boys ('caponado') for castration.[23] Could Spain have been providing Rome with castrati as early as this? We are unlikely ever to know for sure. Establishing historical facts is difficult enough when the issues were recorded overtly; when they were executed covertly, we are

---

[20] Giuseppe Gerbino, 'The Quest for the Soprano Voice: Castrati in Sixteenth-Century Italy', *Studi Musicali* 32(2) (2004), pp. 303–57, at p. 306.

[21] The tangled identity of this singer, and the knotty history of the Renaissance castrati in general, is eloquently unraveled by Gerbino in 'The Quest for the Soprano Voice'.

[22] Richard Sherr, 'Gugliemo Gonzaga and the Castrati', *Renaissance Quarterly* 33(1) (1980), pp. 33–56, at p. 35.

[23] 'La cual todo mandarin guarder de aquí adelante, e que tomen un mozo tresado, que nombrará el señor provisor, caponado, que tiene buena voz, por mozo de coro.': cf. Angel Medina, *Los atributos del capon* (Madrid, 2001), p. 48.

left with little more than conjecture. Suspicion has always hung over the nature of the Spanish sopranists: we even catch a whiff of this in the entry on the Sistine Choir from the first *Grove* dictionary, in which the soprano falsetto voice is described as coming 'from Spain, in which country it was extensively cultivated, by means of some peculiar system of training, the secret of which has never publicly transpired'.[24] Incidentally, the assertion that illustrious Spanish composers such as Escobedo, Morales and Victoria were also falsettists is perhaps based on a misreading of Burney's *General History*.[25] Following a mention of Spanish falsettists, Burney refers to Andrea Adami's list of Spanish composers. Admittedly Burney's text on this issue is open to misreading, but the prosaic truth is that neither Adami, the Sistine diaries, nor any other contemporary source, make reference to the specific voices of these men.

Unpicking the evidence of these various clandestine references, it is tempting to wonder whether in Italy the terms 'falsettist' and 'sopranist' were no more than euphemisms for 'castrato'. Undoubtedly the terms were used as terminological cloaks for certain castrati, but that was not their sole use. From Naples in 1545 there survives a fulsome report of a *commedia* in which 'the music was truly heavenly; it was outstanding because Dentice with his falsetto and Brancaccio with [his] bass performed miracles.'[26] Revealingly, there were two Dentices, Luigi and Fabrizio, involved in this performance. Fabrizio, who is described in the report as 'son of Luigi', was only a child at the time, and played one of the female lead characters. By implication, then, the falsettist was Luigi who, as a father, could not have been a castrato. Luigi, incidentally, was a well-travelled musician, and the suggestion has been made that amongst his attested travels to Spain and the Low Countries, he also made a secret visit (with Lassus) to the court of Henry VIII in England. However intriguing this possibility, there are good reasons to believe that it is more fiction than fact.[27]

Proven fatherhood aside, there is another good reason why some of the Italian sopranos could not have been castrati: from the letters of agents trying to secure their services from Spain and elsewhere, it becomes apparent that there were simply not enough castrati to go around. They were a great rarity, with salary demands to match. Girolamo Negri, reporting back to Mantua from Spain, remarks that there were 'not more

[24] Sir George Grove (ed.), *A Dictionary of Music and Musicians (a. d. 1450–1880)* (London, 1878–99), vol. 2, p. 521.

[25] Giles, *History and Technique of the Counter-Tenor*, p. 40: cf. Charles Burney, *A General History of Music from the Earliest Ages to the Present*, ed. Frank Mercer (London, 1935), vol. 2, p. 240.

[26] 'Onde la musica fu veramente celeste; e massime perchè il Dentice con il suo Falsetto, ed il Brancaccio col Basso ferno [fecerono] miracoli.': Richard Wistreich, *Warrior, Courtier, Singer: Giulio Cesare Brancaccio and the Performance of Identity in the Late Renaissance* (Aldershot, 2007), pp. 24–5.

[27] Wistreich, *Warrior, Courtier, Singer*, pp. 32–41.

than six really excellent ones' in the whole country.[28] If the Duke of Mantua balked at their salary demands, the average Italian cathedral could not have even entertained the idea of engaging castrati. This is borne out by Lodovico Grossi da Viadana, choirmaster at the cathedral of Mantua at the end of the sixteenth century. In the preface to a publication of his sacred works Viadana writes:

> in these *Concerti* falsettists will make a better effect than the natural Sopranos, because the boys normally sing carelessly and with little grace, and furthermore because listened to from distance it sounds better; but there is no doubt, one cannot pay a good natural Soprano with just coppers; and they are rare.[29]

Viadana's words are initially confusing – though the reason for this confusion is itself telling: loathe to use the word 'castrati', he uses the paradoxical term 'soprani naturali'. In one sense, of course, castrati are completely *un*natural, but Viadana follows the ethos of the time, in which it was the policy of the church to ask no questions about how a eunuch came to be so; rather, Viadana simply observed that the men in question sang with their natural speaking voice, and not in falsetto. Yet in avoiding the term 'castrato', Viadana brackets these singers with boys, since they were also 'natural' sopranos. Through the semantic thicket, Viadana's meaning is clear: the pecking order for a choir soprano line is castrati if possible, but if not, falsettists rather than boys. Robert (Gregory) Sayer, an English Benedictine who died in Venice in 1602, wrote that 'now the voices of the castrati are so desirable for singing the praise of God that they are beyond price'.[30]

Nor should we imagine that Italy was alone in its demands for Spanish sopranists. Documents from the Habsburg Court Chapel in Prague tell us that it employed a number of 'discantisten' (soprano) singers from Spain, one of whom, Martín de Lara, was with the chapel from 1570 until 1612.[31] The nature of these singers is not specified, but since falsettists could be

---

[28] Sherr, 'Gugliemo Gonzaga and the Castrati', p. 36.

[29] 'Che in questi Concerti faranno miglior effetto i Falsetti, che i Soprani naturali, si perche per lo più i Putti cantano trascuratamente, e con poca gratia, come anco perche si è atteso alla lontananza, per render più vaghezza; non vi è però dubbio, che non si può pagare con denari un buon Soprano naturale; ma se ne trovano pochi.': Lodovico Grossi da Viadana, *Cento concerti ecclesiatici* (Venice, 1602), p. 3.

[30] Gregory Sayer, *Clavis regia sacerdotum, casuum conscientiae* (Venice, 1615); facsimile available online at <http://reader.digitale-sammlungen.de/en/fs1/object/display/bsb10497192_00178.html> [accessed 25 April 2014]. Cf. P. Defaye and J. P. Sauvage, 'Les Castrats: hypothèses phoniatriques', *Les Cahiers d'O.R.L.* 19(10) (1984), pp. 925–30.

[31] Cf. Carmello Peter Comberiati, *Late Renaissance Music at the Habsburg Court* (New York, 1987), p. 30.

trained anywhere, we might initially infer that there was indeed something distinctive about these Spaniards: that they were castrati. On the other hand, one of the discantists, Peter de Nasera, is elsewhere listed as a bass; assuming that both these designations were accurate, Nasera could hardly have been a castrato. The evidence, then, points in both directions – towards the Spanish discantists' including both falsettists and castrati. However untidy this dual meaning of 'discantisten' may be, in one way it makes obvious sense of the situation. After all, with castrati being at such a premium across the Continent, it would hardly be surprising to find falsettists filling the demand for sopranists. And so it proves.

The case of Luca Conforto is particularly interesting. Conforto was a member of the Cappella Sistina from 1581–5, and was later eulogised by Pietro della Valle: 'I remember the falsettist Gio. Luca, a great singer of throat articulations and passage work, who could sing as high as the stars.'[32] In 1586, despairing of finding a suitable castrato in Rome, Scipione Gonzaga wrote to the Duke of Mantua concerning Conforto's voice:

> He usually sings soprano, but when he was in the papal chapel he always sang, so I understand, contralto, perhaps to avoid joining his falsetto to the natural voices of the castrati.

In a letter a week later Gonzaga clarifies his meaning, saying that when Conforto sang contralto he did so 'in full voice' ('voci piene').[33] Aside from further underlining the pre-history of castrati in Rome, where they sang alongside falsettists, these comments also emphasise that falsetto could be a facet of any singer's technique. A comment about a Neapolitan courtier, Ettore Gesualdo, is revealing of a similar versatility: 'With regard to music [...] he has a rather good tenor voice. He also sings soprano, but his voice in this range is not as true, although he sings gracefully.'[34]

The acceptance of adult sopranists in Rome, Cambrai and elsewhere did not mean that boys were universally dispensed with as polyphonists. Staffing, or partly staffing, a soprano line with boys had financial benefits,

---

[32] 'Mi ricordo di Gio: Luca Falsetto, gran Cantore di gorge, e di passaggi, che andava alto alle stele.': Pietro della Valle, 'Della musica dell'età nostra' (Rome, 1640), in *Lyra Barberina Amphichordos*, ed. Giovanni Battista Doni (Rome, 1763), vol. 2, p. 255 (my translation): cf. Richard Wistreich, 'Reconstructing Pre-Romantic Singing Technique', in *The Cambridge Companion to Singing*, ed. John Potter (Cambridge, 2000), pp. 178–91, at pp. 180–1.

[33] '[...] e di soprano tuttavia nel tempo che egli stette in cappella di N. S.re canto sempre, si come intendo, il contralto, forse per non accoppiar il suo falsetto alle voci naturali de'castrati.': Sherr, 'Gugliemo Gonzaga and the Castrati', p. 43.

[34] 'Quanto alia musica canta la parte sua a libro in quella piu vaga maniera che possa farlo un gentilhuomo. Ha voce di tenore assai buona. Canta anco il soprano ma la voce in questa parte non e tanto sincera, benche egli sia graziosa.': cf. Antony Newcomb, 'Carlo Gesualdo and a Musical Correspondence of 1594', *Musical Quarterly* 104(4) (1968), pp. 409–36, at p. 434.

as well as ensuring a future generation of musically literate singers. In this sense, the adult-only Cappella Sistina was exceptional. Elsewhere in Italy soprano lines were more commonly taken by an *ad hoc* mixture of boys and adult men. At St Mark's in Venice, as at Cambrai, a grey area between the adults and boys was occupied by the *zaghi cantadori* – a group of older boys and young men training for the priesthood, who were trained musically by the *maestro di cappella*.[35] This fluid state of affairs might seem unusual when compared to our own culture in which, primarily for social reasons, distinctions between boys and men in choirs are more rigidly maintained.

'Voce mutate'

W E now come to the species 'voce mutate' – a twin-boled tree of words which, in miniature, seems to encapsulate much of the problem we have in defining the 'counter-tenor' as a whole. As with the term 'counter-tenor', 'voce mutate' comprises two conjoined words which (language being language) we instinctively assume to carry a singular meaning. In fact, the term 'voce mutate' branches out into a variety of languages, and this should alert us to a geographical spread which (allied to a significant historical spread) in turn signals different contexts and thus different meanings. Sure enough, when we examine these contexts, we realise that 'voce mutate' is a misleadingly simple term carrying meanings which are often subtly (and sometimes radically) different. In trying to trace these meanings, readers should be warned that they will discover no clearly formed tree, but rather a dense thicket.

At the root of the term are two Latin words: firstly 'vox', which most obviously translates as 'voice', but in musical contexts is also used to mean 'part', or even 'note'; and 'mutare', which can carry the meanings of 'moved', 'changed', 'varied' and 'transformed'. Just as 'contra-tenor' first crops up as a term to indicate a part (not a voice) below (not above) the tenor, so when 'vocum mutatio' first appears in treatises, it indicates nothing to do with changing voices, but with the renaming of notes when moving between different hexachordal scales. Such specific references can be traced back to early fourteenth-century writers like Jacob of Liège, but they really have their roots in theories of solmisation (attributing syllables to notes in scales – do, re, mi, etc.) which date back to around 1100. So when Tinctoris, in the early Renaissance, offers the definition 'mutatio est unius vocis in aliam variatio', he is not telling us that one voice can change into another, but rather repeating the medieval meaning that 'mutation is the changing

---

[35] Masataka Yoshioka, 'Singing the Republic: Polychoral Culture at San Marco in Venice (1550–1615)', unpublished Phd dissertation (University of North Texas, 2010), p. 49; available online at <http://digital.library.unt.edu/ark:/67531/metadc33220/m2/1/high_res_d/dissertation.pdf> [accessed 4 April 2014]

of one pitch name into another.'[36] The context in which Tinctoris writes this (in a chapter on moving between hexachords) makes his meaning unequivocal. Other writers, sadly, are less easy to decipher, and we need to bear in mind a variety of possible meanings in the contexts that follow.

Confusingly, from the period just before Tinctoris we find an example of 'voces … mutatae' which seems to mean something else entirely. In the constitution of the choir-school of Notre Dame in Paris, around 1410, comes the following passage:

> Furthermore, the master of singing is to teach the boys at the appointed times: plainsong primarily, and also counterpoint and some good, decent discants, but no dissolute or improper songs; and he should not make them expend so much effort on such things that they fail to progress in grammar. Let it be particularly noted that in our Church discant is not in use, but is prohibited by the statutes, at least for those voices that are called changed [voces quae mutatae dicuntur].[37]

This calls to mind the twelfth-century Cistercian prohibitions we read earlier. The most obvious reading is that, whilst boys may sing upper parts (so long as these are not ostentatious), any such singing by 'changed voices' is prohibited: in this context, 'mutatae' suggests men singing in falsetto. The only other possible reading is that 'voces' means 'parts' or 'notes' – as the word could do in later musical history – but there is no evidence elsewhere in the statute that the author had this usage in mind; nor does this passage make obvious sense with such a reading.

Also from the middle of the fifteenth century, the motet *Gaude virgo* by the northern French (or possibly Belgian) composer Battre makes an intriguing reference to 'mutate voces'. The upper part in the opening section of the work is marked 'mutate voces'; in the following section, parts of similar written range are marked for boys – 'pueri' (see Ex. 4).[38] The apparent implication here is that 'mutate voces' sang in the same range as the boys, but were somehow distinct from them. Again, this would point to them being falsettists or (if we admit the possibility of their existence in northern Europe at this time) castrati. The only other reading of this scoring

---

[36] Johnannes Tinctoris, *Expositio manus* (Naples, c. 1475), chap. 7. Translation by Ronald Woodley.

[37] 'Porro Magister cantus statutis horis doceat pueros. Planum canabus, et contrapunctum, et aliquos discantus honesto; non cantilenas dissolutas, impudicasque, nec faciat eos tantum insistere in talibus, quod perdant in grammatica profectum. Altento maxime, quod in Ecclesia nostra, discantus non est in usu, sed per statuta prohibitus, saltem quoad voces quae mutatae dicuntur.': Jean Chartier, *L'Ancien chapitre de Notre-Dame de Paris et sa maîtrise, d'après les documents capitulaires (1326–1790)* (Paris, 1897), pp. 67–8. Translation by Hugh Griffith.

[38] Cf. Fallows, 'Specific Information on the Ensembles', pp. 122–3.

Ex. 4 H. Battre, *Gaude virgo,* opening

is that the word 'mutate' is actually an instruction to the singer(s) of that part to 'move' the line down by an octave. Although within a hundred years the words 'mutate voces' would refer to precisely this manner of transposed performance, it has to be said that from the time of Battre no theorist is yet known to offer such an explanation of the term. And in this case, such an octave shift would result in the harmonic *faux-pas* of parallel-fifth and second-inversion chords. The most likely reading of this performance indication, then, is that it suggests falsetto singing at a time and place not far removed from Dufay's Cambrai.

Terms related to 'mutate voces' are found elsewhere in Europe: for instance, in Portuguese 'tipre mudado' translates as 'changed soprano', and seems to refer to a specific type of singer – most likely a falsettist or a castrato. A 1604 document from a church in Lisbon refers to 'a very good changed Soprano that sang with much grace'.[39] However, the Italian term 'voce mutata', which has commonly been translated in the same way, may well refer to something else altogether. Writing in Bologna in 1516, Pietro Aron makes quite explicit that 'vocum mutate' singing soprano parts are not falsetto voices, but 'manly singers' who would ordinarily sing alto or bass parts. In Aron's text, the potential ambiguity of 'mutatae' is compounded by that of 'voces'.

> On the manner and composition for voices that are said to be changed [vocum quae mutate dicuntur]. Chap. 46

> Indeed, since vocal works are sometimes composed for four parts in which all the voices are said to be changed, I will explain how this ought to be done. Voices of this kind are said to be changed for the reason that they are not capable of reaching the pitch attained by boys. The cantus itself in this kind of composition, because it is customarily constituted as a low part, may not be able to be sung by a boy's voice, or sung in falsetto; rather, it is sung by a manly voice, that is, by those who customarily sing alto or bass.[40]

Aron goes on to explain that this kind of composition is created by reducing the overall compass of the parts so that the work can be sung by men's (modal) voices alone. Whilst Aron's words are directed at composers, later Italian theorists address their remarks to performers also, suggesting how existing works can be adapted for a low-voice ensemble. But perhaps our modern concepts of 'composer' and 'performer' are themselves victims of mistranslation.

Certainly the word 'comporre', which often appears in conjunction with 'mutare', is open to misreading. 'Comporre' is often translated as 'to compose', but can also carry the meaning 'to arrange'. Writing a little later than Aron, the Italian theorist Nicola Vicentino makes clear his distinction between the words 'comporre' and 'compositione' in the chapter heading, 'Modo di comporre a Quattro voce, diverse compositione, à voce piena, & à voce mutata'. Vicentino goes on to describe how music with soprano parts

[39] 'Muito bom tipre mudado que cantava com muita graça [...]': *Boletim da segunda classi*, Academia das Sciências de Lisboa 11 (1918), item 180, p. 158; available online at <http://archive.org/stream/boletima11acaduoft/boletima11acaduoft_djvu.txt> [accessed 4 April 2014].

[40] 'De modo et compositione vocum quae mutate dicuntur. Cap. XLVI. Verum, quia Cantilenae non nunquam vocibus quattuor idest partibus omnibus componi solent: quae voces mutatae dicuntur quomodo id fieri debeat, edisseram. Voces eiusmodi ob id quidem mutatae appellantu[r], quod secundum aliarum pueriliumvocum ascensum attolli nequeunt: Cantus enim ipse in eiusmodi cantilenis: quia gravioribus solito in partibus constituitur: cum puerili voce, vel ficta cani non possit: virili canitur eorum scilicet: qui vel Altos, vel Bassos canere consueverunt.': Pietro Aron, *Libri tres de institutione harmonica* (Bologna, 1516), p. 52.

could be realised in performance with lower male voices by the simple expedient of transposing the top line down an octave to make it a tenor part.[41] In other words, in this context Vicentino's chapter heading could be freely translated by us as 'a way of arranging various four-part works, with a normal complement of voices, or with transposed parts'. Describing a similar method of low-voiced compositions, Zarlino, writing in Venice around the same time, confirms that 'this style of composing/arranging is termed 'for changed voices' or 'for equal voices'.[42]

Emerging from this semantic thicket, we might conclude these remarks on 'voce mutate' by noting (not without irony) that in the space of 150 years the term itself mutated – from a way of describing notes in a scale, to a description of a type of voice, to being a technique for composers and a strategy for performers.

High Male Singing in the Secular World

So far in this chapter the discussion of the falsetto voice in the Renaissance has focused exclusively on music in church. This is because almost all the evidence about individual singers takes the form of financial, or contractual documents. And, whereas a church singer was a professional who might have had his activities documented, no such paper trail exists for the singers (largely amateur) of secular music. This is not to say that we have no evidence for the use of falsetto in secular music. We do, but from an altogether different angle – narrative texts written by musical theorists.

Men such as Giovanni Maffei or Thomas Morley, who offer us these words about Renaissance musical practice, rarely emerge from modern musical histories with any great credit. Three charges are frequently levelled against the theorists. Firstly, they are often cast as scathing reactionaries. Subsequent history may have proved some writers to be musically conservative, but we should remember that only with the benefit of hindsight can this judgment be made: at the time they were writing they (and those whom history has deemed to be 'progressives') were at the coal face, arguing in the dark about the best way forward. The second charge against the theorists is that their words are frustratingly vague. Here we have another anachronistic complaint: writers may not tell us quite what we want to know, but that does not necessarily mean they were being vague. They were writing not for us but for their contemporaries, and those contemporaries would have had no need to read the very thing we most seek – common knowledge. Finally, and most fundamentally, there is the collective noun we know these men by: 'theorists'. This is today often used as a mildly pejorative term, implying men incapable of putting thoughts

---

[41] Nicola Vicentino, *L'antica musica ridotta alla moderna prattica* (Rome, 1555), p. 84.

[42] 'Il qual modo di comporre si chiama a Voci mutate, overo a Voci pari.': Gioseffo Zarlino, *Le institutioni harmoniche* (Venice, 1558), 3, p. 263.

into action. But, applied to the Renaissance, such a usage is inaccurate. The 'theorists' whose words we will read below were also practical musicians. Maffei might have been a medical doctor by profession, but he was also an accomplished musician. Many others, such as Morley, Finck and Zarlino, were both professional composers and performers. We should remember that until the nineteenth century the composer's chief method of guiding the performer was not by littering the score with expressive directions, but by setting out a more generalised ethos for interpretation in the form of a treatise or introduction.

What, then, did the theorists say about singing, and falsetto in general? Inevitably they all reveal different tastes and agendas, but one recurring theme is the difference between styles of singing required for church and chamber. This is concisely expressed by Zarlino:

> One sings one way in churches and public chapels and in another in private chambers, such that there [in churches] one sings in a full voice [...] and in chambers one sings in a more submissive way without any shouting.[43]

Whereas modern singers are trained to make the voice fuller (and louder) as it ascends, by depressing the larynx, the theorist Hermann Finck suggests that Renaissance singers were encouraged in the opposite direction: 'the higher a voice rises the quieter and lovelier should the note be sung'.[44] But did singers ever have to ascend high in their ranges? Taken at face value, the music itself suggests that they had to reach neither the top nor bottom of their voices, since most parts have a total range of around a tenth. Vicentino writes explicitly about limiting this written range: 'for the convenience of singers and in order that every common voice can sing its part easily [...] no ledger lines should ever be added to the five lines of the stave.'[45] Understandably, commentators have interpreted this to mean that, compared to their Baroque successors, Renaissance composers were 'restricting [...] each voice to a very moderate range'.[46] There is another

---

[43] 'Ad altro modo si canta nelle chiese & nelle capelle publiche, & ad altro modo nelle private camere: imperoche ivi sic anta a piena voce; non però se non nel modo detto di sopra; & nelle camere sic canta con voce piu sommessa & soave, senza fare alcun strepito': Zarlino, *Le institutioni harmoniche*, p. 204.

[44] 'Quaelibet vox quo magis intenditur, eo submissior et dulcior sonus usurpetur.': Hermann Finck, *Practica musica* (Wittenberg, 1556), bk 5; available online at <http://www.chmtl.indiana.edu/tml/16th/FINPRA_TEXT.html> [accessed 4 April 2014]. Translation from MacClintock, *Readings*, pp. 62–3.

[45] 'Per commodita de i cantanti, & acciò che ogni voce commune possi cantare la ma parte commoditamente [...] mai si dè aggiognere righa alcuna, alle cinque righe, ne di sotto, ne di sopra, in nissuna parte, ne manco mutar chiavi': Vicentino, *L'Antica musica*, p. 80.

[46] Mauro Uberti, 'Vocal Techniques in Italy in the Second Half of the 16th Century', *Early Music* 9(4) (1981), pp. 486–98, at p. 491.

possible explanation, though, for why the ranges of Renaissance vocal music appear so small in comparison to those in the period immediately following, when the Italian monodists would write ranges of up to three octaves.

What perhaps tends to be ignored here is that an early Baroque monody was accompanied. This implies a relatively fixed pitch, and with it the security that in writing a high or low note on paper, something very close to a particular frequency would be required in performance. The Renaissance composer could make no such assumptions. Without obligatory instruments of fixed pitch, his seemingly limited written range was a way of leaving unaccompanied singers the leeway which their practical music-making would have demanded. When the five or six parts of a madrigal were divided up amongst a disparate group of singers and players, or a piece was pitched inadvertently high, some voices were presumably required to operate above their comfortable range. When this situation presented itself, a logical implication of Finck's dictum is that, rather than extend the chest voice (and volume) upwards, singers might move into head voice and falsetto.

The Neapolitan physician Maffei is explicit about the existence of falsetto:

> And if a person in his own way wants to fake it [the high voice] with the voice called *falsetto*, he can do so by making the movement of the air faster. And this way of faking a voice is granted only to a man.[47]

Yet for Maffei falsetto is not an end in itself, but a means to what he considers most useful in a singer – flexibility. And here Maffei is equally explicit about wide vocal ranges being a feature of Renaissance music – in performance if not in writing. He extols those 'who sing bass, tenor, and every other voice with great ease, and decorating, diminishing, perform passagework now in the bass, now in the mezzo, now on high – all beautiful to hear'.[48] Maffei's description seems to refer to a wider-ranged and more highly ornate music than we will find in any written secular source of the time. This should alert us to the gulf between what was written down and what was sung out: with Renaissance secular music, evidently, all is not as meets the eye. In other words, just by writing parts with a range of three octaves the early seventeenth-century Italian monodists did not discover the extremes of the vocal range, any more than Franco of Cologne discovered rhythm by writing down melodies in mensural notation.

[47] '[...] e per mancamento di soprano fingesse la voce, chiamata falsetto, potria con fare il movimento dell'aere piu veloce, à posta sua farlo. E questo modo di fingere la voce fu solo à l'huomo conceduto.': Maffei, *La lettera sul canto*, p. 26. Translation from MacClintock, *Readings*, p. 42.

[48] '[...] poi se ne trovano alcuni, ch'il basso, il tenore, et ogni altra voce, con molta facilità cantano; e fiorendo, e diminoendo con la gorga, fanno passaggi, hora nel basso, hora nel mezzo, et hora nell'alto, ad intendere bellissimi.': Maffei, *La lettera sul canto*, p. 29. Translation from MacClintock, *Readings*, p. 43.

The language of the theorists can be as deceptive as the written music of the composers. When they make a distinction between modal 'chest' voice ('voce di petto') and falsetto, their meaning is clear. But for some vocal commentators there also existed a 'head' voice ('voce di testo') register. The problem with this extra register is that 'head voice' indicated different things to different theorists. By this term some writers seemed to mean a light, high modal voice which feels (to the singer at least) that it is focused in the sinuses. Others, however, seemed to regard 'head voice' and 'falsetto' as synonymous. Take the Venetian musician Zacconi:

> Those voices that are merely of the head are the ones that are emitted with a sharp quality, and are penetrative without causing fatigue in their production: for the way in which they fall nobly on our ears, even if there are other voices which are bigger and more noble, these will always yield to the superiority of the others [i.e. the purely head voices].[49]

Zacconi's description is not without its ambiguities, but a voice that is penetrative without causing the singer fatigue surely indicates falsetto rather than a quietly intermediate modal register. Elsewhere, Zacconi pragmatically endorses feigning, rather than forcing, high notes: 'Similarly, in singing high notes quietly one should not force them if they do not come out conveniently; because it is better to feign or omit them.'[50] Zacconi also makes a useful distinction between single-register voices (chest or falsetto) and the middling voices.[51] These latter, he tells us,

> are partly chest and partly head voices. They receive their names because of the effect produced, as if they are half the first type and half the second. It is said, however, that when they sing more in the chest than in the head, they are even more beautiful.

---

[49] 'Quelle voci che sono meramente di testa sono quelle che escano con un frangente acuto & penetrativo senza punto di fatica del producente: le quali per l'acutezza loro percuotano si gagliardamente l'orecchie nostre, che se bene ci sono delle altre voce maggiori & più gagliarde; sempre quelle appassiscano al'altre superiore.': Lodovico Zacconi, *Prattica di musica* (Venice, 1592), fol. 77v. My translation.

[50] 'Similmente nel cantar piano nelle alte non si debbono sforzare et comodamente non via rivano; perche meglio è di fingerle o di taccerle.': Zacconi, *Prattica di musica* fols 52v–55v. Translation from Uberti, 'Vocal Techniques', p. 494.

[51] 'In fra queste tre forte de voci se ne trovano alcune che sono mezzane; cioè che sono parte di petto, & parte di testa. & alcun alter che sono parte di petto & parte obtuse: & queste vengano cosi chamate per l'effetto che di loro si sente, che sono mezze d'una forte & mezze de un'altrare però redutto le voci, in queste voci mezzane: si dice, che quando le tengano più della voce di petto che di testa deletteranno piu sempre che non fa ranno quelle di petto & obtuse [...]': Zacconi, *Prattica di musica*, fol. 77v. My translation.

We will do well to remember Zacconi's model singer – a chest voice with a falsetto extension – when we come to the 'new' Italian vocal method of Tosi a century later.

Since there are references to falsetto singing in both sacred and secular contexts, it would be easy to assume that the technique had a similar role in all Renaissance music. And at least to the eye, both types of music make similar demands: compare five-part motets and madrigals by composers of the later sixteenth century, and one will find far more similarities than dissimilarities in their vocal ranges, overall compass, and musical style. But in terms of their original performance practice (and particularly the use of falsetto) these similarities are deceptive. For all the exceptions to the rule there is still much truth in the traditional view – that sacred music was predominantly sung publicly, chorally and unaccompanied, whereas secular music was predominantly private, solo-voiced, and with instrumental involvement. However, the most fundamental difference between the forces with which madrigals and motets might have been performed – and the difference which relates most to the use of falsetto – lies not in the number of voices per part, or instruments, but in the gender of the performers.

Although women were barred from singing in church, paintings and texts such as Castiglione's *Il Cortegiano* (1528) make it plain that they had a significant role to play in secular music-making.[52] Very occasionally this role was professional and performance-oriented – the *Concerto delle donne* at the court of Ferrara being an obvious example – but more often it was in domestic music-making that women sang. Indeed, the majority of domestic madrigal singing, for which no specific records exist, presumably featured amateur women as sopranos, rather than professional falsettists or castrati. When this was the case, any use of the kind of falsetto described by Zacconi must have been at the top end of parts sung by men predominantly in chest voice. This becomes even more probable when we consider the repeated advice of the theorists that one should sing more quietly in the chamber than in the church, and more quietly as the voice ascends. So, whereas falsetto in church (at least on soprano lines) was publicly projected by specialist sopranists who rarely used their modal register, any falsetto in the chamber would have been sung by gentlemen feigning notes they could not reach with any refinement in their modal registers. In this crucial sense, on the Continent during the Renaissance the single word 'falsetto' embraces two quite different styles of singing. At least by the end of the period, in the European church one could hear something resembling the modern falsettist; in the chamber, however, we would still do better to keep in mind the submissive voices of those gathered around the dying Dufay.

---

[52] Baldassare Castiglione, *Il libro del cortegiano* (Venice, 1528), bk 3, chap. 8, available online at <http://www.letteraturaitaliana.net/pdf/Volume_4/t84.pdf> [accessed 25 April 2014].

Are We Too Loud?
The Impact of Volume on Singing Styles

> After dinner Grace Moore offered to sing, and we put out our cigarettes [...] Now the drawing room at Number Three is large, but not enormous, and we were not quite prepared for what happened. She went to the piano, and began with a bit from 'Butterfly' and the first few notes shook the chandeliers, nearly blowing us from our chairs. She has a voice of tremendous volume, but to my mind no very great beauty. We literally vibrated until she adapted her notes to the size of the room.
>
> Sir Henry Channon[1]

WHEN Grace Moore, primadonna of the Metropolitan Opera in New York, was heard by the diarist 'Chips' Channon at a private party in 1936, she unwittingly provided a pithy example of how modern singing technique and the tastes of previous ages grate. The 'Number Three' in question was the London residence of the Duke and Duchess of Kent in Belgrave Square: this 'not enormous' drawing room, then, was quite literally the aristocratic salon – albeit in its dying day. Moore had developed her voice to fill the world's largest opera house, and to judge from Channon's description, in this intimate context she appeared as the proverbial elephant dancing on a sixpence. Humour aside, this raises a serious – if basic – question: how loud is loud? And how does volume influence the way in which we sing?

Already discernible in this history of high male singing is the contention that in earlier centuries men often incorporated both modal and falsetto into their vocal delivery, thus using a fundamentally different method from that used by singers today. The evidence for this, though, has so far been an undercurrent, more felt than seen: a clerical dictat, the migration of an individual singer from one part to another, or the range of a certain alto part – instances such as these may suggest another approach to singing, but they do no more than that. With the exhortation of Lodovico Zacconi, that one should feign rather than force high notes (see p. 64), the argument for a different vocal technique bubbles up to the surface. And for the next three centuries, in the words of vocal pedagogues and critics, there it will stay.

In theory, most of us will have little difficulty with accepting that singers from a different age used different methods to achieve similar ends. In practice, most of us (or at least most of us who sing) will have a great deal

---

[1] *Chips: The Diaries of Sir Henry Channon*, ed. Robert Rhodes James (London, 1993) p. 63.

of difficulty accepting this. Why? Put simply, for the last 150 years or more, anyone who has learnt to sing is likely to have been taught that when the voice ascends it must be more strongly supported, to facilitate resonant, well-projected high notes. Even leaving aside the intervention of teachers, most Romantic and post-Romantic vocal music will make this same demand: the highest note in a song, or in an individual phrase, will tend to mark an emotional apex, and often with it the composer's request for maximum volume. Modern operatic promoters candidly refer to this as the 'money note'. To put into practice the advice of Zacconi, then, is to fly in the face of what we have ourselves been taught, and what later music (and the industry which surrounds it) demands.

Sheer volume of sound is a very recent mammon. In the late eighteenth century Mancini commented on contemporary taste by saying that 'in our day [...] the tendency is to judge a singer's merits by the range of his voice.'[2] This maximal range, he noted, was achieved by deploying both registers available to the singer. Far from being a priority, volume could only impair the imperceptible transition between registers (which is what Mancini himself regarded as the true mark of a singer). The transmission between a man's modal and falsetto voices is nowadays often referred to as a 'gear-change', and this is an analogy worth pursuing. When we manually change gear in a car, we need to reduce the engine revolutions to allow the synchromesh to coordinate the different spinning speeds of the gear wheels. In the same way, the only reliable method of vocally 'changing gear' is to do so when our modal voice does not require excessive air pressure to support the sound. In other words, vocally we need to change gear with a reduction in volume – with our foot off the gas, metaphorically speaking. A significant key to facilitating the vocal gear-change, then, is diminished volume. If we can establish that singers in earlier centuries typically produced less sound, we will be some way to understanding how they evidently managed (at least better than most modern singers can manage) the vocal transition from their modal to falsetto voices.

Perhaps this is self-evident. Whereas listeners at the back of a modern opera house or concert hall require performers who can sing with a large and sustained volume throughout their range, listeners in a stone-walled chapel or a domestic salon required no such thing. Therefore, in earlier times people presumably sang more quietly than they do today. Yet how, apart from lazily stating that this is a truism, can we really gauge the volume – and implicitly the way – in which people sang?

---

[2] 'A giorni nostri si vuol raffinare maggiormente, ed anche, forzando la natura, si esige che la voce de' cantanti si estenda a maggior numero di voci, talchè èstimato il cantore di maggior pregio dal maggior numero ed estensione di corde.': Giambattista Mancini, *Pensieri, e riflessioni pratiche sopra il canto figurato* (Vienna, 1774), p. 78: cf. Mancini, *Practical Reflections on the Figurative Art of Singing*, ed. and trans. Pietro Buzzi (Boston, 1912), p. 59.

Here, the words of contemporary commentators and theorists will help us little. Zarlino, we saw earlier, tells us that:

> one sings in one way in churches and public chapels and another way in private rooms. In [the former] one sings in a full voice, but with discretion nevertheless [...] and in private rooms one sings with a lower and gentler voice, without any shouting.[3]

We can debate the implications of Zarlino's 'discrezione' and 'strepitò' *ad nauseam*, but since his concept of full ('piena') and lower ('somessa') are not absolutes but relatives, such debate will tell us little. Zarlino, and presumably his readers, knew roughly what volume levels he meant, but we fool ourselves if we imagine that the levels on our decibel gauge are necessarily the same as his. We need to look elsewhere, then, for evidence of the volumes at which people sang.

The development of instruments is highly suggestive of a parallel development in vocal capacity. Keyboard, wind and string instruments have all grown in both volume and sustaining powers. This change, we might note, has largely taken place since the mid-nineteenth century, thus running historically parallel to a development in vocal technique (which we shall observe in due course) away from the combination of modal and falsetto techniques. Of Renaissance instruments used to accompany singers domestically, a consort of viols, or a lute, will be happily matched by a single small voice. True, cornets and sackbuts require greater vocal strength to balance them, but when wind instruments accompanied singers it was more often in church where, according to Zarlino, singers sang relatively loudly. Not necessarily loudly by our standards, though: with their narrow bores, early wind instruments were much softer than our modern trumpets and trombones. And when they did accompany, iconography suggests that wind instruments were generally balanced by a number of singers, rather than by a soloist. A similar picture presents itself for both the Baroque and Classical periods, in which virtually every instrument was quieter than its modern counterpart.

Inevitably, the dynamic capacity of instruments and the size of performing venues had a symbiotic relationship. From royal chapels, to domestic rooms and salons, to the venues of the first operas, by and large early music was performed in acoustics which were relatively intimate. Obviously a smaller room will always suit a smaller voice. Venue size itself, though, can be a misleading factor in suggesting how loudly people sang. The west end of a great cathedral, for instance, is much further from singers in the quire than the back wall of any modern opera house is from

---

[3] 'Ad altro modo sic anta nelle Chiese & nelle Cappella publiche; & ad altro modo nelle private Camera; imperoche ivi sic anta à piena voce; con discrezione però... & nelle Camere sic anta con voce più sommessa & soave, senza fare alcun strepitò': Gioseffo Zarlino, *Le institutioni harmoniche* [1558] (Venice, 1588–9), 3, p. 253; cf. Wistreich, 'Reconstructing Pre-Romantic Singing Technique', p. 181.

its stage. But, whereas today's opera singer is obliged to be heard clearly by every egalitarian patron, the chorister's audience was rather different: historically, that audience is less the humble congregant at the back of the nave than the cathedral's hierarchy gathered around the singers in the quire, or even closer, in the form of an omnipresent God. Even leaving aside the unprovable issue of the intended listener, one thing that is certain is that a long stone building will convey sounds much more efficiently than an upholstered theatre. A number of years ago I was standing in the cloister of Le Thoronet, a Cistercian monastery in rural Provence. As I stood there outside the main church, the building began to ring with the sound of what I took to be a choir of female voices singing a melismatic chant. Entering the church, I found a single female guide with a smallish voice, demonstrating the acoustic to a group of visitors. When we read the early Cistercian demands for full and virile singing, we should again remember that all such descriptions are relative.

Let us be more specific about one way in which Zacconi's transition into falsetto would have been easier in earlier performing contexts. Whereas acousticians today design performing spaces to offer minimal reverberation, earlier designers were commonly guided by an entirely different aesthetic. At one extreme stands the stone-clad church. But even at the other extreme, in terms of acoustics, domestic music-making was far from what we, in an age of fitted carpets and soft furnishings, might understand by the term: in *De cardinalatu*, Paolo Cortese advises cardinals to furnish their music rooms with empty vases to improve resonance.[4] And quite apart from the question of volume, a resonant building (of any size) influences a responsive singer in other ways. By projecting a modally produced high note relatively loudly into a lively acoustic, as its sound decays the singer can then stealthily shift upwards into falsetto. The gear-change, here masked by the continued resonance of previous notes, is difficult for listeners to detect. In a dry, more typically modern acoustic, however, the same sleight-of-larynx will be glaringly obvious.

There is one other reason why earlier generations of musicians would have been inclined to produce less volume. This underlying reason is worth airing, even though it has little to do with music, and is quite impossible to gauge. Ambient noise level – the aural background to our everyday lives – has increased dramatically with population growth and the invention of the internal combustion engine. Whilst it is impossible to quantify the precise effect of this increase historically, it is self-evident that a lower ambient noise level will require a proportionally lower decibel level of someone wishing to be heard. The obvious rejoinder here is that since the majority of music is performed indoors, where ambient noise level is negligible, this is a non-issue. There may be a more subtle relationship at work, though, in

---

[4] 'Quid cubiculum musice debet habere vasa musica I pariete col locata ad consonantiam': Paolo Cortese, *De cardinalatu* (Rome, 1510), p. 56.

which exposure to lower ambient noise is reflected in a quieter approach to singing. One of the reasons why a single small voice at Le Thoronet was so audible to me outside the building was that, because of its rural seclusion, there was virtually no ambient noise. In the 2005 documentary *Die große Stille*, filmed at the secluded abbey of the Grand Chartreuse in the Alps, it is striking that the monks' liturgical singing is restrained almost to the point of inaudibility. On a personal visit to the English Jesuit monastery of Glasshampton (another virtually silent order in a secluded location) I noticed the same approach to chant: further, visitors to services were asked to respect this approach by themselves singing very quietly. Monastic settings such as these are atypical to us, but in the centuries before the industrial revolution, acoustically they would have represented something closer to the norm – even for urban environments.

As a last example of how remarkable (and by implication unusual) loud singing was before the last century, we might read a 1685 diary entry by Sir John Evelyn. Having begun this chapter with the words of Sir Henry Channon, Evelyn's description carries a particular resonance:

> I also heard Mrs. Packer (daughter to my old friend) sing before his Majesty and the Duke, privately [...] [her voice] was so loud as took away much of the sweetness. Certainly never woman had a stronger [voice] or better ear could she possibly have governed it. She would do rarely in a large church among the nuns.[5]

Individually, it would be fanciful to suggest that these strands of evidence prove that people generally sang more quietly in earlier centuries. But taken together, the witness of instruments, buildings and ambience point to a manner of singing which would make the demands of Zacconi and others infinitely more practicable than we might at first think.

---

[5] *The Diary of John Evelyn*, ed. Austin Dobson (New York, 1906), vol. 3, p. 137.

CHAPTER 4

Late Medieval and Renaissance England

S o far, in our geographical scan to find areas in which falsettists operated during the Renaissance, England has been notable by its absence. Notable, because the view we have received through Deller and his early followers is that the historical home of the falsettist was not the Continent, but England. As we have seen, part of this received view is skewed, since the falsettist certainly was known in mainland Europe from the early Renaissance onwards. But was the falsettist known in England at the time, or does that part of the picture also need amending?

Perhaps the first point to make here is a bald statement of fact: not one reference to falsetto singing has so far come to light from England during the Renaissance. Indeed, between those ambiguous prohibitions in the middle of the twelfth century, and a remark by Thomas Campion in 1613, falsetto singing as a definable phenomenon seems to vanish without trace for over four hundred years. If falsetto singing existed at all in England, one place we might expect to find mention of it would be in the words of the Lollards and Reformers, since in their efforts to condemn the ceremonies of the church, men such as John Wycliffe, and later writers John Bale and Thomas Becon, painted gaudy word-pictures, painstakingly detailing every perceived exoticism and excess. In *Of feynid contemplative lif*, a late fourteenth-century treatise by Wycliffe (or a follower of his), the 'vain tricks' of singers are listed as 'high crying' (by which he seems to mean loud singing, as this gives listeners 'aching heads'), as well as 'discant, counternote, and organum, and small breaking' (or 'smale brekynge', as Wycliffe refers to ornamental divisions of longer notes). However, though 'feynid' and 'false' are very much part of the author's vocabulary in other contexts, they do not feature with regard to singing.[1]

As late as the middle of the sixteenth-century, John Bale offers much the same list as he catalogues musical excesses in the Catholic church (the 'verye synagoge of Sathan'): 'descante, prycksonge, counter point, & faburden'. To these Bale adds a fantastic litany of 'lasciviouse' sonorities:

> harpes, lutes, and fydeles, the swete voyce of musycyanes that synge wyth virginales, viales, and chymes, the armonye of them that pype in recorders, flutes, and drones, and the shirle [shrill] showte of trompettes, waites, and shames [shawms] [...] swete orgones containinge the melodiouse noyse of all manner of instruments and byrdes'.[2]

---

[1] Cf. Rob C. Wegman, *The Crisis of Music in Early Modern Europe, 1470–1530* (New York, 2005), pp. 21–3.

[2] Cf. Wegman, *The Crisis of Music*, p. 106.

Again, womanly, false and feigned singing are notable by their absence. Nor is this absence simply a matter of vocabulary, since no one has yet identified other terms which, during this period, seem to serve as substitutes for 'falsetto'. The absence of words does not, in itself, indicate the absence of a reality. Might it be that 'So commonplace did its use apparently become, that the word falsetto is hardly mentioned'?[3] For this to have been the case, though, logic suggests that the strength of the circumstantial evidence would be inversely proportional to the weakness of the written evidence. As we shall see, this is very far from being the case.

The Old Hall Manuscript and Eton Choirbook

TODAY, when we perform English music from the early fifteenth century, whatever pitch we choose – high, medium or low – one of our outer male voice-types (bass or falsettist) will be made redundant. So which of these two voices was the later medieval choirmaster unfamiliar with? There is no definitive evidence in the music itself, and those who have argued strongly one way or the other may have revealed less about the subject than they have about their personal preferences. In particular, the music historian (and occasional falsettist) Roger Bowers has suggested that the falsetto range was not used in chant and so *would* have been used in polyphony, but that the lower bass register was not used in chant and so *would not* have been used in polyphony: in other words, identical assumptions are made, but opposite conclusions are drawn from them.[4] Theory aside, one basic practical consideration makes it highly improbable that falsettists could have had a significant part to play in medieval polyphony. If falsetto was not a standard feature of chant performance (as Bowers and the monastic prohibitions suggest), we have to imagine that for day after day in the regular liturgical cycle, singers used only their modal voices. Then, on the relatively rare feast days when polyphony was performed, for the few minutes that a piece of this exposed and virtuosic music might last, some of these singers were expected suddenly to switch into their falsetto registers. Few singers could cope with this challenge. None would welcome it.

With so little information about the falsetto voice available from the late Middle Ages, musical historians have looked to the adjoining periods for suggestive evidence. And just as twelfth-century texts have been projected forward, so has evidence from the later fifteenth century been traced backwards. In the case of English music, Roger Bowers – whose knowledge of the archival sources is unparalleled – has noticed an apparent continuity

---

[3] Peter Giles, 'The Male Alto or Countertenor in the English Cathedral Choir Tradition: A Unique Survival?', *Der Countertenor: die männliche Falsettstimme vom Mittelalter zur Gegenwart*, ed. Corinna Herr and Arnold Jacobshagen (Mainz, 2012), pp. 39–54, at p. 39.

[4] Bowers, 'To Chorus from Quartet', pp. 13–14.

Ex. 5 Clefs and ranges in works by Old Hall and Eton Choirbook composers

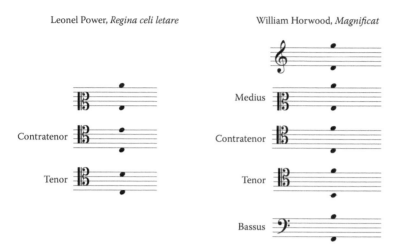

between the scoring of the central three parts in the late fifteenth-century music of the Eton Choirbook, and (from around a hundred years earlier) the three-part music of John Dunstable, Leonel Power and the composers of the Old Hall manuscript (see Ex. 5).[5] On paper this continuity does look convincing. In Ex. 5, not only do the three parts in question share the same clefs, but there is a similarity of ranges, and two of them share names. If we can establish that the continuity went beyond the medium of parchment, and into the medium of actual sound, it would suggest that the original singers of these lines in both types of music shared vocal attributes. This is potentially significant for the role of the falsettist in early English music, since Bowers suggests that the original pitch levels of both Old Hall and Eton music roughly correspond to our own, and that therefore Power's top line, and the second line down in the Horwood, were both taken by the equivalent of our male alto.

Straightaway, however, two stumbling blocks appear. Firstly, we have absolutely no method for gauging the performing pitch(es) of early fifteenth-century English polyphony (and only the haziest clues for music of the Eton Choirbook); secondly, even if we could verify that their pitch levels were similar to our own, physiological evidence suggests that fifteenth-century singers would *not* have had the same ranges as modern singers. There are also much larger obstacles to accepting this link. Although the singers of Power's top line were undoubtedly adult males, the supposedly linked *medius* part in the late fifteenth century was (as we shall shortly see) commonly sung by boys: in other words, the parts for which we

[5] Bowers, 'To Chorus from Quartet', p. 24.

have good evidence that there was no performing link were the very parts which Bowers has earmarked as the falsettist's continuous domain. Lastly, we need to note that although the scorings above were common, they were far from being standard in the way that our own SATB arrangement has become. In the collected modern editions of Power and his great contemporary John Dunstable, only twenty of some seventy-seven works exhibit the same scoring and clefs as *Regina celi*. And out of forty-nine complete pieces in the Eton Choirbook, only twenty-nine are for five-part choir, and of these, only ten exhibit the same clefs in their interior parts as the Horwood *Magnificat*. A one-size-fits-all theory of vocal scoring, then, will not suffice for either period, let alone for both periods together.

As for the 'choirs' which actually sang this music, there is good evidence that the standard performing ensemble of Power and his contemporaries was just four adult soloists: the Eton choir, on the other hand, really was a 'choir' – consisting of ten boys and seven men. The ensembles, then, were fundamentally different, and the four soloists of the older performance practice, whatever their vocal techniques, would have been subsumed in the larger whole of the Eton choir. The apparently neat 'continuity' between the ensembles, and in particular the kinds of voices used on the early upper and later *medius* parts, extends no further than the parchment on which it is occasionally evident. To use a comparison from a later period, the viol music of Dowland and string sinfonias of Purcell may share identical clefs, and even similar names, in some of their interior parts, but we would be wrong to infer from this that there is any continuity between their original performing ensembles.

The Early Tudor Mean Part

O N the Continent, the falsetto voice had come into being during the early Renaissance as the highest voice in the polyphonic texture. Yes, boys were trained to sing polyphony, but rarely were they trusted with singing the top line on their own. At Cambrai, for instance, they shared the soprano line with adult males, and in the Cappella Sistina, after brief experiments, boys were dispensed with altogether. In Europe, then, the adult sopranist was never far away. In England this state of affairs did not develop. (We will have to wait until we reach 1660 before finding the first (and only) evidence of men and boys sharing a soprano line.) From at least as early as the 1430s, boys in England were being trained to sing polyphony.[6] Evidently this training was a success, because by the 1470s composers felt able to expand the sonic range of their polyphony, with boys singing the upper (treble) and lower (mean) parts at the top of what became a fairly common five-part texture. The reasons for English and Continental practices differing on the fundamental issue of performing upper parts are

[6] Bowers, 'To Chorus from Quartet', p. 13.

difficult to establish. They are worth briefly exploring, though, because they are significant for our subsequent history. Centuries later, when religious ideology persuaded many European church choirs into admitting women, and therefore dispensing with boys, falsettists or castrati, in England there was no such choral revolution: by then, boys were part of the musical and social fabric of the major English churches. So why, going back to the fifteenth century, did the English favour boys' voices, rather than men's, on the upper lines of their polyphony? This is a question it seems impossible to answer with any certainty. Was it purely the result of an aesthetic whim? Perhaps it is more revealing to pose the question the other way round: since both English and European churches had similar existing structures in the early Renaissance, with boys already singing chant, why did the Europeans prefer to add falsettists rather than extend an existing resource by exclusively using boys? Was it simply that Continental ears had been exposed more to castrato and falsetto singing in their contact with Mediterranean lands? This seems probable, if unprovable. Whatever the reason, as a top part the falsetto voice found favour in Europe in a way it did not in England. Did the English, though, know the falsetto voice on a lower part?

When the revival of Tudor church music took hold in the early twentieth century, choirmasters took the pragmatic decision to fit the scores they now had to the singers in front of them. As far as their altos were concerned, the part in earlier Tudor music which best fitted their vocal ranges was termed 'mean' or 'medius'. Before the 1970s, it was assumed that this had originally been a part composed with falsettists in mind. Gradually, though, evidence came to light that suggested this part was originally written for lower boys' voices. Chapel records from Gloucester to Northumberland explicitly or implicitly linked boys with the mean part. There are hints in the music, too: one source of John Taverner's 'Meane Mass' is annotated 'for iiij men and a childe': in this context the 'childe' could only be the 'meane'. And later in the period, as we shall see, there is a particularly detailed description of the mean as a boys' part. Recently, though, it has been suggested that the mean was also sung by falsetto altos. Does the following record, from Chichester Cathedral around 1526, tell us this?

> Four lay clerks having mutually blending voices and learned in music, of whom one at least is always [to be possessed] of a natural and audible bass voice; while let the voices of the other three be sweet and melodious, so that by the joint application of their voices they may naturally and freely encompass fifteen or sixteen notes.[7]

---

[7] 'Quod sint ibidem perpetuo quatuor clerici laici concinnas voces habentes et musice docti, quorum unus ad minus semper sit basse naturalis et audibilis vocis, aliorum vero trium voces sint suaves et canore ita quod a communi vocum succentu possint naturaliter et libere ascendere ad quindecim vel

The question is, which voices are expected to encompass the range of sixteen notes (or two octaves)? If it is the three parts above the bass, then this might indeed suggest that at Chichester, as the Reformation approached, the top adult voice sang the mean part, most likely in falsetto. If, on the other hand, 'the joint application of their voices' referred to all four men, the mean part must have been sung by the boys. Although it has been used as a prime piece of evidence that the mean part in England was sung by men in falsetto, in reality the document is ambiguous. When weighed against the mass of other evidence that the mean part was sung by boys, this Chichester document would barely affect the scales.

Tudor Pitch Levels

PERHAPS, then, the Tudor composers commonly expected to hear the falsettist on the line beneath the mean. The obvious attraction of this theory is that this line beneath the mean is the part marked 'counter-tenor'. Could this have been something akin to the counter-tenor we now know? For traditionalists, it would be hugely reassuring if such a continuity could be established. But can it? The argument that the counter-tenor (or alto) part in English Tudor music was originally a falsetto part is bound up with the issue of pitch. Before we take a deep breath and dive into these turbulent waters, perhaps an explanation of the issue's significance for the counter-tenor voice is needed. To those with only a casual interest, the intensity of debate on this issue can appear disconcerting: can the difference, for instance, between $a' = 435.4$ and $a' = 440$ (about a fifth of a semitone) really affect the essential quality of the music in performance?

The answer is that it most certainly can. It does, too, because as we shall see, throughout the revival of Tudor polyphony, tiny errors and misreadings like this have been compounded. This might sound like a simple case of Chinese whispers, but the advancement of pitch arguments may not have always been quite so innocent. In an attempt to force complex and contextual historical evidence into the mould of modern singers and choirs, individuals have adopted perspectives which minimise or hide ill-fitting data. Modern editors might offer the excuse that unequivocally rounding up (or down) equivocal data is a necessity inherent in our system of musical notation (which allows a G or a G♯ but nothing in between). Musical historians, dealing in the written word, have less of an excuse. Whatever the justification, the reality is that stark demarcations in pitch have ultimately determined the voices used. Essentially, on the counter-tenor line modern performers have the option of a lower pitch with tenors, or a higher pitch with falsettists. Although choral directors might try to temper the effect of their choices, implicitly one option will tend towards performances

---

sexdecim notas.': cf. Bowers, 'To Chorus from Quartet', p. 35. I am grateful to Dr Bowers for sharing with me the Latin original.

which sound rich and human, whilst the other will sound more ethereal and suprahuman. (Or – remembering that each listener's experience is subjective – one option which sounds muddy and earthbound, and another which is thin and cold-blooded.) So for the music's final receiver – the listener – pitch really does matter. And for the modern falsettist the argument matters, because unless a Tudor high pitch is shown to have some authenticity, he is left without a natural place in the polyphonic matrix.

On paper, with its standard top note being *g'*, the counter-tenor part in most Tudor polyphony appears to be written for what we would think of as tenors. Yet as long ago as 1873, when Sir Frederick Gore Ouseley published his collection of sacred works by Orlando Gibbons, he mooted the theory that the original pitch of English Tudor church music was more than a tone above the pitch of his own day.[8] Another way of expressing 'more than a tone' is 'between a tone and a minor third', from which it was a short step to 'as much as a minor third'. This argument was subsequently developed by others – most notably by David Wulstan, who not only gave the fullest written exposition of what became the 'minor third' theory, but from the late 1960s also addressed its practice as director of the Clerkes of Oxenford.[9]

The rationale for this theory we will come to in a moment, but we might ask, at this point, how universally any pitch 'standard' can be applied in earlier music. Wulstan himself applied the minor third transposition to music from every town and time of Tudor polyphony – from Fayrfax in London to Tomkins in Worcester. Noting similar ranges in the vocal parts, he assumed a single standard pitch for the whole period. Actually, it is easy to overstate the consistency of vocal ranges. Comparing settings of a single text from across the Tudor period gives us some idea of these ranges (see Ex. 6). Aside from the top boys part, which almost entirely vanishes after the Reformation, the other noticeable change is the steady rise of the counter-tenor range, which will become significant when we look at the high male voice in seventeenth-century England.

In any event, although similar written ranges might suggest similar sounding ranges, they can do no more than suggest. As on the Continent, the majority of polyphony in Tudor England would have been sung unaccompanied, and aside from a few alternatim settings such as Tallis's organ hymns, there is no evidence that until after the Reformation any vocal music was pitched with reference to another instrument. If choirs were rarely accompanied by organs, or even took their pitch from them, then would the pitch at which an instrument played have had any bearing on the pitch at which voices sang? The answer is that it probably

---

[8] Frederick A. Gore Ouseley (ed.), *A Collection of the Sacred Compositions of Orlando Gibbons* (London, 1873), p. iii.

[9] Edmund Fellowes, *English Madrigal Composers* (Oxford, 1921), pp. 70–3; Peter le Huray, *Music and the Reformation in England, 1549–1660* (London, 1967), pp. 112–14; Wulstan, *Tudor Music*, pp. 192–249.

Ex. 6 Written vocal ranges in Tudor *Magnificat* settings
(in approximately chronological order)

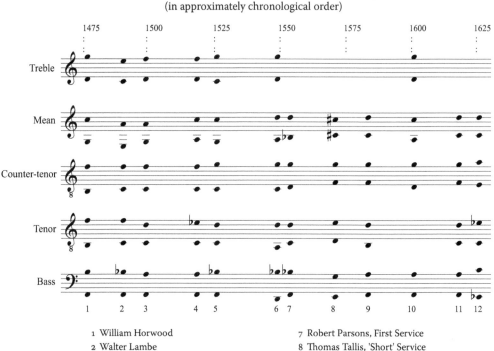

1 William Horwood
2 Walter Lambe
3 Robert Fayrfax, 'Regale'
4 Nicholas Ludford, 'Benedicta et venerabilis'
5 John Taverner, for six voices
6 Robert Parsons, Latin setting

7 Robert Parsons, First Service
8 Thomas Tallis, 'Short' Service
9 William Byrd, Second Service
10 Thomas Weelkes, Service 'for trebles'
11 Orlando Gibbons, 'Short' Service
12 Thomas Tomkins, Fifth Service

Note: in works where a pair of parts share the same clef, the composite range is shown.

would: whilst organ pitch may not have directly informed vocal pitch, the moment a choirmaster had some notion of what constituted c' – courtesy of the instrument he played as a soloist – it would surely have given him a relative (or even 'perfect') pitch when he came to intone the choir. Also, it is worth noting that when the organ did become a feature of choral performance, in verse anthems and services after the Reformation, the written pitch ranges of the lower voices corresponded closely with those in earlier unaccompanied music: again, this suggests some measure of pitch consistency. The key word here is perhaps 'some': however neat the theory of an absolute and universal pitch standard may have made the 'minor third' argument, practical considerations imply that such a definite standard could not have existed. Perhaps the term pitch *band* would be a more realistic concept for us to carry forward.

Had the 'minor third' theory been based on evidence from around the country, a better argument could be made for its universality, but in fact the argument revolved around a single organ. The instrument on which evidence for the theory hinged was the long-since destroyed 1614 Dallam organ of Worcester Cathedral. With the surviving measurements of this instrument in mind, Ouseley noted that 'an open pipe two feet and a half in length will not produce our modern F, but a somewhat sharp G.'[10] Actually, estimating pitch standards from organ specifications alone is not as exact a science as one might suppose: the tin content of the pipe's metal, its thickness, the arching of its mouth, and the temperature of the church – these are just some of the factors which can influence a pipe's pitch, but which are never communicated in a single measurement of length.

Because Edmund Fellowes published the majority of his editions of Tudor music in upward transpositions of a minor third, it is commonly assumed that his own calculation regarding the Dallam organ was that its C was the equivalent of a 'modern' A. This, though, is not true. In writing, Fellowes (following Ouseley) actually made the tempered suggestion that Tudor choir pitch (taken from the Dallam organ) was 'more than a tone higher than ours'. What did he mean by 'ours'? Fellowes explained that the pitch 'which is now most commonly employed in this country' (and from which he made his comparisons with Tudor pitch), was what he termed 'flat pitch' of $a' = 435.4$, and not our $a' = 440$. Perhaps this has been overlooked by later commentators and editors, who have stated with less and less equivocation that Tudor pitch was 'about a minor third higher than today's standard'.[11] At this pitch, the counter-tenor part regularly ascends to a modern bb' – above the comfortable range of most modern tenors; and although at this pitch the same part (which goes down to the f and eb below c') lies uncomfortably low for falsettists, they seem to be the only practical solution. Hence, in our own time the Clerkes of Oxenford, and later the Tallis Scholars and the Sixteen (two influential groups both directed by pupils of Wulstan) established the practice of have counter-tenor lines sung by falsettists. Although this practice still remains, as a theory it has gradually been eroded.

The first part of the theory to crumble was the pitch-level of a minor third above $a' = 440$. The most recent and comprehensive study of early seventeenth-century organ pitch has included specifications from Dallam's Worcester organ and various other now-defunct instruments.[12] This study suggests that the pitch of the Worcester organ was only 'one to two semitones sharp' of $a' = 440$, and that other organs had similar, if not identical, pitches. Though still above modern standard, in this slightly lower pitch band the counter-tenor part edges closer to the range of the modern tenor, and away from that of the falsettist. In the discussion that

---

[10] Ouseley (ed.), *Sacred Compositions of Orlando Gibbons*, p. iii.

[11] Wulstan, *Tudor Music*, p. 202.

[12] Andrew Johnstone, '"As it was in the beginning": Organ and Choir Pitch in Early Anglican Church Music', *Early Music* 31(4) (2003), pp. 506–24. The practical and theoretical work of Dominic Gwynn and the Early English Organ Project has also been central to expanding our knowledge of pitch in the Tudor church.

follows, the term 'high pitch' assumes this band of a semitone to a tone above modern pitch, and not a minor third.

The second part of the theory to show flaws was the assumption that parts ascending to ab' or a' would have been too high for tenors to sing. Here, it was a clearer understanding of the implications of physiology and historical human heights (covered in Extempore 2) which suggested that by comparing a modern male with a Tudor male we were simply not comparing like with like. With an average height of around 167 cm (some 10 cm shorter than the current average), Tudor men were likely to have had modal voices easily capable of realising parts which would cause modern tenors major problems.

In truth, even before the high-pitch theory was called into question, other evidence strongly pointed towards the Tudor counter-tenor having originally been a tenor and not a falsettist. The music itself holds a significant clue. English composers in the Tudor period were presented with a situation not unlike that of today, with boys singing the uppermost part, or parts. This being the case, it seems musically reasonable that in writing imitative polyphony composers should have set the ceiling of the counter-tenor range exactly an octave below that of the treble part. And yes, this is the case in much of the Latin music of composers such as Tallis and Sheppard: in other words, perhaps there was a purely musical reason why the range of the counter-tenor part was kept at a level which is low for falsettists. Yet if this is really an explanation for a low falsettist range, it falls to the ground in a number of works, such as Sheppard's *Gaude, gaude, gaude Maria*, in which the ceiling of the counter-tenor parts, even in imitative entries, is (perversely) a ninth below that of the treble part. At high pitch, the upper limit to the counter-tenor range in these cases would be only $f\sharp'-g'$. What other reason could there be for these low ranges, other than that the counter-tenors in question were unable to sing higher? To take this one step further, if these counter-tenors really were falsettists we must ask what kind of singers they were who could not be trusted above an $f\sharp'$ or g'? Even today, this pitch level would be a minimum requirement for tenors, let alone falsettists.

Now let us look at the lower part of the counter-tenor range. Compared to the ranges written by modern English composers (who were known to have been writing for counter-tenors, and at a pitch we can be sure of), even a tone above modern pitch the bottom notes in Tudor counter-tenor parts lie extremely low. Modern falsettists, faced with this music at high pitch, are forced to switch downwards into chest voice for low-lying passages. In his beautifully produced editions, David Wulstan presented Tudor polyphony a minor third above written pitch. Yet even at this pitch, in a work such as Sheppard's first setting of *Dum transisset sabbatum* (Ex. 7), the multiple ledger lines of the alto parts provide a real test of the calligrapher's art. As for the test provided to the falsettist, it is not simply the lowness of the notes that causes a problem, but their lowness in relation to the other parts. In the third bar of Ex. 7 the second alto part descends below the

Ex. 7 John Sheppard, *Dum transisset sabbatum*: excerpt from the Oxenford
Imprint edition by David Wulstan, transposed up a minor third

tenor and bass, whilst the treble sails two and a half octaves above. For a
modal singer, interweaving with other modal voices is straightforward: for
the falsettist, having to produce exposed bass notes with his less-preferred
vocal technique, it is not so easy.

Ultimately, it is not the lowest part of the Tudor counter-tenor
range which causes most problems for falsettists, but the middle, in the
troublesome border area of chest and head registers. At high pitch a huge
number of entries in this music begin in precisely the awkward area just
below *c'* in which the 'gear-change' is normally effected. For instance, at
written pitch, *g* is the most frequent starting note for counter-tenor parts in
the 1575 *Cantiones sacrae*: at high pitch this exposes the most problematic
part of the falsettist's range. Would Tallis and Byrd – both practical
musicians – have continuously exposed their colleagues to such an
unnecessary technical trial? The difficulty most modern falsettists have with
this hybrid range has led to the convenient theory that Tudor counter-tenor
parts call for a technique and style which has been 'lost'.[13] Yes, techniques
do change with time, but in this case there is a much simpler explanation:
pitch and physiology. The high pitch theory may bring the counter-tenor
part of the mid-to-late Tudor period clos*er* to the range of the modern
falsettist, but the line remains clos*est* to that of the modern tenor. And for
his Tudor equivalent, shorter in physical stature but higher in vocal pitch,
there is no reason to believe that the upper notes of the counter-tenor part
would have caused any problems.

[13] Peter Phillips, 'Performance Practice in Sixteenth-Century English Choral
Music', *Early Music* 6(2) (1978), pp. 195–9, at p. 194.

Charles Butler and the 'sweet shrill voice'

T HIS question of physical stature and vocal pitch also accounts for another curiosity of English Tudor music – and one worthy of a brief digression, as it has a knock-on effect on the counter-tenor part. At high pitch, the treble part in phrase after phrase of much of the Latin music of the period goes up to (and hovers around) $g\sharp''-a''$. In our own time, experiments with boys singing Tudor polyphony at high pitch have been very rare, and even more rarely successful. More common have been performances by adult female sopranos. But whether with boys or women, to modern ears, in performance this range has proved nothing but remarkable. Reviews of modern performances at high pitch seem magnetically drawn to the stratospheric range of the treble part, and indeed the Tudor 'high treble' has become accepted terminology. Yet from the entire Tudor period, only one reference to the high range of trebles has survived – and that one carries a very significant qualification. In the fullest description of the treble voice, Charles Butler says that 'The Treble [...] is to bee sung with a high cleere sweete voice.'[14] Yet elsewhere Butler remarks that there are 'soom Trebles that arise aboov this ordinari compas'.[15] Evidently to the boys of Butler's time – and by implication to those who heard it – the standard treble range was high, but not uncomfortably so. This suggests that what we think of as high, and what Tudor commentators thought of as high, are not the same. The obvious reason for this difference in perception is the physiological capacity of Tudor and modern singers.

Despite its late date, Butler's 1636 description of vocal types is perhaps the strongest documentary evidence of singing styles in the Tudor period, and has been drawn into the front-line of those arguing for and those arguing against the existence of the falsetto voice. The irony here is that it dates from long after the deaths of almost all the great Tudor composers. As with the evidence of the Dallam organ at Worcester, we should be wary of applying evidence dating from the seventeenth century to the early Tudor era, of which Butler had no direct experience. That said, Butler had sung in the choir of Magdalen College, Oxford, from 1579 to 1585, and there are more references to music from the 1575 *Cantiones sacrae* of Tallis and Byrd than to that of any other composer. Moreover, when he wrote his *Principles*, Butler was a Hampshire country parson, far removed from the hub of modern performance. So, while we cannot apply his observations to pre-Reformation Tudor music, we should bear in mind that the highest choral standards he is likely to have known would have been at Oxford in the early 1580s. Further, in the preface to his *Principles* Butler refers to the present day as 'these giddy and new-fangled times', which should perhaps alert us to the nostalgia of a man looking back at the music-making

---

[14] Charles Butler, *The Principles of Musik* (London, 1636), p. 42.

[15] Butler, *The Principles of Musik*, p. 9.

of his youth. Butler's description of vocal types reinforces this image of a backward-looking commentator, since it refers to the five-part vocal scoring of the pre-Reformation period – a vocal scoring which had all but died out in music for the new Anglican rite. It seems reasonable, then, that despite its date we can apply Butler's definitions to choral practice at least as far back as the 1570s. But interestingly, Butler refers to the treble as 'the highest part of a boy or woman': since there is no record of women being used in the church choirs which sang this music, perhaps we might also apply his definitions to the kind of private devotional music-making at which post-Reformation Latin music (such as the 1575 *Cantiones*) was sung.

So what does Butler say about the voices of the time, and about the counter-tenor in particular? Firstly, his descriptions of the bass part as being that of the lowest man's voice, and of the upper two parts as being those of higher and lower boys (or women's) voices, are unequivocal, and tally with all other evidence from the period. When modern all-male choirs sing the music of the early Tudor period, they tend to do so at written pitch, with the mean part being sung by falsettists. As a modern practice this is understandable, but as we have seen, almost all documentary evidence from the Tudor period confirms that the mean part was sung by boys' voices: from the whole of the period there is not one direct reference to an adult male singing the mean part.

More equivocal, perhaps, are Butler's definitions of the tenor and counter-tenor parts:

> (b) The Tenor is so called, becaus it was commonly in Motets the ditti-part or Plain-song: which continued in the same kind of notes (usually briefs) much after one plain fashion: uppon which the other partes did discant in sundry sortes of Figures, and after many different ways: or (if you will) becaus neither ascending to any high or strained note, nor descending very low, it continueth in one ordinari tenor of the voice and therefore may be sung by an indifferent voice.

> (c) The Countertenor or Contratenor, is so called, becaus it answereth the Tenor, though commonly in higher keyz: and therefore is fittest for a man of a sweet shrill voice. Which Part though it have little melodi by itself; (as consisting much of monotonies) yet in Harmoni it hath the greatest grace: specially when it is sung with a right voice: which is too rare.

Before looking at Butler's notional counter-tenor, let us study its context, by looking closely at the implications of his definition of the tenor. 'An indifferent voice' strongly suggests what we would call a baritone. 'Neither ascending to any high or strained note', implies, since there is no disclaimer elsewhere, that one man's part *did* ascend to high and, if not actually 'strained', at least unrestrained notes.

This part could only be the counter-tenor, yet as we have seen, even at high pitch this part lies very low for falsettists, and for them its general tessitura could hardly encourage unrestrained singing. To be sure, one essential characteristic which generally distinguishes the falsetto voice (even in its higher range) from that of the tenor is its apparent ease of production. Butler's definition of the counter-tenor part as being best suited to a man of 'sweet shrill voice' has been used to support the theory that this part was taken by falsettists.[16] Nowadays, when applied to individuals the word 'shrill' is most-often used pejoratively to describe an edgy female voice. The falsetto voice, too, has often been likened to a female voice. Linked by the word 'edgy', it has been suggested that 'falsetto' and 'shrill' are synonymous.[17] However tenuous this link appears, it is difficult to find any other reason why modern commentators could have associated 'shrill' with the Tudor counter-tenor part. The etymology of the word certainly suggests no such reading. In the early seventeenth century 'shrill' was simply used to describe loud (sometimes high) sounds – a meaning which could hardly be applied to the falsetto voice in its low to mid-range. In 1581, the priest Gregory Martin describes clerical assistants using their speaking voices to announce the nature of particular relics to a Roman church full of visitors: 'Two other of shrill and sounding voices [...] to pronounce and tel the people what everie relike is.'[18] Interestingly, when 'shrill' was used to describe musical instruments these were typically military pipes and trumpets – witness the words of John Bale at the start of this chapter. Again, these instruments hardly call to mind the tone of the low falsettist.

A further clue that the English counter-tenor was not a falsetto voice comes in an early seventeenth-century description of a song in a masque by Thomas Campion:

> Here standing on a smooth green, and environed with the horse-men, they present a song of five parts [...] the Robin-Hood men feign two trebles; one of the Keepers with the Cynic sing two counter-tenors, the other Keeper the bass [...][19]

Note that the men singing treble 'feign' their parts but those singing counter-tenor, evidently, do not. As we shall see in Chapter 5, this use of the word 'feign' to signify falsetto would, during the seventeenth century, become standard in England. This reference is our first strong evidence of falsetto singing in England, but before we regard it as signifying a more widespread practice, we should bear in mind its context: like the earlier references to falsetto in the Feast of Fools in Sens, this singing was part of a comical 'rude entertainment'.

[16] Wulstan, *Tudor Music*, pp. 233–4.
[17] Wulstan, *Tudor Music*, p. 245.
[18] Gregory Martin, *Roma Sancta*, ed. George Bruner Parks (Rome, 1969), p. 52.
[19] Thomas Campion, *A Relation of the Late Royall Entertainment...* (London, 1613), pp. 6–7; available online at <http://special-1.bl.uk/treasures/festivalbooks/BookDetails.aspx?strFest=0244> [accessed 4 April 2014].

It is tempting to summarise the situation in England simply by noting that, taken together, the evidence of pitch, physiology and written accounts suggest that the falsetto voice was not known during the Tudor period. We should not reach this conclusion, however, without noting that there was at least a whiff of change in the air by the end of the period. Perhaps Butler even hints at this, and we will return to his words in a moment. Arguably the greatest myth of English Tudor church music (and one which even this sentence appears to peddle) is that it can be referred to as a single entity. Let us remember that this was a period of more than a century, during which English music moved from the medieval to the Baroque, with the small matter of a religious revolution in the middle. Not surprisingly, aesthetics changed, and with them musical styles and performance practices. Vocal scoring certainly changed, and perhaps by implication the individual voice types. At least on paper the counter-tenor part altered significantly during the period. In the music of the Eton Choirbook its range, ascending only to a written *f'*, is virtually indistinguishable from that of the tenor part. By the pre-Reformation polyphony of the mid-sixteenth century the tenor and counter-tenor are distinct, with the upper part ascending more commonly to a written *g'*, mirroring a rise in the range of the treble part an octave above. In the music of the late Tudor composers, written *g'* is the common ceiling of the counter-tenor part, with even the occasional *a'*. This historical rise occurred against a relatively stable written range in the bass. (The bass, incidentally, is always the part likely to have been most constant in sounding pitch: whereas the upper limits of adult male voices are variable, depending on the choice of modal or falsetto techniques, the lower limits have no such possible extension.)

The implication of this is that not just the written range, but the sounding range of the counter-tenor part rose incrementally during the Tudor period. With this in mind, we can now look at Butler's final words on the counter-tenor: 'it hath the greatest grace: specially when it is sung with a right voice: which is too rare'. If the 'right voice' he describes was what we would think of as the tenor, what was the nature of the other voices – not 'right' – which he had heard singing this part? Could this be a rather grudging acknowledgement that, at the time of writing, Butler was aware of certain men singing at least the top notes of the range in falsetto? This will be our point of departure when we come to the existence of falsetto in Restoration England.

Before we leave the question of English sacred music, one final conundrum needs addressing. If Tudor choirs did generally perform at a higher pitch than our own modern standard, and if we are interested in recreating their performance practice, should we not adopt a similar pitch to theirs – even if this means replacing their tenors with our falsettists? The answer to this conundrum perhaps lies not with the performers but with the listeners. To late twentieth-century listeners performances a tone or more above modern pitch, even with falsettists on the counter-tenor line, have rarely proved other than remarkable; with tenors on the counter-tenor line the sonority of performances at high pitch would be sensational.[20] However there is no evidence that to sixteenth-century ears the 'ordinari compas' of the music was in the least exceptional. The reason for this would now seem to be obvious: the shorter physiological stature of the sixteenth-century male and his correspondingly higher voice would have made 'high pitch' performances unremarkable for singers, and thus unremarkable for listeners also. If we want to reproduce the effect – as opposed to the actuality – of the first performances of Tudor sacred music, we need to re-create the falsetto-less choirs of the original ensembles. With this ensemble in place, we then need to perform at a pitch which sounds as 'ordinari' to modern ears as did the original to Tudor ones.

Of course, by implication the same principle can be applied to Continental Renaissance music. Again, pitch may have been generally higher than our own, but if we attempt to replicate this by asking singers to operate above their comfortable ranges, or by rearranging parts with historically inappropriate voices, we are surely moving further away from the effect of the original performances. Yet this is precisely the way modern choirs most often sing this music. Specialist early music choirs, and all-male church choirs, commonly perform Renaissance music with boys or women singing soprano, and falsettists on the alto line. True, boys (and castrati) did sing soprano in the Renaissance, but there are two good reasons to suggest that they would have done so in the lower part of their possible ranges: firstly, if falsettists were also singing this part, as the evidence suggests they often were, it must have been sung at a mutually manageable pitch: secondly, if the alto part was taken by modal-voiced singers, then this again implies a limit on how high, relatively, the music could have been pitched. It is worth remembering that outside the modern English tradition, boys' voices are commonly used on lower-lying parts. Suffice it to say that, without exception, every piece of Continental polyphony from the Renaissance can be comfortably sung by a combination of modern basses, baritones, tenors and falsettists. The effect of Renaissance polyphony at this pitch is perhaps more akin to dark velvet than bright silk, but as long as the contemporary theorists' mantra of clarity is heeded by the singers, the details of the music are still audible. Before leaving the contradictions between historical and modern performance practice, it remains to underline one salient point: that nowhere in Renaissance England or Europe did the falsettist commonly sing the alto part.

[20] Although Andrew Parrott and his Taverner Choir come close to this actuality (and effect) when performing early Tudor polyphony a semitone above modern pitch, with high tenors on the counter-tenor line.

Dowland and the Lutenists' Cantus Voice

ASIDE from the alto lines of church music, if there is one aspect of Renaissance music we commonly associate with the sound of the falsettist it is the music of John Dowland and his fellow English lute song composers. In modern times, Deller was the first to stake a claim on this territory, and his followers have shown no signs of relinquishing their hold. Is there any evidence, though, that Dowland and his contemporaries wrote with the falsetto voice in mind? Taken at face value, there is little in the music to suggest this, since commonly the cantus part (as the vocal part is termed) goes up to a soprano *f"*. Certainly at modern pitch, for modern falsettists, this has proved uncomfortably high, and common practice for Deller and his followers has been to transpose the music down a fourth. Could this kind of pitch have been what the lutenist composers expected to hear? The pitch levels Dowland knew (which can tentatively be gauged by the optimal tension of lute strings) were indeed lower than our own, but by around a tone, and not a fourth. It is true that various sizes of lutes existed, and obviously these had different optimal pitches, but larger, lower-pitched instruments were far from common. Nor is there evidence that individual players used a battery of different instruments to accommodate different vocal ranges. The instruments, then, do not suggest the low pitch adopted by Deller and others. Neither does the written music: lute parts do exist in different keys, but again, such instances are very rare. Perhaps, then, the key to a low performance pitch lies in the skills of the players. After all, musicians of the period were adept at transposing. Yet when performers transposed they were doing so from staved notation: to do so from lute tablature was not remotely practicable.

There is one other factor we need to consider before ruling out the possibility that the lutenists were writing for falsettists. If the shorter men of the period generally had higher voices, then there is no reason why this would not also apply to falsettists. Combined with a pitch level around a tone below our own, shorter human height might bring many lute songs into the possible falsetto range of the Renaissance singer. But by the same token, these factors would also have brought baritones (and middling female voices) into play. These latter options are surely far more likely. After all, Dowland was writing for publication, and as such for the widest possible amateur market. Even if there was any evidence that falsettists were known in England at the time, Dowland's greatest commercial opportunity could hardly have been to target this particular voice.

There is only one surviving contemporary source which associates the lute-song repertory with the counter-tenor voice. Of a masque by Campion, we find the following description: 'this song was sung by an excellent counter-tenor voice, with rare variety of division unto two unusual instruments, all being concealed within the arbour.'[21] This undoubtedly connects a counter-tenor with a solo song of one of the lutenists. However, its uniqueness hardly suggests that the connection was commonplace. And in any event, from the weight of other evidence we have amassed, the type of counter-tenor referred to was what we would think of as a tenor, and not a falsettist. In short, the evidence suggests that the lutenist composers were not writing for any particular vocal type, and certainly not for a falsettist.

I F the picture we have created of the Renaissance falsettist in England and the Continent is not as sharply defined as we might like – more Monet than Michelangelo – that perhaps represents the historical reality in the truest way possible. At every step the Renaissance singer will confound our preconceptions of stratified vocal scoring, our calibrated idea of pitch, and our modern approach to performance practice. Perhaps one historical example will illustrate the ad-hoc nature of Renaissance performance.

In January 1506 the Habsburg court of Philip the Fair, including his cosmopolitan musical entourage, set sail from the Netherlands to Spain. Within days the entire party was shipwrecked on the English coast. Henry VII, hearing of this, received Philip and his court at Windsor, where musicians of both sovereigns entertained the company over the Feast of Candlemass. Although in this case the causes may have been unusual, musical blind dates such as this were far from uncommon. There are similar records of the Habsburg chapel singing with other chapels in their travels across Europe, from Austria to Spain. Nor was this cross-cultural exchange exclusive to the Habsburg chapel: examples abound from every part of Europe and every decade of the Renaissance. When rulers came together, meetings between their musical establishments were staged to symbolise harmony on a political level. Yet for all the documented occasions of disparate musicians coming together to perform, we have no evidence that they ever rehearsed beforehand. Presumably they must have arranged who would sing and play which parts, but if they went beyond this point, no records survive. The matters that early vocal ensembles spend time preparing today – the coordination of pronunciation and consonants, decisions on accidentals arising from *musica ficta*, establishment of tempi, balance, blend and dynamics – were evidently of no great concern to Renaissance musicians. Nor was the nature of the ensemble. Many Renaissance choirs changed in size and disposition from one year to the next. In the records of any one institution we might find boys replaced by castrati and falsettists, or a tenor who then appears as a bass, or a bass substituted for by a trombonist. To a modern choral director the implied realities of performance practice in the Renaissance are likely to be an anathema. From our own age it is perhaps impromptu meetings of folk or jazz musicians, at which various routes towards a vaguely shared goal are

---

[21] Campion, *A Relation of the Late Royall Entertainment*, p. 10.

explored, and journeying takes precedence over arriving, that would best resemble the Renaissance performance ethic.

Only in this context of perpetual flux can we realistically place the figure of the Renaissance falsettist. Or perhaps we should clunkily (but more accurately) say 'singers of the Renaissance who used falsetto': in Europe, if not England, the period was musically peopled by a great variety of singers whose voices came under this umbrella term.

Reserved Spaniards:
Cultural Stereotypes and the High Male Voice

> A performance of Victoria's Requiem comes to mind, in which I mistakenly attempted to impose an English restraint upon certain passages. Only when the full-blooded Spanish texture was allowed to come into its own did the piece become more comfortable to sing and the performance achieve a more obvious reflection of the intentions of the composer.
>
> David Wulstan[1]

WHETHER based on nation, race, gender or occupation, stereotyping is a practice which we lapse into more than we might care to admit. Be it the restrained Englishman or the full-blooded Spaniard, at some time most of us will use this type of broad brush to tar a group of people. Perhaps its dubious value can best be gauged by our willingness to typecast others, but not ourselves. On British roads most drivers will be wary of white vans, which are regarded as synonymous with cavalier driving. Yet the same drivers, if and when they find themselves behind the wheel of a white van, are unlikely suddenly to see themselves as irresponsible. This is not to say that stereotypes are wholly erroneous. Like clichés, they are unlikely to gain currency without some basis in reality. Yet how widely we can use that currency is another matter. Stereotypes are not universally applicable, even in our own time and country. And if typecasting is an unreliable way to pass judgment on those we experience at first hand, what possible value can it have in judging people outside our own orbit? It is quite possible that men driving white vans in Jakarta today are thought of as models of highway probity. Similarly, perhaps to Englishmen of half a century ago, their deliverymen had a reputation for courteousness on the road.

If stereotyping is such dangerous territory, is it something we need engage with? In an ideal world perhaps not, but those interested in the history of performance practice have little option. For our purposes, in establishing what types of high male voices were favoured at a particular place and time, and how they were used, it helps if we can form a picture of that society. In the background of that picture, giving it depth, we will need to sketch in the social, political and cultural motivations of those involved. Our foreground will be based on the most specific evidence we can find – a review of a singer, a vocal treatise, or an impression from a listener. Ultimately, though, however specific these individual observations are, we will need to distil them into a composite image. So, remembering that this

---

[1] Wulstan, *Tudor Music*, p. 185.

is more art than science, and that interpretation will always have the final say after observation, now let us examine some stereotypes of particular significance.

Post-war England is a good place for us to start, since it was the formative moment in the modern counter-tenor revival. Despite the fact that it was an era of great change, the culture of England in the late 1940s was frugal, and not just for consumers. When one listens to the clipped voices of BBC broadcasters from that period, or to the deferential responses of their subjects, one senses formality and emotional restraint. The English – at least its higher classes – not only recognised this quality in themselves, but viewed it as a virtue. In this context, it is easy to see why the falsetto voice was immediately recognised as quintessentially English: certainly in the case of Deller, here was a voice which favoured quiet subtlety over voluble histrionics. The fact that in the later twentieth century, emotionally effusive Italy should produce a wealth of ringing tenors but no falsettists, seemed to complement this view. Granted, bombastic Englishmen and restrained Italians could always be found, but exceptions qualify a stereotype rather than discount it. Following Deller, the notion that England was a nation of counter-tenors, and that the Mediterranean was the home of tenors, was quickly established. Until recently it persisted.

Since its subjects are relatively easy to define, any snap-shot of the present has an undeniable validity. The problem with our picture of the present – of English restraint, Mediterranean vigour, and (if we care to widen the image) French suavity and Germanic forthrightness – comes the moment it is projected backwards in time. What tells us that the same stereotypes can be applied to the era of Rossini and Bizet, let alone the Renaissance worlds of Victoria and Tallis? Staying with England for the time being, to what extent can we link the worlds of Deller and of the earlier English composers his voice came to be associated with? When the Deller Consort recorded a disc of music by Thomas Tallis in the mid-1950s, reviewers who noted the 'authenticity' of the singing would have been aware that the composer and director had both been members of the same institution – Canterbury Cathedral choir. If we know that they shared the same environment and cultural tradition, then does it not suggest that they shared the same musical and vocal sound-world? In other words, whilst falling short of firm evidence, would not such similarities quietly imply that a restrained falsettist such as Deller might have had a place in Tallis's sound-world?

Of course, there are threads which seem to link the worlds of those two men – and not just physical ones. They also spoke the same language, shared a belief in the same God, and praised him in the words of the same liturgy. If these physical and cultural factors were indeed constants, then surely the worlds of Tallis and Deller would have fitted the same broad stereotype of English restraint? What we imagine to be constants, though, are often no such thing. Take the physical environments both men knew at Canterbury. Although from the outside the building would have appeared the same, the choir stalls Deller sang in date from the century after Tallis's death. And, lest this seem trivial, the new choir stalls point to a changing function for the institution itself. When Tallis went to Canterbury in 1540 England was undergoing a religious revolution. For musicians everything changed, from the language they sang in to the place they sang from. Tallis was born into a medieval world and died in a humanist one. In truth, there was far more upheaval in the life of Canterbury Cathedral during Tallis's working life than there was between his death and the arrival of Deller some 350 years later. English 'restraint' is understandable in a status quo of the kind Deller knew, but is not as easy to sense in the maelstrom Tallis experienced.

To move to a specific illustration of Tallis's Canterbury, whilst in service there, he would have witnessed conservative members of the clergy plotting against their Archbishop, Cranmer. At the funeral service for Cranmer's reformist chaplain in the Cathedral, the bell-ringer seized the censer and poured the hot coals over the new grave.[2] The plotters were later arrested on suspicion of heresy. Later still, of course, Cranmer himself was to be burnt at the stake for his religious convictions. Evidently the 'comfortable words' of Cranmer's Prayer Book, which centuries later Deller sang as part of a cosy tradition, had been anything but comfortable in their creation. Even outside the church of the English Reformation we sense a passion and lack of restraint. In 1560 Bishop John Jewel wrote from London that 'You may now sometimes see at St Paul's Cross, after the service, six thousand persons, old and young, of both sexes, all singing together and praising God.'[3] This picture of volatility and fervour underlines how misguided it is for us automatically to assign the stereotype of Deller's age to the age of Tallis. As we have seen in the last chapter, the direct evidence suggests that English counter-tenors of the late-twentieth and mid-sixteenth centuries were not of the same vocal species. The indirect evidence of cultural stereotypes only supports the theory that they were different.

As well as the context, the sound of Cranmer's words changed dramatically between the ages of Tallis and Deller. On paper, words appear to be a constant. Yet just as their meaning will shift over time, so will their sound. Pronunciation, then, is a hidden variable, and one which has a direct bearing on the stereotypes we unwittingly create, particularly for singers. Opera singers often point to the open nature of Italian vowels as being a direct aid to emotionally direct performances of Verdi and Puccini. By implication, languages with relatively closed vowels – modern French being an example – encourage subtlety and nuance. Yet in the life of one language we can often find both ends of the spectrum. Whereas the covered, muted

---

[2] Cf. Diarmaid MacCulloch, *Thomas Cranmer: A Life* (London, 1996), p. 312.

[3] Hastings Robinson (ed. and trans.), *The Zurich Letters: Comprising the Correspondence of Several English Bishops and Others ...* (Cambridge, 1842), vol. 1, p. 71.

vowels of modern English may lend themselves to a restrained approach to Tallis's English-texted works, the pungent colours of Elizabethan English provide no such encouragement. A similar dichotomy exists with the French language. Attempts at the style of French Lully would have heard in *Le Bourgeois Gentilhomme*, with rolled r's, diphthongs and voiced final consonants, suggest a far more vibrant sound-world than one might hear today from the Comédie-Française.[4]

However suggestive it might be, the evidence of cultural environments and historical pronunciation will never tell us directly how people sang at a given time and place. The specific observations of commentators, though freighted with their own agendas and sometimes contradicting each other, are harder to dismiss. In the eighteenth century, for instance, countless writers stereotyped Italian and French singers, and not in the way we, today, might expect. Take Jean-Jacques Rousseau, writing in 1753:

> French singing demands full lung power, the full range of the voice, louder, our singing masters tell us, swell the sounds, open the mouth, use the whole of your voice. Softer, say the Italian masters, don't force, sing freely, make your notes soft, flexible and flowing, save the outbursts for those rare and fleeting moments when you must astonish and overwhelm.[5]

Neither can we dismiss such observations as cultural inferiority or the mere sniping of neighbours, since even the neutral observer offers similar observations. In Lyon, Charles Burney 'was more disgusted than ever at French music after the dainties my ears had long been feasted with in Italy', having to endure 'such screaming, forcing and trilling as quite turned me sick'.[6]

An Italy besotted with castrati and falsettists, and soft high singing, is difficult to equate with the country of red-blooded tastes we know today. A similar, but perhaps even more remarkable case is that of Spain. The nation we now associate with the machismo of the bull-fighter was, as we have seen, the same country which in the early Renaissance had exported

---

[4] For a flavour of earlier French pronunciation, readers are referrered to the magnificent work of Benjamin Lazar, online at <http://www.youtube.com/watch?v=suPosOis4Qc> [accessed 4 April 2014].

[5] 'Le chant Françoise exige tout l'effort des poumons, toute l'étendue de la voix; plus fort, nous disent nos Maîtres, enflez les sons, ouvrez la bouche, donnez toute votre voix. Plus doux, dissent les Maîtres Italiens, ne forcez point, chantez sans gene, rendez vos sons doux, flexibles & coulands, reservez les éclats pour ces momens rares & passagers où if faut surprendre & déchirer.': Jean-Jacques Rousseau, *Lettre sur la musique françoise* (Paris, 1753), p. 30. Original and translation quoted from Andrew Parrott, 'Falsetto and the French', *Basler Jahrbuch für historische Musikpraxis* 26 (2002), pp. 129–48, at p. 138.

[6] Charles Burney, *Music, Men, and Manners in France and Italy ...* [1770], ed. H. Edmund Poole (London, 1974), p. 220.

male sopranos to the rest of Europe. Here we sense a grinding of tectonic plates as we bring these images of modern and early Spain alongside each other. Neither do we find much help from contemporary observations as we try to mesh these realities together. Spain was never part of the Grand Tour, as were Italy and France, and visitors were relatively rare, particularly as the period of most interest to us is before 1600. The Swiss student Thomas Platter wrote, in 1599, that 'The Spaniard is sad by nature, taciturn, uncommunicative, slow in his enterprise [...] always stiff and affected, he knows neither the gaiety nor the affability of the French.'[7] Spanish gravity was a vein mined by many others (with a consistency which might indicate veracity but which, we should always bear in mind, might simply indicate plagiarism). James Howell, for instance, in his *Instructions for Forreine Travell* (1642), noted that the Spanish were 'reserved and thoughtful'. Yet interesting as these occasional visitors are, they tell us little that is useful about any music they might have heard. To glean anything about musical matters we are left with passing remarks such as that by the Renaissance German theorist Ornithoparcus, who notes that when singing 'the Spanish weep'. Granted, a pithy quip such as this (albeit one which resonates with other, non-musical observations) is hardly an ideal basis for recreating the sound-world of Victoria. If, though, our only other option is to casually transplant a modern blood-and-thunder stereotype, we are surely better to perceive the Renaissance Spaniard in the words of his contemporaries.

By doing so we may see Victoria and his countrymen as rather lachrymose and austere. Yet this hardly accounts for the earlier Spanish predilection for falsetto and castrato voices, let alone the exotic instruments which were heard in and around Iberian churches. Where did these traditions spring from? Here, observations from commentators will not help us, since they are virtually non-existent before the sixteenth century. To appreciate this earlier Iberia, we are left to rely on what we know of the ethnic mix and cultural kaleidoscope of the peninsula before 1600. When the Berber Muslims from North Africa invaded Spain during the eighth century, they brought with them a sound-world and culture new to Europe. Moorish Spain introduced many new instruments to the West (such as the oud, which was to spread through Europe as the lute); as we have seen, the Moors also brought eunuchs to Europe. By 1492 the Moorish invaders had been finally routed and forced to leave, but just as they left behind them mosques such as the Mezquita in Córdoba, which became appropriated as a

---

[7] 'Sie sindt von nature alle zimblich melancholisch unndt de{ß}wegen auch langsam in ihren fürnemmen, understehndedt nicht baldt ettwas [...] Sie sindt zum zächen unndt wolleben nitt so gesellig als die Frantzosen [...]': Thomas Platter, *Beschreibung der Reisen durch Frankreich, Spanien, England und die Niederlande ...* (Basel, 1968), p. 380. Translation from Sean Jennett (ed. and trans.), *Journal of a Younger Brother: The Life of Thomas Platter as a Medical Student in Montpellier at the Close of the Sixteenth Century* (London, 1963), p. 227.

Catholic cathedral, so they left a musical legacy which included a penchant for the high adult male voice, and which became a vital part of Western culture. Only when we shelve our modern perception of Spain, and replace it with this exotic cultural mix, does the known reality of its falsetto and castrato history sit more easily.

Occasionally, of course, we might come across a historical perception of a country, or a culture, which seems to chime with our own view. Take Charles Burney's withering comment on German musicians being too loud: 'Sound can only be augmented to a certain degree, beyond that it is noise.'[8] Or the final words from Burney's journals of his European travels: 'Music, if I may hazard the thought, seems *play* to the Italians, and *work* to the Germans.'[9] The temptation, on finding a historical observation which accords with one of our own, is to nod, as if it were only to be expected. When we bear in mind the cross-currents of history, perhaps we should rather assume dissimilarity and raise our eyebrows at similarity. Only very rarely does the evidenced history of the high male singer match with the picture we create when we idly project modern stereotypes backwards in time.

---

[8] Charles Burney, *The Present State of Music in Germany, the Netherlands and United Provinces* (London, 1773), vol. 2, p. 203.

[9] Burney, *The Present State of Music*, p. 302.

CHAPTER 5

Baroque Europe

THE Grand Tour, that ill-defined rite of passage which for two centuries allowed young gentlefolk to experience the cultural legacies of the Mediterranean, offers up a literature with rich pickings for the musical historian. These travelogues are significant not just for what they tell us of music abroad but also, by implication, for what they tell us of the music the writers knew at home. When in 1770 Charles Burney heard the strident voice of a Neapolitan 'counter-tenor [...] one of the most powerful I ever heard – it made its way through the whole band [numbering a hundred] in the loudest and most tumultuous parts of the choruses', he was unwittingly telling us as much about English performance practice as Italian.[1]

Granted, for centuries men had made passing reference to music they heard abroad. But invariably these comments were written by professionals, and freighted with strong (if unspoken) agendas: a cleric writing for members of his order, or an ambassador reporting to his patron, might note a style of singing, but with the implication that it would (or more often would not) be desirable at home. Unravelling the objective ear from the subjective mind in these cases is never easy. But from the seventeenth century onwards listeners experienced foreign music in a spirit of relative naivety. Thomas Coryat, the eccentric Englishman sometimes credited with establishing the Grand Tour, might have had royal connections in England, but he makes it clear in the account of his European travels that he is commenting as a private man, and not as a politician.

Italy and the 'supernaturall voice'

FOR our purposes Coryat, with his innocent ear, is by far the most important of the early tourists, because his visit to Venice in 1608 yields up the most famous of all historical descriptions of the falsetto voice. Largely because of the influence of Monteverdi and the Italian monodists, by this time the musical centre of gravity had shifted from Rome to northern Italy, and in plotting the course of the falsettist during the early Baroque, much of our attention will be focused on this small geographical area. Coryat found himself in Venice on 16 August, the Feast of San Rocco. On that day he heard, at the Scuole San Rocco, a performance featuring many of the finest musicians in Venice:

> This feast consisted principally of Musicke, which was both vocall and instrumental, so good, and delectable, so rare, so admirable, so super-excellent, that it did even ravish and stupifie all those strangers

---

[1] Burney, *Music, Men, and Manners in France and Italy*, p. 160.

that never heard the like [...] Of the singers there were three or foure
so excellent that I think few or none in Christendome do excell them,
especially one, who had such a peerless and (as I may in a manner say)
such a supernaturall voice for such a privilege for the sweetness of
his voice as sweetness, that I think there was never a better singer in
all the world, insomuch that he did not onely give the most pleasant
contentment that could be imagined, to all the hearers, but also did
as it were astonish and amaze them. I alwaies thought that he was a
Eunuch, which if he had beene, it had taken away some part of my
admiration, because they do most commonly sing passing well; but
he was not, therefore it was much the more admirable. Againe it was
the more-worthy of admiration, because he was a middle-aged man,
as about forty yeares old. For nature doth more commonly bestowe
such singularitie of voice upon boyes and striplings, than upon men
of such yeares. Besides it was farre the more excellent, because it
was nothing forced, strained or affected, but came from him with
the greatest facilitie that ever I heard. Truely, I thinke that had a
Nightingale beene in the same roome, and contended with him for
the superioritie, something perhaps he might excell him, because
God hath granted that little birdie such a privilege for the sweetnesse
of his voice, as to none other: but I thinke he could not much. To
conclude, I attribute so much to this rare fellow for his singing, that
I thinke the country where he was borne, may be as proude for
breeding so singular a person as Smyrna was of her Homer, Verona of
her Catullus, or Mantua of Virgil. But exceeding happy may that Citie
or towne, or person bee that possesseth this miracle of nature.[2]

Who, then, was this 'miracle of nature'? Fortunately, in the Venetian State
Archives survive documents stating whom Coryat heard performing at the
Scuole on that day. Amongst the illustrious cast – which included Giovanni
Gabrieli – were three adult male sopranos. Two of these – Vido Rovetta
and Bartolomeo Barbarino – were known as falsettists. The third, however,
was a Spanish castrato, Mattia Fernando. Bearing in mind the clandestine
operations of castrati in Italian churches during the Renaissance, we might
wonder whether Coryat was really listening to a falsettist. In other words,
were the 'falsettists' actually undisclosed castrati? Or, come to that, had
Coryat been deliberately misled by an evasive guide, and was he listening
to the castrato Fernando? Had Coryat's visit been thirty years earlier, these
scenarios would have been distinct possibilities. But since the Papal Bull
of 1589, when castrati were officially sanctioned, there would have been
less reason for such secretive manœuvres. And in fact, in this case we
can be fairly confident that the designation is accurate. Coryat describes
the 'supernaturall voice' as belonging to a man 'about forty yeares old', and

---

[2] Thomas Coryat, *Coryat's Crudities; Hastily Gobled up in Five Moneths Travells
in France, Savoy, Italy* ... (London, 1611; repr. 1905), p. 389.

whereas the castrato Fernando was a young man, first employed at St Mark's in 1603, the two falsettists were indeed about forty. Both older men were illustrious singers and, to judge from their surviving compositions, virtuoso ones.[3]

Coryat's description is obviously informative of practice in Italy during the early Baroque. It is also suggestive of practice in England. If the falsetto voice was familiar to him, surely we might expect him to relate the singer he has heard in Venice to falsettists he has encountered in England, in the same way that he relates the singer to 'eunuchs', 'boyes' and 'striplings' he has heard. It is noticeable that Coryat does not actually possess a technical term to describe the singer. Certainly the term 'counter-tenor' is notable by its absence. This, and the fact that he remarks on the phenomenon in such an astonished manner, sits uneasily with the notion that the falsettist was a feature of English choral practice at the end of the Tudor period.

Coryat's words add weight to the argument that the falsettist was still only a Continental voice at the turn of the seventeenth century. Not just in Venice, but Rome too, falsettists were still to be heard. As part of the jubilee celebrations in 1600, at the Oratory of the Arciconfraternita all'Ave Maria, were heard 'the most rare falsettists', including 'the most pleasing Signor Lodovico – a very light falsetto – who with *gorgie* and *passaggi* showed how much he is valued in this profession.'[4] Even in Italy, though, the role of the falsettist was under threat. The church's acceptance of castrati, and the consequent rise in their numbers as a production-line of native Italian castrati swung into operation, clearly threatened the livelihood of falsettists. At the Cappella Sistina in Rome, any remaining falsettists had been replaced with castrati by 1601.[5] Although this process happened naturally, as falsettists left the choir, we may wonder what became of the successors to their tradition. At less well-endowed churches in Italy, where castrati could not be afforded, falsettists still found employment. But we should remember that falsetto was not the only method available to an aspiring singer when his voice broke: without a strong demand for falsettists, there would have doubtless been less encouragement for them to develop this method. In these circumstances potential falsettists were more likely to nurture their modal voices instead.

---

[3] Denis Arnold, 'Music at the Scuola de San Rocco', *Music and Letters* 40(3) (1959) pp. 229–41, at pp. 237–8.

[4] 'falsetti rarissimi [...] molto leggiadro per falsetto il Signor Lodovico gratiasissimo, che con gorga e passagi mostrava quanto valesse in questa professione.': cf. Richard Wistreich, '"Il soprano e veramente l'ornamento di tutte l'altre parti": *Soprani, Castrati, Falsettisti* and the Performance of Late Renaissance Italian Secular Music', in *Der Countertenor: die männliche Falsettstimme vom Mittelalter zur Gegenwart*, ed. Corinna Herr and Arnold Jacobshagen (Mainz, 2012), pp. 65–78, at p. 70.

[5] Gerbino, 'The Quest for the Soprano Voice', p. 321.

Yet almost as soon as Pope Sixtus's bull threatened to close Italian church doors on falsettists, they were opened up again for a straightforward musical reason. Opera, which took the peninsula by storm from the start of the seventeenth century, soon acted as a magnet for the better castrati, ultimately offering them vast financial rewards. Aside from the Roman churches and a handful of other lavish institutions, the church simply could not match the financial lure of the opera house. Significantly, the role of La Musica in Monteverdi's 1607 *Orfeo* – the first voice heard in the first great opera – was sung by a castrato, Giovanni Gualberto Magli. As a signal of the way in which the theatre was to attract singers from the church, the role of Euridice was taken by a castrato who sang in the ducal chapel, Girolamo Bacchini. Granted, the protagonist's role was taken by a tenor, but even this was soon to change. By the time of Monteverdi's late opera *L'incoronazione di Poppea*, the part of Nero was written for a castrato. And for nearly two hundred years this casting, with castrati filling the primary operatic roles, was the norm.

Despite the fact that castrati and falsettists occupied much the same territory in church, this transferability never existed in the opera house. (Here, it may be worth stating that the first major operatic role known to have been written for a falsettist was the part of Oberon in Britten's *A Midsummer Night's Dream*, first performed by Alfred Deller in 1960.) In 1739 Charles de Brosses writes that in Italian opera houses alto parts were sung by low female voices.[6] *Persona non grata* in the opera house, then, the falsettists were left with the church as their only viable employment, where they had fewer castrati (or at least, fewer of the best castrati) to compete against. To judge by the reports of English travellers to Italy in the seventeenth century, though, castrati had not disappeared from Italian churches: in 1659 Francis Mortoft heard '3 or 4 Eunuchs and singing Masters' at the Jesuit Church at Genoa, and 'at least 20 Eunuchs' at St Peter's in Rome; John Raymond and John Jackson made similar observations.[7] The only word of caution we need sound here is that, as Englishmen, these travellers were probably not familiar with high falsetto singing. It is possible, then, that amongst the singers they assumed to be castrati, were also falsettists.

What parts did falsettists sing in the early seventeenth-century Italian church? From Coryat's description it is fairly clear that they were still sopranists. But did falsettists also sing alto parts? This is a significant question for modern performers addressing the question of pitch and

---

[6] '[...] voix de femmes en bas-dessus [...]': Charles De Brosses, *Lettres écrites d'Italie à quelques amis ...* (Paris, 1858), p. 317. Translation from Parrott, 'Falsetto and the French', p. 130.

[7] Michael Tilmouth, 'Music and British Travellers Abroad, 1600–1730', in *Source Materials and the Interpretation of Music: A Memorial Volume to Thurston Dart*, ed. Ian Bent (London, 1981), pp. 358–69, at pp. 359–60.

transposition in a work such as Monteverdi's 1610 *Vespers*. Many have been reluctant to accept evidence which points to a low pitch in this music, partly because it makes the alto line (which they assume to have been a falsetto part) uncomfortably low. Yet Monteverdi himself seems to indicate that he expected his altos to sing in a high modal voice. In a letter from Mantua to Duke Vincenzo Gonzaga, dated June 1610, he writes:

> I was entrusted by Messr Pandolfo [del Grande] (on behalf of your Serene Highness) with hearing a certain contralto, come from Modena and desirous of service with your Serene Highness; so I took him straightway into S. Pietro and had him sing a motet in the organ gallery. I heard a beautiful voice, powerful and far-reaching; and when he sings on the stage he will make himself heard in every corner very easily and without strain, a thing that Brandino [Antonio Brandi, another Mantuan male alto] could not do as well.[8]

Nowhere here do we find the word falsetto, or any likely synonyms. Rather, Monteverdi admired the 'powerful and far-reaching' voice. And whilst he notes his lack of strain (which could apply to any falsettist or to a naturally high modal voice), his comment about Brandi's strain suggests that this other (anonymous) alto was what we would think of as a more forced tenor. Monteverdi's reference to the Modenese alto's potential for opera (in which falsettists had no known role) lends weight to this reading.

Taking into account transposition implied by clef-combinations, Monteverdi's alto parts have a narrow written range of around *g* to *g'*, with occasional extensions a tone above and, more usually, below; his tenor parts have a core range from *c* to *f'*, again with occasional extensions. The likely pitch standard Monteverdi knew would have been roughly a semitone above our own. Bearing this in mind (and the historically omnipresent factor of shorter human height) we can see that both the tenor and alto parts were written for modal voices – the former intermediate (the equivalent of our baritone), and the latter high (the equivalent of our tenor). In this sense, although the male alto was on the verge of changing, at the very start of the Baroque period he was fundamentally similar to his Renaissance predecessor. By 1639, though, we have confirmation that in Rome, at least, things were changing. The visiting French viol player André Maugars comments that 'There are a great number of castratos for

---

[8] 'Da messer Pandolfo m'è statto comesso da parte de l'Altezza Serenissima Sua ch'io senta un certo contralto venuto da Modena desideroso egli di servire all'Altezza Serenissima Sua; così dilongo l'ho condotto in Santo Pietro e l'ho fatto cantare un motetto nel'organo, e ho udito una bella voce, gagliarda e longa, e, cantando in sena, giongerà benissimo, senza discomodo, in tutti I lochi, cosa che non poteva così bene il Brandini.': Claudio Monteverdi, *Correspondance, préfaces et épîtres dédicatoires*, ed. and trans. Jean-Philippe Navarre and Annonciade Russo (Mardaga, 2001), p. 42. Translation from Denis Arnold and Nigel Fortune (eds.), *The Monteverdi Companion* (New York, 1968), p. 26.

the Dessus [soprano] and Haute-Contre [alto], very beautiful and natural tenors, and very few low basses.'[9] Other French commentators, whose words we will come to in due course, become a rich source of information on changing Italian vocal practices in the eighteenth century.

We should, incidentally, be wary of misreading Monteverdi where, auditioning a prospective bass for St Mark's in Venice, he notes that his 'voice goes into the tenor with ease.'[10] Since the 'tenor' of the time was an intermediate modal voice, Monteverdi is only observing that the bass also had what we would term a baritone range. His range may have been wider than average, yes, but there is no evidence here that he had an unusual modal range, or even that he sang partly in falsetto. Monteverdi's fellow innovator Giulio Caccini certainly did not think falsetto desirable (although he himself was a tenor, which might be significant). In the preface to his *Le nuove musiche*, Caccini comments that 'faked voices cannot give rise to the nobility of good singing, which comes from a natural voice suited to all the notes.'[11] In other words, Caccini acknowledges the existence of 'voci finte', but expresses a strong personal dislike for them. This may remind us of the medieval clerics' disapproval of falsetto, but there is an obvious difference: whereas the clerics had a formal authority to prohibit falsetto, Caccini had none.

Italian Influence in the North

F URTHER north, writing in Germany for 'the training of young boys in school in the current Italian manner of singing', Michael Praetorius appears to adopt and adapt Caccini's words.[12] He states as a requisite that the singer 'must choose one voice, such as cantus, altus, or tenor, etc., that he can sustain with a full and bright sound without falsetto'.[13] Praetorius's mention of 'junge Knaben in Schulen' in connection with lower

---

[9] 'Il y a un grand nombre de Castrati pour le Dessus et pour la Haute-Contre, de fort belles Tailles naturelles, mais fort peu de Basses creuses.': André Maugars, *Lettre à un curieux* (Rome, 1639), p. 16; available online at <http://www.chmtl. indiana.edu/tfm/17th/MAURES_TEXT.html> [accessed 4 April 2014]; cf. E. Thoinan [A. E. Roquet]: *Maugars: célèbre joueur de viole ...* (Paris, 1865), p. 35. Translation from MacClintock, *Readings*, p. 122.

[10] 'La voce sua ariva ad un tenore con gratezza del senso.': cf. Wistreich, 'Reconstructing Pre-Romantic Singing Technique', p. 184.

[11] 'Ma dalle voci finte non può nascere nobiltà di buon canto: che nascerà (invece) da una voce naturale comoda per tutte le corde': Giulio Caccini, *Le nuove musiche* (Florence, 1602): cf. Uberti, 'Vocal Techniques', p. 495.

[12] 'Und junge Knaben in Schulen an die jetzige italienische Art und Manier im singen zu gewehnen seyn': Michael Praetorius, *Syntagma musicum*, vol. 3: *Termini musici* (Wolfenbüttel, 1618), titlepage. Translation my own.

[13] 'Ein Sänger [muß] [...] eine Stimm als *Cantum, Altum,* oder *Tenor &c.* erwhlen welche er mit vollem und hellem laut ohne Falsetten': Praetorius, *Syntagma*

vocal parts raises an obvious question of translation: in seventeenth- and eighteenth-century Germany (and we need to remind ourselves of this when we come to Bach and his singers) the school system took boys into their early twenties. So, we might more meaningfully translate this as 'young college boys', particularly since Praetorius was evidently including boys whose voices were changing and who could sing lower parts. Johann Andreas Herbst, writing in Nuremburg, echoed Praetorius' sentiments regarding tone, urging singers to use a 'loud, bright sound without using falsetto'.[14]

These appear to be unequivocal anti-falsetto statements. It would, though, be misleading to treat them too literally. At the same time that they were written, falsettists were a feature of musical life in Germanic lands – even in choirs which Praetorius himself knew. Although Praetorius clearly expected that the 'altum' would sing without falsetto, he did not imagine that, when sung by non-castrated adult men, the 'cantum' could be sung without falsetto. This much is clear from Praetorius's earlier illustration of vocal ranges, where the soprano part is annotated 'eunuchus, falsettista, discantista'.[15] The standard range Praetorius gives for this highest part stretches nearly an octave and a half, from *c'* to *f"*. Praetorius also suggests that the two notes above this standard ceiling are possible as exceptions. When we read the words of Praetorius, his stance on falsetto singing may seem confused and confusing. Yet even today we can find musicians who direct choirs with falsettists whilst at the same time being ambivalent towards the voice. We should hardly be surprised to find similar contradictions in other eras.

Aside from the direct information he provides about falsetto, when Praetorius refers to the 'Italian manner' he indirectly points to another significant development. At least from the time of Dufay onwards Italy had been a net importer of both musical and performance styles, but by the early Baroque the balance had shifted. Whereas in 1562 Andrea Gabrieli had travelled north to Munich to visit and study with Lassus, by 1608 it was a German, Schütz, who was in Venice studying with Andrea's nephew Giovanni. From this encounter Schütz brought back to Germany the new Venetian polychoral style, taking this to the Dresden court, where he influenced Praetorius. Compositional style aside, as the Baroque period progressed, it was from Italy that there emanated a vocal method which is of huge significance for any study of high male singing, in that it encouraged

---

musicum, vol. 3: cf. Wistreich, 'Reconstructing Pre-Romantic Singing Technique', p. 180.

[14] 'Erwehlen welche er mit vollem und hellem laut / ohn falseten (daß ist halbe und erzwungener Stimme) haltentöne.': Johann Andreas Herbst, *Musica practica sive instruction pro symphoniacis* (Nuremburg, 1642), p. 3: cf. Stark, *Bel Canto*, p. 36.

[15] Michael Praetorius, *Syntagma musicum*, vol. 2: *De organographia* (Wolfenbüttel, 1618), p. 20.

the limited use of falsetto by all singers. To understand this seminal method, and the place of falsetto singing in the later European Baroque, we should now look at the most influential singing pedagogue of the period.

Tosi and the bel canto

P IER Francesco Tosi was a castrato who sang in Italian churches and opera houses as a young man, before travelling to London in 1693. For the rest of his life he was to work throughout Europe as a singer, composer and teacher. In reality, Tosi was only one of a number of contemporary Italians to proselytise a similar method – which would in time become known as *bel canto*. Tosi's influence, though, was uniquely widespread: his *Opinioni de' cantori antichi* was published in Bologna in 1723, translated into English some twenty years later, and into German in 1757.[16] Even as late as 1774 Giambattista Mancini (also a castrato) makes clear his debt to Tosi in his *Pensieri e riflessioni*.[17] Tosi's influence, then, was both far reaching and long lasting. His significance for us is that he freely discusses falsetto as a technique for aspiring students. Firstly, though, we need to establish what kind of singers Tosi's readers were. Nominally at least, his treatise was aimed at aspiring castrati (and their teachers), but Mancini states that Tosi's method (and his own) was valid for all voices. Tosi's translator into German, Agricola, makes a similar comment. In practical terms Tosi, in common with many other castrati, taught all types of singers. In particular, the list of famous tenors taught by castrati is surely significant.[18] As we shall see, until the emergence of the *tenore di forza* in the nineteenth century, when the taste for castrati began to wane, it was tenors who became heirs to their modal-falsetto technique.

However narrow his nominal audience, then, courtesy of his translators and proselytisers around Europe, Tosi's message was widely heard. It is worth reminding ourselves that the castrato, whatever our historically remote perception might be, in reality had modal and falsetto parts of his voice – like any other singer. There is no reason, then, why Tosi's method could not be universally applied. We might bear this in mind when we read Tosi's words on falsetto:

> A diligent Master, knowing that a *Soprano*, without the *Falsetto*, is constrained to sing within the narrow Compass of a few Notes, ought not only to endeavour to help him to it, but also to leave no Means

---

[16] Pier Francesco Tosi, *Opinioni de' cantori antichi* (Bologna, 1723): cf. *Observations on the Florid Song*, ed. Michael Pilkington, trans. J. E. Galliard (London, 1987).

[17] Mancini, *Pensieri, e riflessioni pratiche*: cf. Mancini, *Practical Reflections on Figured Singing …*, ed. and trans. Edward Foreman (Minneapolis, 1967).

[18] John Potter, 'The Tenor-Castrato Connection, 1760–1860', *Early Music* 35(1) (2007), pp. 97–110.

untried, so to unite the feigned and the natural Voice, that they may not be distinguished; for if they do not perfectly unite, the Voice will be of divers Registers, and must consequently lose its Beauty.[19]

As for how this skill could be learnt, Tosi comments that:

Among the Women one hears sometimes a *Soprano* entirely *di Petto*, but among the Male Sex it would be a great rarity, should they preserve it past the Age of Puberty. Whoever would be curious to discover the feigned Voice of one who has the Art to disguise it, let him take Notice, that the Artist sounds the Vowel *i*, or *e*, with more Strength and less Fatigue than the vowel *a*, on the high Notes.[20]

Frustratingly, beyond this neither Tosi nor any of his many followers offer detailed guidance on how the unity of registers was to be achieved. The closest we have to practical advice comes from Mancini, who is worth quoting at some length:

Take, for instance, a student who has a strong chest voice, and head tones out of proportion, weak and feeble. In such a voice the break of two registers comes from C-sol-fa-ut [C] of the soprano and goes to D-la-sol-re [D] on the fourth space. In, such cases the head voice is in need of help, because it is separated from the chest, and the way to correct it is to have the pupil at once undertake and fix in his mind in his daily study, to keep the chest tones back as much as he can, and to force the voice little by little against the head just there where it seems to be most unfriendly to him, and thus fix it and develop it with the same strength that the chest tones have already naturally developed.

Here is where the student and the teacher both must be very much in earnest. The student's part is to keep that portion of the voice under control that is in itself robust and sprightly, and to render the other portion strong that is by nature weak. On the part of the teacher it means this: After he has kept the student for some time in this work

---

[19] 'Un diligente Istruttore sapendo, che un Soprano senza falsetto bisogna, che canti fra l'angustie di poche corde non solamente proccura d'acquistarglielo, ma non lascia modo intentato acciò lo unisca alla voce di petto in forma, che non si distingua l'uno dall'altra, che se l'unione non è perfetta, la voce sarà di più registri, e conseguentemente perderà la sua bellezza.': Tosi, *Opinioni de' cantori antichi* (Bologna, 1723); *Observations on the Florid Song*, ed. Pilkington, trans. Galliard, p. 23.

[20] 'Nelle Femmine, che cantano il Soprano sentesi qualche volta una voce tutta di petto, nè Maschj però sarebbe rarità se la conservassero passata, che abbiano l'età puerile. Chi fosse curioso di scoprire il falsetto in chi lo sa nascondere badi, che chiunque se ne serve esprime su gli acuti la vocale *i* con più vigore, *e* meno fatica dell' *a*.': Tosi, *Opinioni de' cantori antichi*, p.38; *Observations on the Florid Song*, ed. Pilkington, trans. Galliard, p. 23.

and he sees that the pupil starts to attack the head tones with more strength and flexibility, then he must let him sing the chest tones with the usual strength, so as to find out to what degree the difficulty has been overcome. It may be the case that the blending of the two registers has not as yet reached an ideal in evenness, nevertheless, I beg the teacher and student to not lose faith, because I am sure in the end success will crown the effort, that it has diminished the pain and effort in taking the notes of so unfriendly a register.[21]

This may still fall some way short of a 'method', but Mancini advises the scholar (and master) not to 'lose courage' in the attempt: practice, he suggests, will make perfect.

Mancini's optimism was tempered by others: the eighteenth-century German musician Johann Samuel Petri suggested that in reality successful blending of registers was seldom achieved: 'Only a few learn to use a good falsetto which is not differentiated appreciably from the chest voice.'[22] Critics provide numerous references to singers who failed to achieve a seamless break between their modal and falsetto registers. Petri himself describes this in the low range of a particular soprano falsettist: 'his falsetto did not reach there, and all at once he fell into his piercing and robust tenor voice. I was shocked, and my entire pleasure in his lovely soprano voice was utterly destroyed.'[23] We will meet examples of the inverse – of primarily

---

[21] 'Datemi per cortesia uno scolare, che abbia gagliarde le voci di petto, e fuor di proporzione debolissime quelle di testa. In questo caso in una simile voce la separazione dei due registri seque dal C-sol-faut del Soprano, passando al D-la-sol-re della quinta riga. Ciò supposto, essndo la voce di testa bisogna d'ajuto, perchè separata da quella di petto, il mezzo più certo per ajutarla ad unirsi con questa, si è, che lo scolare, senza perdita di tempo, intraprenda, e si presigga nel suo studio giornaliero la maniera di ritenere le voci di petto, e di forzare a poco a poco la corda nemica di testa, per rendere quelle nel miglior modo possible eguali a questa. ¶ E quì conviene, che sieno solleciti il maestro non meno, che lo scolare, poichè per parte dello scolare trattasi di soggettare una porzione di voce, che in se stessa è gagliarda, e di rendere vigorosa un' altra porzione, che di natura è debole. Per parte del maestro trattasi, ch'egli con ingegno, dopo d'aver tenuto lo scolare in questo esercizio un certo dato tempo, ed avvedutosi, che lo scolare forza e flessibilità, deve allora ordinargli di dare alle voci di petto la consueta forza, per rilevare ed indagare accortamente a qual segno sia ridotta la corda nemica.': Mancini, *Pensieri, e riflessioni pratiche*, p. 90. Translation from Mancini, *Practical Reflections*, ed. and trans. Buzzi, pp. 109–10.

[22] 'Man lehre ihn daß Falsett oder die sogenannte Fistelstimme brauchen, und der natürlichen oder Bruststimme egal machen, damit er in einer Arie, die ihm etwas zu hoch ist, nicht einen Uebelstand mache durch Heruntersebung oder vielleicht mislingende Berkehrung der Melodie.': Johann Samuel Petri, *Anleitung zur practischen Musik* (Lauban, 1767), pp. 61–2. Translation from Stark, *Bel Canto*, p. 66.

[23] 'Hier reichte sein Fallsett nicht, sondern es fiel auf einmal seine scharfe und starke Tenorstimme ein. Ich erschrack, und mein ganzes Bergnügen über seine

modal singers failing to negotiate a change into falsetto – in subsequent chapters.

The insistence by Tosi and his school on the seamless incorporation of falsetto into the technique of modal-voiced singers certainly resonates with other methods originating in Italy (the first of these probably being Zacconi's, which we discussed in Chapter 3). These other methods were not specifically addressed to castrati. Although in earlier periods we have found suggestions that falsetto was used to extend the modal voice, Tosi is the first explicitly to state this as a technique rigorously to practise and perfect. Right through until the nineteenth century this technique became standard throughout most of Europe, and not just in domestic music-making. Such a use of falsetto also represents the greatest gulf between pre- and post-Romantic vocal techniques.

One of the benefits of Tosi's treatise being disseminated so widely was that many of his translators offer revealing glosses on the text. John Galliard, Tosi's first English translator, finds it necessary to clarify Tosi's terminology:

> *Voce di testa* comes more from the throat than from the breast and is capable of more volubility [than *voce di petto*]. Falsetto is a feigned voice which is entirely formed in the throat, has more volubility than any, but of no substance.

Here the clarifier may need clarifying, since in our age 'volubility' often implies someone who is loudly vocal. In Galliard's day a voluble singer – from the Latin 'volubilis', meaning something turning round – was simply one capable of rapid passagework.

Tosi's German translator is even more revealing. Agricola, himself a composer (and, in his teens, a copyist to J. S. Bach) states that 'like Tosi himself, the Italians [literally 'foreigners'] often confuse what one should actually call the falsetto with the name of the head voice'.[24] Going on, Agricola then defines his understanding of falsetto:

> Some adult male singers have nothing but pure falsetto notes, and these singers are actually called falsettists. Their lower notes are generally more out of tune and softer. With such singers, the following can contribute to the attainment of the whole range of a high voice in exclusively falsetto notes (namely, that a tenor can sing a full soprano and a bass a full alto): that they make the effort, from

---

schöne Diskantstimme war vernichtet, und selbst ben Wiederholung des vorher so schönen ersten Theils fiel mir immer wieder daß garstige rauhe a ein.': Petri, *Anleitung zur practischen Musik*, p. 206. Translation from Stark, *Bel Canto*, p. 63.

[24] 'Die Wälschen pflegen aber oft, wie auch Tosi hier selbst öfters thut, daß was man eigentlich Falsett nennen sollte, mit dem Namen Kopfstimme zu verwechseln.': Johann Friedrich Agricola, *Anleitung zur Singkunst* (Berlin, 1757), p. 34: cf. Agricola, *Introduction to the Art of Singing*, ed. and trans. Julianne C. Baird (Cambridge/New York, 1995), p. 76.

the time in their youth when the high voice is about to change into the deeper one, to continue to force out the high notes in the manner described above; and thus, through practice, to effect a greater capability in the muscles that contract the windpipe than in those which expand it. Physiology demonstrates that this is possible. All singers are capable of adding some falsetto notes to their upper range in the natural voice, even if they do not wish to make a profession of purely falsetto singing.[25]

Agricola, having criticised Tosi for failing to discriminate between *voce di testa* and falsetto, then muddies the waters by suggesting that the very lowest notes in the chest voice were also sung in falsetto. Quite what he meant by this has baffled many of his readers since. Following Agricola, a futile debate ensued amongst German theorists – particularly Hiller and Marpurg – about the precise definition of the vocal registers. Perhaps in all this the most telling comment is Agricola's when he notes that 'it is just as difficult to find two people whose voices are completely the same in every aspect as it is to find two people with the same figure.'[26] Much the same could be said of the opinions of vocal theorists.

One section of Tosi's text which helps explain why he and his contemporaries valued the addition of falsetto to the modal technique, is his comment on pitch:

the teacher should accustom the student to the pitch of Lombardy and not that of Rome, not only so that he may acquire and maintain

---

[25] 'Einige erwachsene Mannspersonen haben, wenn sie singen, nichts als lauter Falsetttöne; und diese nennet man eigentlich 'Falsettisten.' Die tiefern Töne werden diesen gemeiniglich sauerer, und sind schwächer. Bey dergleichen Sängern kann etwas zur Erreichung des ganzen Umfangs einer hohen Stimme, in lauter Falsetttönen, nämlich daß ein Tenorist einen völligen Sopran, und ein Bassist einen völligen Alt singen kann, etwas beytrage, daß sie sich von der zeit an, da sich in dern Jugend die hohe Stimme in die tiefere verwandeln wollte bemühet haben, immer die hohen Tone noch, auf oben beshriebene Art, heraus zu swingen, und folglich, durch die Uebung, den musteln welche, die *Luströhre zu sammenziehen, ein Gröseres Bermögen juwege gebracht haben, als denen welche die Luströhre erweitern. Da*ß dieses möglich sen, ist aus der Physiologie klar. Alle und jede Na*türliche Stimmen, wenn sie auch nicht von puren Falsettsingen Profession machen, können in der höhe einige Falsettöne angeben.'*: Agricola, *Anleitung zur Singkunst*, pp. 35–6; *Introduction to the Art of Singing*, ed. and trans. Baird, p. 76.

[26] 'Wie aber nicht leicht zweere Menschen gefunden werden, deren ausserliche Gestalt einander in allern volkommen gleich ist. Also werden auch nicht leicht ihre zweere angetrossen, deren Stimmen einander, in aller Betrachtung, volkommen gleich waren.': Agricola, *Anleitung zur Singkunst*, p. 36; *Introduction to the Art of Singing*, ed. and trans. Baird, p. 77.

the high notes, but also to spare him the difficulties that high-pitched instruments may cause him later on.[27]

The pitch of Lombardy (including Milan) was about three-quarters of a tone higher than a' = 440, whilst Roman pitch was about three-quarters of a tone lower: a journey of three hundred miles, then, could result in the singer being faced with a pitch variance of about a minor third.[28] Agricola offers an explanation of this issue:

> It might seem that one or one and a half semitones would hardly make such a difference to a singer; but in that point in the voice where the natural voice divides from the falsetto, experience often proves the contrary. Many a passage or a sustained note or a certain word can be uncomfortable in one tuning and comfortable in another. Under such circumstances, the happiest singers are those in whom the unification of the natural voice and the falsetto does not cause much difficulty and who, in case of necessity, have a few extra notes in their high and low registers.[29]

This is worth us pausing to ponder, since in an age of standard pitch we simply do not experience the problem Agricola and Tosi describe. For those of us who are modal-voiced singers, perhaps we should imagine singing a particular song in a key that suits us, and then being required to sing it in public a minor third higher. When we have recovered from the horror of this prospect, we can readily see why the Baroque insistence on the falsetto extension was not so much an aesthetic whim as a practical necessity.

Bach's Altists and Discantists

READING the above, it would be easy to imagine that the written word was the driving force behind the spread of Tosi's method. Treatises are the best evidence that we have today, but it is important to see these texts in their true place. They were, at the time, no more than carts; the actual drivers were the singers themselves, whose performances around Europe persuaded local musicians to seek out the secrets of the new style. Primarily, the singers which Italy exported were the castrati (or 'musici', to adopt yet another euphemism with which they were squeamishly referred to). Under

---

[27] 'Eserciti lo Scolaro studiando sempre sul Tuono di Lombardia, e non su quello di Roma non solo per fargli acquistare, e conservar gli acuti, ma perchè non sia incomodato mai dagli Strumenti alti': Pier Francesco Tosi, *Opinioni de' cantori antichi*, p. 16: cf. Agricola, *Introduction to the Art of Singing*, ed. and trans. Baird, p. 82.

[28] Bruce Haynes, *A History of Performing Pitch: The Story of "A"* (Oxford, 2002), p. 74.

[29] Agricola, *Anleitung zur Singkunst*, pp. 35–6; *Introduction to the Art of Singing*, ed. and trans. Baird, p. 83.

the leadership of Lassus, as early as 1568 the lavishly endowed chapel of the Bavarian court at Munich had employed six castrati. This was no passing fad: Cesare Bontempi, a castrato from St Mark's, Venice, became assistant to Schütz in Dresden in the 1640s; at the same time the Munich cappella was still employing castrati, and in Innsbruck an anonymous English observer at a royal wedding in 1655 noted 'the sweetest harmony of voices [...] the Duke having caused many Eunuchs, that are esteemed the prime of Italy, to be at court'.[30] As in Italy, castrati also played a fundamental role in German opera houses of the time.

As we have already seen, wherever a taste for castrati existed, falsettists were rarely far away. The north-German composer and theorist Daniel Friderici indirectly confirms this: 'Those unskilled cantors therefore err not a little, who, when they cannot sing *fictâ voce* with the discantists, will sooner take the octave and make a tenor out of a discant part.'[31] The implication here is that German sopranists who were not clumsy *did* use 'fictâ voce' – which in this context can only mean falsetto. In court records, the number of adult 'discantists' with German names confirm (since there is no evidence that castration was practised in Germany) that falsettists were commonplace in the seventeenth century.

It is noticeable that the German Praetorius's disparaging sentiments towards falsetto, quoted earlier, seem to echo those of the Italian Caccini. A century later, at the height of the Baroque, we find similar echoes – of key figures in German music simply amplifying Italian methods. By then, though, the prevailing sentiment towards falsetto in Italy had changed from disparagement to endorsement, so it is now this approval of falsetto which we find German writers echoing. Agricola, as we have seen, propagated the pro-falsetto ideas of Tosi, as did another influential writer, Johann Quantz:

> The requirements of a good singer are: that he first of all have a good, clear, pure tone and an equal scale from bottom to top [...] Further, a singer should know how to join the falsetto to the chest voice in such a way that one cannot observe where the latter ends and the former begins.[32]

[30] Tilmouth, 'Music and British Travellers', p. 372.

[31] 'Irren derowegen die ungeschickten *Cantores* nicht wenig / Welche / wenn Sie bey den *Discantisten* nicht können *fictâ voce* singen / alsbald zur *Octava* greiffen / und einen *Tenorem* aus dem *Discant* machen / und nicht wenig *vitia* von *quintem* einfüren.': Daniel Friderici, *Musica figuralis* (Rostock, 1618), p. 47. Translation from John Butt, *Music Education and the Art of Performance in the German Baroque* (Cambridge, 1994), p. 203.

[32] 'Von einem guten Sänger wird erfodert: daß er hauptsächlich eine gute, helle, reine, und von der Tiefe bis in die Höhe durchgehends egale Stimme habe [...] daß ein gutter Sänger daß Falset mit der Brustimme so zu vereinigen wisse, damit man nicht bemerken könne, wo die letze aufhöret, und daß erstere anfängt.': Johann Quantz, *Versuch einer Anweisung Flöte traversière zu spielen* (Berlin, 1752), chap. 18, sec. 11. Translation MacClintock, *Readings*, p. 357.

Although it is convenient to speak of 'Germany' in the Baroque, as if it were a single entity, we may need to remind ourselves that it was anything but. We certainly mislead ourselves if we try to reconstruct a singular 'national' vocal aesthetic during the period. Not surprisingly, Catholic, Lutheran and Calvinist states took very different standpoints. At the court of Weissenfels in Saxony, for instance, the composer and theorist (and comic novelist) Johann Beer preferred adult sopranists: 'It would be better if one could have a pair of castrati or falsettists, because these types show greater judgement, are not as timid as frightened boys, and their singing is more stable.'[33] But although Catholic courts such as Weissenfels, Dresden and Munich employed castrati, Lutheran states did not tolerate them. As sopranos and altos, in various permutations German composers at the time knew of four options – castrati, falsettists, boys, and women. Nowhere is this variety of options better encapsulated than in the performing tradition of a J. S. Bach, since his career embraced both religious cultures. Although modern performers and scholars are slowly arriving at a consensus regarding the minimal number of voices Bach generally had to sing his own music, no such accord has been achieved about the nature of those voices. In particular, a source of debate has been whether Bach's alto parts were sung by boys or falsettists.

At Weimar, where Bach was appointed in his early twenties, court payment records reveal that the court employed a choir of six singers. One of these, Adam Immanuel Weldig, who was then in his forties, is listed in the court records as (the sole) falsettist.[34] Besides Weldig, two tenors and a bass, the chapel also employed two teenage 'discantists' (sopranos).[35] The implication here is that in performing these early cantatas Bach would have known the falsetto voice singing the alto part. This tallies with practice in certain other German courts at the time.

At Leipzig (at least after his first years there) Bach's concertist singers were schoolboys from the Thomasschule. This, together with modern Continental practice, has led to the more widely held assumption that Bach's altos were boys. Yet Bach's altos from the Thomasschule were not necessarily 'schoolboys' as we might understand the term: the maximum age for the 'school' was twenty-three, an age at which many people today have already graduated from university. Age is also a factor in assessing Bach's practice, because of the suggestion that boys' voices then changed later than they do today. As we shall see in Extempore 5, this issue is a

[33] 'Könte man aber ein paar gleiche *Castraten* oder *Falsedisten* haben wär es um so viel besser weil solche Leute mit grössern *judicio*, item nicht so zagicht wie die erschrockene Knaben und dann auch endlich beständiger singen.': Johann Beer, *Musikalische discurse ...* (Nuremburg, 1719), pp. 13–14. Translation by Sylvia Snowdon.

[34] Charles Sanford Terry, *Bach: A Biography* (London, 1928), p. 91.

[35] Joshua Rifkin, 'Bassoons, Violins and Voices: A Response to Ton Koopman', *Early Music* 25(2) (1997), pp. 302–8, at p. 306.

hugely complex one for all historical periods. The evidence about the age of voice maturation in Bach's time, though, is particularly baffling. On the one hand, we find Agricola writing that the male voice changes at about thirteen years of age, and that when this happens, 'hoarseness generally sets in, which often lasts half a year or even longer'.[36] On the other, Martin Heinrich Fuhrmann, a Lutheran cantor in Berlin, said that the usual age at which an alto became a tenor was over eighteen.[37]

At whatever age this process took place, there is supportive evidence for the alto part being sung by boys with unchanged voices. Johann Mattheson, a contemporary of Bach's, writes that 'during mutation the so-called descant voice usually falls to the tenor and the alto to the bass' – which suggests that, in his Hamburg choir at least, altos were boys with unchanged voices. In this respect Mattheson and Fuhrmann agree (although we might note that they disagree about the level at which a boy's alto voice tended to settle in maturity).[38] In a 1729 memo Bach himself complimented Johann Gottfried Neucke, a fourteen-year-old who is listed as an alto, for having a 'strong voice and quite fine proficiency'.[39] But in the *Entwurff* from 1730, Neucke is listed only among the larger group of singers used to sing simple old-style motets, who need more training before they are ready to sing Bach's new cantatas. If all of this is any indication, then Bach's altos in the cantatas may have been older than fifteen and younger than twenty-three. Perhaps, then, Bach would not quite recognise our own distinction between 'boy' and 'adult' alto. Perhaps even the distinction between 'modal' and 'falsetto' is overly sophisticated for singers who probably had little idea, from week to week, of how they were producing their voices. The result of having such alto singers was not always a positive one: 'Seldom can a male voice sing the alto part without harshness. In the protestant churches of Switzerland where four-part music is generally sung, young men take the alto part, but usually with some forcing.'[40] Bach's altos at Leipzig,

---

[36] 'daß [...] ohngefähr um daß vierzehnte Lebensjahr, die hohe Stimme sich in eine tiefere verwandelt [...] meistentheils eine Heiserkeit einzustellen pflegt, welche öfters ein halbes Jahr und noch länger dauert': Agricola, *Anleitung zur Singkunst*, pp. 28–9. Translation from Andrew Parrott, *The Essential Bach Choir* (Woodbridge, 2000), pp. 13–15.

[37] Martin Heinrich Fuhrmann, *Musikalischer-Trichter* (Frankfurt, 1706), p. 36. Original and translation quoted from Parrott, *The Essential Bach Choir*, p. 13.

[38] 'Welches bei der Mutation, von der sogenanten Discant – Stimme gemeiniglich aus einen Tenor, und vom Alt auf den Bass fällt.': Mattheson, *Der vollkommene Capellmeister* (Hamburg, 1739), part 2, 1:7, 95. Translation from Mattheson, *Der vollkommene Capellmeister*, ed. and trans. Ernest C. Harriss (Ann Arbor, MI, 1981), p. 241.

[39] '14 Jahr, hat eine starcke Stimme, u. ziemlich feine *profectus*': cf. Parrott, *The Essential Bach Choir*, p. 160.

[40] 'Selten kann eine Mannsstimme den Alt ohne Härte singen [...] In den Kirchen der protestantischen Schweiz, wo durchgehends vierstimmig gesungen wird,

then, were quite possibly older boys whose voices were in the process of changing; how many arrested their downward progress at the alto line and became falsettists in adulthood' we have no way of knowing. Even so, when we consider the dominant vocal technique of the time – Tosi's blend of modal and falsetto registers – we should bear in mind the possibility that even an 'adult falsettist' such as Weldig might have sounded quite unlike our modern counter-tenors. What we are left with, then, are altos who stubbornly refuse to fit our own neat distinctions, either between boys and men, or between falsettists and modal singers.

Applying the evidence of such hybrid singers to Bach's actual music for alto is interesting. If we imagine that some of Bach's alto and soprano arias were sung not by wholly different voice-types, but by variants of the same late-adolescent model, it may help remove the uncomfortable dichotomy often presented to us with these solos: instead of choosing between adult maturity with polish on the one hand, and childish naivety with roughness on the other, we can imagine (as probably Bach knew) a melding of these qualities.

Is there any justification for bracketing Bach's regular alto and soprano soloists like this? Were they, commonly, youths with shared vocal attributes? And were there parallel situations, in which Bach's altos and sopranos were both *adult* males? Martin Geck has argued that this was indeed the case, especially early on in Bach's time at Leipzig, and in certain high-profile contexts.[41] One work which may have been sung by adult male soloists, Geck conjectures, is the *St John Passion*, with soprano arias as testing as 'Ich folge dir gleichfalls' (Ex. 8).[42] Our initial response to the suggestion that this aria was first sung by a falsettist may well be one of incredulity: no modern falsettist has convincingly demonstrated the range to cope with this high tessitura. However, if the argument is valid that changes in human physiology account for a Renaissance tenor having a higher voice than his modern counterpart, then by the same token we would expect a Baroque falsettist to have what we would deem an unfeasibly high range. And sure enough, Petri tells us of a sopranist (not a castrato, but a falsettist) whose range extended upwards to f'''.[43] Likewise Buxtehude, whose chief sopranist in Lübeck was the falsettist Hans Iwe, and whose soloists appear to have all

---

führen die jungen Mannspersonen den Alt, aber insgemein so, daß die Stimmen etwas übertrieben werden [...]': Johann Georg Sulzer, *Allgemeine Theorie der schönen Künste*, 2nd edn (Leipzig, 1793; repr. 1967), p. 44. Translation from Beverly Jerold, 'Choral Singing before the Era of Recording', *Musical Times* 147, no. 1895 (2006), pp.74–84, at p. 80.

[41] Martin Geck, 'Bach's Sopranos', *American Choral Review* 46(2) (2004), pp. 1–8.

[42] Martin Geck, 'Bach's Art of Church Music and his Leipzig Performance Forces: Contradictions in the System', *Early Music* 31(4) (2003), pp. 559–71, at p. 561.

[43] Petri, *Anleitung zur practischen Musik*, p. 206: cf. Kerala J. Snyder, *Dieterich Buxtehude* (New York, 2007), p. 371.

Ex. 8 J. S. Bach, 'Ich folge dir gleichfalls', from *St John Passion*, bars 48–66

been adult men, wrote soprano parts as high as a *b″*.[44] Returning to Bach's singers, Christian Friedrich Schemelli (1713–61) attended the Thomasschule in Leipzig between the ages of eighteen and twenty-one, when his voice had most probably changed. In a testimonial letter dated 24 February 1740, Bach attests to Schemelli's abilities as a soprano while attending school, noting 'that I was able to make very good use of him as a soprano in the church choirs'.[45] There is no specific evidence that Schemelli was a cantata singer rather than a member of the larger choir which sang older motets,

---

[44] Snyder, *Dieterich Buxtehude*, p. 371.

[45] 'daß Ihn auch bey denen Cantoreyen als Sopranisten gantz wohl habe gebrauchen können': Hans David, Arthur Mendel and Christoph Wolff (eds. and trans.), *The New Bach Reader: A Life of Johann Sebastian Bach in Letters and Documents* (New York, 1998), p. 208.

but Bach's reference at least suggests that he was familiar with (and could approve of) the high falsetto voice.

Bach would presumably have encountered falsetto sopranos as early as his 1705 visit to Lübeck (where Buxtehude's choir was composed of adult males only). Elsewhere in Germany, Telemann appears to have been forced to engage (at significant expense) a male soprano for a memorial service in Hamburg. The term 'subrett sänger' ('coquettish singer'), with which Telemann refers to this man, may refer to his vocal mannerisms, his financial demands, or both.[46]

Telemann's encounter dates from 1765, but by the end of the eighteenth century the practice of using soprano falsettists seems to have vanished in Germany. In one German musical encyclopaedia the entry for 'Discant' specifies that only children, women and castrati can sing the soprano part.[47] This agrees with what we know of Bach's later practices. For instance, the chapel of the Elector of Saxony, to whom Bach dedicated the *B Minor Mass*, appears to have had only adult singers, with castrati and women as sopranos. The virtuoso solo cantata *Jauchzet Gott in allen Landen* may have been written for one of these singers, perhaps the castrato Giovanni Bindi or the female soprano Faustina Bordoni (Italian names both).

Those wanting to establish that Bach had any strong preferences regarding vocal types for the higher parts will be thwarted by a mass of evidence which points in every direction and none. As altos and sopranos, he would probably have been familiar with the voices of boys, changing voices, mature falsettists, women and castrati. In testimonials and audition notes, a large number of Bach's comments on individual singers have survived. Crucially, though, in none of these we will find any indication of his preferences for particular vocal types. In this sense, as we shall shortly see, Bach's attitudes mirror those which his compatriot Handel was to establish on his travels in Italy and England.

The French haute-contre

I N the nebulous vocabulary of the high male voice, no term has acquired a more mythical aura than *haute-contre*. Like certain French culinary terms, *haute-contre* is often airily tossed into discussions by those who have no firm idea of what the words mean (or even what they mean them to mean), but who think that using them displays a level of sophistication. As long ago as the 1860s, the *Grand Dictionnaire Larousse* commented that 'The present generation no more knows what an *haute-contre* is than what a castrato is.' (Although we might comment here that a 'present generation'

---

[46] Georg Philipp Telemann, *Briefwechsel*, ed. Hans Grosse and Hans Rudolf Jung (Leipzig, 1972), p. 47.

[47] '[...] welche nur Kinder, oder die weibliche Kehle, oder Kastraten erreichen.': Sulzer, *Allgemeine Theorie*, vol. 1, p. 744: cf. Jerold, 'Choral Singing', p. 80.

will almost certainly know what a type of singer *is* – but perhaps not what it *has been*.) Nowadays, the most common context for *haute-contre* is when the term does service to describe a light tenor whose upper notes have an unclear technical provenance. Used in this way *haute-contre* might describe the vocal technique of Baroque altos across Europe except, ironically, the one type of singer which we might expect it to describe – the eighteenth-century French *haute-contre*. As a contracted translation of *contratenor altus*, the term *haute-contre* can be traced back to the Renaissance. It simply signified the part above the tenor and below the *dessus* (soprano), in both vocal and instrumental music. Here we shall look at the rise of the *haute-contre*, its eventual fall being dealt with when we look at the nineteenth century.

Just as the term 'counter-tenor' has shifted in meaning throughout history, so *haute-contre* cannot be set in stone. Neither can it be seen in isolation. To understand the French *haute-contre* we first need to survey the surrounding parts: what voices sang tenor and soprano? As we have seen, at the start of the Renaissance it was in northern France that the trend of falsetto sopranos had developed, and although it quickly spread across the Continent, this practice remained a feature of French sacred music throughout the sixteenth century and beyond. Most references to falsetto singing in France during the eighteenth century are placed in the context of soprano parts. At the Chapelle Royale, in 1645, the soprano ('dessus') part was taken by six boy sopranos, two cornetists, and two men described as 'dessus mués' – which is commonly assumed to refer to falsettists. With this term, we walk straight into what looks like a semantic minefield. 'Mués' (or the older French spelling 'muez', as it sometimes appears in records) is the past participle of 'muer' – meaning 'to mutate, or change'. This looks and sounds close to the word 'muet', meaning 'mute', which is a source of potential confusion, because the soprano part was also played by cornetists, who may well have accompanied the singers on the 'cornet muet' (an instrument with an integral mouthpiece which gives the instrument a softer sound).

Since 'dessus' primarily referred to a part and not necessarily a voice, is it possible that the 'dessus mués' were not singers at all, but players of the muted cornet on the soprano line? Or even, as one commentator suggests, that they were musicians who were both singers and players: from a 1631 list of Chapelle Royale musicians Peter Bennett freely translates the entry 'dessus mués ou cornets', as 'falsettists doubling on cornet'.[48] Granted, some of the musicians named in this list are known to have been players and not singers, but, crucially, this does not apply to all the names. In fact, that

---

[48] Peter Bennett, 'Collaborations between the Musique de la Chambre and the Musique de la Chapelle at the Court of Louis XIII: Nicolas Formé's *Missa Æternae Henrici Magni* (1638) and the Origins of the Grand Motet', *Early Music* 38(3) (2010), pp. 369–86, at p. 372.

word 'ou', read literally as 'or', suggests that whatever they were, the 'dessus-mués' were not cornetists. And the 1631 Chapelle Royale list, along with a later one from 1708, confirms that the 'dessus mués' were singers and not players: these lists separate singers and instrumentalists, and include the 'dessus mués' in the former list.[49]

Having established that the 'dessus mués' sang (rather than played) soprano, can we now confirm that they were falsettists? In various languages we have already come across the term 'changed soprano', sometimes referring to a part, and sometimes to a voice. In this list of personnel, though, it clearly refers to performers rather than the part they sang. So what does 'mués' tell us about the performers? Could the word refer to castrati, who were able to sing soprano as adults because of a specific change they had experienced? We can give a definite 'no' to this question, because the 1708 list of eleven sopranos separates the singers into 'Dessus mués, Dessus italiens, enfants'; in a country where (as we shall see) castrati were widely regarded with distaste, 'Dessus italiens' was a euphemistic term for such singers. 'Dessus mués', then, were not castrati, not children, and not cornetists: by implication they were, indeed (with apologies to those who have followed this tortuous route through an apparent minefield only to come back to the point from which we started), falsettists.

France knew of falsetto sopranos, then, but did it also know of falsetto singing on lower parts? Dating from 1668, a passage written by Béninge de Bacilly seems to suggest this:

> Those who have a natural voice scorn the falsetto voices as being false and strident; and the latter hold that the essence of the song [le fin du Chant] is much more apparent with a clear, brilliant voice, such as those of falsetto singers, than with a natural tenor voice [une Voix de Taille naturelle].[50]

Read literally, de Bacilly seems to suggest that modal and falsetto singers were being compared as options for the same part, in which case that part would likely be the *haute-contre*. The words 'du Chant', though, are ambiguous, and Bacilly could easily be referring to singing more generally. Or, since he uses the word 'taille' and not 'haute-contre', Bacilly might have in mind a particular song, but transposed to suit either the lower modal or falsetto voice. However unlikely this explanation might sound, an eighteenth-century writer in the *Mercure de France* makes precisely the same kind of indirect comparison, between a tenor with 'the voice of this

---

[49] These lists can be viewed at <http://arsmagnalucis.free.fr/chapelle-royale.html> [accessed 4 April 2014].

[50] 'Ceux qui ont la Voix naturelle, méprisent les Voix de Fausset, comme fausses & glapissantes; & ceux cy tiennent que le fin du Chant paroist bien plus dans une Voix éclante, telle que l'ont ceux qui chantent en Fausset, que dans une Voix de Taille naturelle [...]': Béninge de Bacilly, *L'Art bien chanter* (Paris, 1668), pp. 35–6. Original and translation quoted from Parrott, 'Falsetto and the French', p. 146.

age' and the 'sourness' of falsettists and 'aridity' of 'voices conserved against the order of Nature'.[51] (This, incidentally, is not the last Frenchman we will meet whose sensibilities will not allow him to write the word 'castrati'.) These references, then, are at best ambiguous, while all the other evidence we shall see firmly tells us that falsetto in France was not a feature of parts below the soprano.

Although there is no doubt that falsetto singing was known in France during the Baroque, whether it achieved any great popularity is another matter. In his anecdotal history of the French Chapel Royal, written in 1770, Marc-François Bêche wrote that during the last century

> some persons who sang falsetto were sometimes added to them [the Italian castrati], but very few. Moreover, it is very bad practice, and the Italians are better value because the falsettists' voices are neither as pleasant nor as durable as theirs.[52]

This low opinion is borne out by the relative anonymity of the falsettists: in France, their role was choral rather than solo.

The kind of mixed soprano lines described above are similar to those found in Italy from the late Renaissance onwards. If we were to deduce from this that the neighbouring countries shared similar vocal performance practices, however, we would be plain wrong. Resolving not to be subsumed by a dominant culture (a trait it has never quite lost), France maintained an individualistic approach to music during the Baroque. As Burney put it, 'There seems to be a most unaccountable Obstinacy in the attachment of the French to their National Music.'[53] In terms of vocal performance, the French public remained aloof from the appetite for castrati. It is true that from the Renaissance onwards castrati were known in France, but they never acquired the prized status they held elsewhere in Europe. They were present at the French court and chapel from the reign of Louis XIV until the Revolution, holding privileges that suggest high esteem in that closeted

---

[51] '[...] la voix de cet âge, que a continué long-temps, par l'art te par le goût de son chant. II a conservé, avec une espèce de voix de taille, la faculté de chanter les dessus, sans l'aigreur du fausset te sens aridité des voix conservées contre l'ordre de la nature.': *Mercure de France*, 5 April 1765. Translation from Lionel Sawkins, 'For and Against the Order of Nature', *Early Music* 15(3) (1987), pp. 315–24, at p. 318.

[52] '[...] on leur a adjoints quelques fois des personnes qui chantoyent le fausset mais tres peu. D'ailleurs, cela est un tres mauvais usage et les italiens vallent mieus parce que les voix des faussets ne sont ny si agreables ny si durables que les leurs.': cf. Lionel Sawkins, 'The Brothers Bêche: An Anecdotal History of Court Music', *Recherches sur la musique française classique* 24 (1986), pp. 192–221, at p. 219. Translation from Andrew Parrott, 'Falsetto and the French', p. 144.

[53] *The Letters of Charles Burney*, ed. Alvarro Ribeiro (Oxford, 1991), p. 80.

environment.[54] But outside the court, castrati only occasionally appeared in secondary roles in opera, and that was the limit of their public success. The taste of the general public lay elsewhere. The castrato Filippo Balatri, performing to a private audience in Lyon in the early eighteenth century, was greeted with ridicule.[55] And Joseph de Lalande (uncannily echoing the sentiments of the Cistercian monks we met in Chapter 2) claimed the moral high ground when comparing French and Italian tastes:

> The repugnance which the Italians have for strong and loud voices, such as our own baritones and even *haute-contres*, necessarily makes them look to the castrati for their pleasures. It is better for human nature to be accustomed like us to find pleasure in voices that are natural, male, radiant, in possession of their full power: it is custom alone that decides our pleasures; our custom is better and our pleasures more natural.[56]

Lalande, it should be said, was only one of many French writers to state this preference for male voices of 'full power'. Quantz, who as a German we may assume to be a more dispassionate source, confirms this national distinction: 'The Italians and several other nations unite this falsetto with the chest voice, and make use of it to great advantage when singing: with the French, however, it is not customary.'[57] Antoine Bailleux demands that the voice comes 'directly from the chest, for fear that in passing into the head or into the nose it degenerates into falsetto'.[58] And elsewhere, Bailleux advises that 'in singing one should always use a plain voice, without

---

[54] Sawkins, 'For and Against the Order of Nature'.

[55] Stewart, 'Voice Types', p. 130.

[56] 'La répugnance qu'ont les Italiens pour les voix fortes & dures, telles que nos basse-tailles & même nos hautes-contres, leur fait regarder comme nécessaire à leurs plaisirs l'usage des *Castrati*: il vaut mieux cependant pour la nature humaine que l'on foit accoutumé, comme nous, à trouver du plaisir dans les voix naturelles, mâles, éclatantes, & qui ont toute leur force; c'est l'habitude seule qui décide des plaiftrs; la nôtre est plus heureuse, & nos plaisirs plus naturels.': Joseph de Lalande, *Voyage en Italie* (Paris, 1796), vol. 7, pp. 196–7. Translation from Parrott, 'Falsetto and the French', p. 139.

[57] 'Die Italiäner, und einige andere Nationen vereinigen dieses Falset mit der Brustimme, und bedienen sich dessen, bey dem Singen, mit grossem Vortheile: Bey den Franzosen aber ist es nicht üblich.': Quantz, *Versuch einer Anweisung Flöte traversière zu spielen*, chap. 4, sec. 17. Translation from Parrott, 'Falsetto and the French', p. 135.

[58] '[...] directement de la poitrine, de crainte que passant dans la tête ou dans le nez elle ne degenere en fausset par la sourdité.': Antoine Bailleux, *Solfege pour apprendre facilement la musique vocale, etc.* 3rd edn (Paris, 1760), p. 116. Translation from Fuss (ed.), *Inside/Out*, p. 218.

ever passing from the natural voice to the falsetto, or head voice, unless absolutely necessary.'[59]

The aversion which the French had for the castrati, then, was related to their aesthetic distaste for non-modal singing in general; and their predilection for full, 'manly' voices is significant when we look at the singers they favoured as *haute-contres*. In the operas of Lully, the majority of male parts are for low voices, albeit with the leading role being for *haute-contre*. At modern sounding-pitch the tessitura of these *haute-contre* parts is *f* to *g'* (occasionally *a'*), but with Lully consistently favouring the lower part of the range. Of Antoine Boutelou, reputedly the favourite *haute-contre* of Louis XIV, Laborde wrote that he

> combined the best voice with the noblest and the most agreeable manner of singing. His voice was not high, and he went to B flat [*bb'*] in passing; the sound was so full, so beautiful and so touching, that one cannot hear him without one's soul being affected.[60]

Although in the generation after Lully the range of *haute-contre* parts rose slightly, the nature of the voices performing them remained 'full'. Perhaps the most famous *haute-contre* of the late Baroque was Pierre Jélyotte, who sang the leading male roles for Rameau in most of his operas. According to a contemporary, Dufort de Cheverny, 'his tone was that of a perfect *haute-contre*, and certain sounds were as bright as they were leaving a newly-minted bell [...] His voice in *Pygmalion* covered the chorus'.[61] Another anonymous contemporary confirms this, as well as suggesting that vocal power was not confined to this one singer: 'One takes more pleasure in hearing a large voice than a small one; [...] Mlle LeMore [LeMaure], Mr Muraire, Mr Geliotto [Jélyotte], Mrs Benoit and Maligne and others [...] have rendered themselves charming by the beauty and large volume of

---

[59] 'De chanter toujour à voix plaine, sans jamais passer de la voix naturelle au fosset, ou voix da téte, sans necessité absolue.': Bailleux, *Solfege pour apprendre*, p. 126. My translation.

[60] 'Célèbre haut-contre [...] joignait à la plus belle voix la maniere de chanter la plus noble & la plus agreeable. Sa voix n'était pas haute, & il n'allait au *si b* qu'en passant; mais le son en était si plein, si beau & si touchant, qu'on ne pouvait l'entendre sans en avoir l'ame afectée.': Jean-Benjamin de Laborde, *Essai sur la musique ancienne et moderne* (Paris, 1780), vol. 3, pp. 506 and 498. Translation from Mary Cyr, 'On Performing 18th-Century Haute-Contre Roles', *Musical Times* 118, no. 1610 (1977), pp. 291–5, at p. 292.

[61] '[...] son timbre était d'une haute-contre parfaite, et certains sons étaient aussi brillants que s'ils sortaient d'une cloche d'argent [...] Sa voix, dans Pygmalion, couvrait le chœur.': Arthur Pougin, *Un Ténor de l'Opéra au XVIIIe siècle* (Paris, 1905), p. 215. Translation from Cyr, 'On Performing 18th-Century Haute-Contre Roles', p. 292.

their voices.'[62] Rousseau saw this vocal style in another light: 'The general
disposition of French composers is always to force the voices in order to
make them shout rather than sing.'[63] Burney, who like Rousseau preferred
Italian voices to French, offers a similar gloss on a singer he heard at the
Parisian Concert Spirituel in 1770: 'the principal counter tenor had a solo
verse [...] which he bellowed out with as much violence as if he had done
it for life, while a knife was at his throat.'[64] This, incidentally, is one of the
many instances in Burney's writing which implies that his point of reference
– the English counter-tenor – was a primarily modal voice.

How, we might wonder, was it possible that Italian and French alto
(*haute-contre*) parts – which on paper appear to be similar – could have
been sung with such different techniques? The answer to this riddle lies
chiefly in the respective performing pitches of the two countries. Writing
home about voices he has heard in Italy, de Brosses says:

> There are in an opera company three or four soprano voices, and a
> contralto or *haute-contre* male or female, and a tenor or baritone for
> the role of kings. The bass voice is not widely used [...] These first
> three types of voices, [soprano, contralto or *haute-contre*, and tenor
> or baritone] are a third or a fourth higher than ours. The *hautes-
> contres* are rare and prized; they go to b [*b'*], and are not of the same
> type as ours: no type of French voice could render their song well.[65]

Lalande, who travelled in Italy in the 1760s, confirms this – albeit with a
bewildering matrix of comparisons:

> I have said that the tenor of the Italians was the haute-contre of
> the French; at least the tenors hardly differ if they choose to sing

---

[62]   'qu'il y avoit plus de plaisir à entendre une grande voix qu'une petite: Je lui
ajoutai encore que l'on faisoit mention de *Mademoiselle Le More, de Mr.
Muraire, de Mr. Gelliotto, de Mrs Benoit & Maligne*, & autres qui se sont rendus
charmans par la beauté & le grand volume de leur voix [...]': Anon., *Dissertation
sur la musique francaise et italienne par Mr. l'A*** P******* (s.l., 1754), p. 36.
Translation from Parrott, 'Falsetto and the French', p. 138.

[63]   'L'esprit general des Compositeurs François est toujours de forcer les *Voix*
pour les faire crier plutôt que chanter [...]': Jean-Jacques Rousseau, 'Voix',
Dictionnaire de musique (Paris, 1768), p. 545. Translation from Parrott, 'Falsetto
and the French', p. 139.

[64]   Burney, *The Present State of Music*, p. 26.

[65]   'Il y a dans un opéra trois ou quatre voix de dessus, et un *contralto* ou haute-
contre, mâles ou femelles, avec un *tenore*, ou taille pour les rôles de rois. Les
voix de basse ne sont point en usage [...] Ces trois premiers genres de voix ont
une tierce ou une quarte d'élévation plus que chez nous. Les hautes-contre sont
rares et prisées; elles vont à *si-mi*, et ne sont pas du même genre que les nôtres;
aucune espèce de voix française ne pourrait bien rendre leur chant': De Brosses,
Lettres écrites d'Italie, p. 362. Translation adapted from Cyr, 'On Performing
18th-Century Haute-Contre Roles', p. 291; and MacClintock, *Readings*, p. 274.

without making monkeys of the castrati, with their endless roulades and ornaments which disfigure the work of composers. The [Italian] tenor goes from *C* to *g'* in full voice and to *d''* in falsetto or fausset: our *haute-contre*, ordinarily, after *g'* goes up in full voice to *b♭'*; while the tenor after *g'* enters into falsetto; but that is not without exception: Babbi [an Italian tenor, as were the next two singers mentioned] goes up to *c''* in full voice, the same as Caribaldi did until the age of 48. Amorevoli, who was a little older, went up to *d''*. In Paris, Geliot [Jélyotte] had the compass of Amorevoli, and Legros [a French *haute-contre*, as were the next three singers to be mentioned] had that of the first two [Babbi and Caribaldi]; these qualities of voice, in all countries, are very rare: Lainez goes up to *a'* forced, Rousseau to a *b'* somewhat forced, Dufrenoy up to *g'* forced; all those who succeeded Legros are obliged to shout to reach the pitch of the *haute-contre*, except Rousseau, but he has a much smaller sound. Thus, Geliot and Legros would have been called tenors [by the Italians] and not contraltos, although one is accustomed to translate this word as *haute-contre*. The contraltos are women's voices of second soprano [second dessus], which go from *a'* to *c''* in full voice, and to *f''* in falsetto, as opposed to the ordinary compass of women's soprano which is from *d'* to *e''* in full voice and to *c'''* in falsetto.

The castratos who have soprano or *dessus* voices have the same compass as the women; others are contraltos, or second *dessus*; we have many of them in Paris among the singers of the choirs; they are often put in unison with the *hautes-contres*, but they are never made to sing alone.[66]

---

[66] 'J'ai dit que le tenore des Italiens étoît la haute-contre des François; du moins les tenori n'en différeroient presque pas s'ils vouloient chanter sans faire les singes des castrats, par la quantité de roulades & de broderies, qui défigurent l'ouvrage des compositeurs. Le tenore va de ut à sol en pleine voix, & jusqu a re en falsetto ou fausset: notre haute-contre, ordinairement après le sol, monte en pleine voix jusqu'au si b au lieu que le tenore après le fol entre dans le fausset; mais celan'eft pas sans exception: Babbi montoit jufqu'à ut en pleine voix, de même que Caribaldi, jusqu'à l'âge de 48 ans. Amorevoli, qui étoit un peu plus ancien, alloit jusqu'à re. A Paris, Geliot avoir la même étendue qu Amorevli, & Legros avoit celle des deux premiers; ces qualités de voix, dans tous les pays, sont très-rares: Lainez va jusqu'au la forcé, Rousseau jusqu'au la b un peu forcé, Dufrenoy jusqu'au sol forcé; tous ceux qui ont succédé a Legros, sont obligés de crier pour arriver au ton de la haute-contre, excepté Rousseau; mais il a le timbre plus petit. Ainsi, Geliot & Legros auroient été appelles tenori & non pas contralti quoiqu'on ait cou-tume de traduire ce mot par haute-contre. Les contralti sont des voix de femmes en séconds dessus, qui vont depuis la jusqu'à ut en pleine voix, & jusqu'en fa en fausset; au lieu que l'étendue ordinaire des voix de femmes en dessus est depuis re jusqu'en mi en pleine voix, & jusqu'en ut en fausset. ⁋ 'Les castrats qui ont la voix de soprani ou dessus, ont la même étendue que les femmes; d'autres sont des contralti, on séconds dessus; nous en

Aside from his explicit comparison of Italian and French voices and methods, Lalande also offers us a glimpse of future changes: Legros, a modal 'shouter' to whom he refers, was Gluck's favoured *haute-contre*. We shall discuss Legros, along with 'those who succeeded him' and – crucially – *how* they succeeded him, in the next historical chapter.

Lalande also alerts us to a change in Italian vocal practice as the Baroque period progressed. In describing a vocal scene of female contraltos, and tenors using falsetto at the top of their ranges, he presents a very different picture from the one painted at the start of this chapter. The greatest difference, of course, is that Lalande (like de Brosses) was writing of what he heard at the opera house and not in the church. Outwith convents and orphanages for girls, Lalande would not have found female contraltos in Italian churches: low castrati and modal-falsetto altos were still the order of the day there. But by the end of the Baroque, church music in Italy had become a sidewater – and one which often eddied backwards to the style and practices of Palestrina. The real thrust of Italian music-making was in the opera house, and here the castrati acted as a magnetic force. It was not so much that they fostered a taste for high voices as such, but for voices with perfect control over a wide range. Yes, the castrati were noted for their power, but this was at its most striking when thrown into relief by quiet singing. Their favoured calling card, the *messa di voce*, is the most obvious example of this. When the great Italian Siface visited London, John Evelyn most admired 'his holding out & delicatenesse in extending & loosing a note with that incomparable softenesse, & sweetnesse'.[67] It is in the context of this kind of acclaim that we can best appreciate why the method and aesthetic of the castrati were adopted by other singers: why, for instance, the Italian tenors whom Lalande heard in the 1760s now employed a falsetto extension. By the end of the Baroque, Tosi's modal-falsetto technique was established throughout most of Europe, as an attribute desired of baritones and tenors as well as of altos and sopranos. Only in France did this fashion fail to establish itself. And even there, as we shall see in the next historical chapter, towards the end of the eighteenth century Tosi's technique was to flourish.

avons beaucoup à Paris parmi les chanteuses des chœurs; on les met souvent à l'unisson des hautes- contres, mais on ne les fait jamais chanter seules.': Lalande, *Voyage en Italie*, vol. 7, pp. 204–5. Translation adapted from Cyr, 'On Performing 18th-Century Haute-Contre Roles', pp. 291–2.

[67] *The Diary of John Evelyn*, ed. Esmond S. De Beer (London, 1959), p. 864.

Into Man's Estate:
Changing Boys' Voices and Nascent Falsettists

Many choirmasters are timid about 'bringing the boys through the break' and developing the counter-tenor alto. But the process is simple and almost guaranteed.

William J. Finn[1]

Y this stage in our history, it has become clear that the question of whether someone sang with a modal *or* a falsetto voice is often a spurious one: with countless singers from Ziryab to Amorevoli, the answer is not one voice or the other, but probably *both*. Related to this, there is another insidious false dichotomy which we should now bring out into the open, and that is the question of whether certain singers were boys *or* men. Sometimes the answer is clear – Coryat's 'middle-aged man', for instance, or perhaps Bach's fourteen-year-old Neucke – but often the distinction is less obvious. From medieval Cambrai to our own day, we find numerous singers who seem to wander across an ill-defined border region between these two states.

For us, there are two obvious reasons why we instinctively find the idea of accomplished adolescent male singers difficult to accept. The first is that modern society tends to insist on an artificially clear demarcation between children and adults. The second is that received wisdom suggests that when a boy's voice begins to change, he should sing no more until his adult voice has stabilised. So today, when we read of historical singers in their late teens still singing soprano parts, we tend to assume that their voices were unchanged. This, in turn, has led to the commonly held belief that in earlier centuries voices changed at significantly higher ages. Taken together, these factors have fogged our understanding of how a great many males have sung high. Navigating through this fog is not easy. The problem with understanding the history of vocal mutation is not just that the data is incomplete and inconsistently acquired. More fundamentally, mutation is in itself a complex process – psychologically as well as physiologically.[2]

---

[1] William J. Finn, *The Art of the Choral Conductor*, vol. 1: *Choral Technique* (Boston, 1939), p. 143.

[2] Cf. Martin Ashley and Ann-Christine Mecke, '"Boyes are apt to change their voice at about fourteene yeeres of age": An Historical Background to the Debate about Longevity in Boy Treble Singers', *Reviews of Research in Human Learning and Music* 1 (2013), available online at <http://rrhlm.org/index.php/RRHLM/article/view/13> [accessed 3 April 2014].

Can we establish any reliable historical data for the ages at which boys' voices changed? Encouragingly, in *The Problemes of Aristotle* we come across the question, 'Why are boyes apt to change their voice about fourteene yeeres of age?' However, our relief at finding a precise mutation age from Antiquity lasts only as long as it takes for us to wonder why we are reading this question in an Elizabethan spelling. Sure enough, in the primary source of this information, Aristotle's *Generation of Animals*, the age is not specified; it therefore appears to have been added by the anonymous Elizabethan translator on the basis of his own observations.[3] But even if it fails to give us the information it promises, *The Problemes of Aristotle* does at least seemingly offer us a figure for the mutation age in late Tudor England. And happily, this figure tallies precisely with the most thorough research of Tudor choir records.[4] The most reliable recent study suggests that by the time of Bach the age of mutation was fifteen to sixteen.[5] And by the early twentieth century, returning to England, oral histories (the ambiguities of which we will address in a moment) suggest an age-range of fifteen to seventeen.[6] The line which these figures plot on a graph seems roughly to shadow a similar U-shape we observed in the line of historical heights. And yes, it might seem to follow that when nutrition is poor, growth is minimal and maturation is slow (and vice-versa). But the historical data on vocal maturation is too flimsy for us to confirm this with any certainty. And it needs to be said that such a conclusion is rebuffed by research on the period since 1845, which suggests that no such link exists.[7] In short, attempts to specify historical mutation ages leave us with more questions than answers.

The most obvious problem with assessing the ages at which boys' voices changed throughout history is that such records as we have tend to be based on nothing more scientific than the ages at which individuals stopped singing soprano in choirs. This method is unreliable because, as we shall see, it introduces the huge variable of human agency. Put simply, the question which these figures pose, but which we cannot answer, is this: who stopped whom singing, and why? For all its glaring faults, the method of charting boy trebles' retirement ages continues to be relied upon, and it is on this basis that the current age of mutation is anecdotally said to stand at around

---

[3] Bruce R. Smith, *The Acoustic World of Early Modern England: Attending to the O-Factor* (Chicago, 1999), p. 227.

[4] Roger Bowers, 'The Vocal Scoring, Choral Balance and Performing Pitch of Latin Church Polyphony in England, c. 1500–58', *Journal of the Royal Musical Association* 112 (1987), pp. 38–76, at p. 48.

[5] Ann-Christine Mecke, *Mutantenstadl: der Stimmwechsel und die deutsche Chorpraxis im 18. und 19. Jahrhundert* (Berlin, 2007).

[6] Stephen Beet, *The Better Land: In Search of the Lost Boy Sopranos* (Portlaw, Co. Waterford, 2005).

[7] Cf. Martin Ashley, *How High Should Boys Sing?: Gender, Authenticity and Credibility in the Young Male Voice* (Farnham, 2009), p. 67.

twelve. A recent scientific survey in Germany, however, suggests that (at least in 1995) the average vocal mutation age is not twelve, but fourteen.[8] This research, significantly, is the work of phoniatricians and paediatricians, whose method of assessment was based on acoustical and physiological analysis, thus minimising the variable of human agency. Results from a similar observational study amongst British choirs in 2012 'appeared to support the belief' that the mutation age was dropping, but pointed out that however scientific its methods, no such study could entirely divorce itself from the influence of changing social norms.[9]

At this point, though, we should perhaps take a step back from the statistical vortex of variables and trends, and consider just how complex is the issue of vocal mutation in males. A clue to the way that voice mutation has been over-simplified lies in the traditional use of the word 'break' to describe the change. 'Break' suggests that the child's voice snaps instantaneously into that of the adult, but more commonly the process is gradual, and for a time both voices exist simultaneously. A clear and colourful description of this process comes from William J. Finn, an American choirmaster in the 1930s.

> The well-trained soprano-boy has not only an easy compass of two full octaves [*c'* to *c'''*], he has also an effective middle register [...] his voice in this range [*f'* to *f''*] should be of rich, round, albeit spiritual timbre. This part of his soprano voice can be retained during the months when adolescence first attacks his childhood and begins stealthily to purloin his boyish attributes. Later, when the change into man's estate has been completed and his natural voice will have become fixed in the lower octave, the former voice, with modifications of the original, may still function as high as [*d''*] and in many cases, higher.[10]

In developing future male falsettists for his choir, Finn saw a value in retaining the upper voice through adolescence. We have already discussed two choral institutions – Dufay's in Cambrai and Bach's in Leipzig – in which something like the practice Finn describes was adopted. Doubtless we have passed over many others in which it took place unremarked. We now come to the single best-known – and perhaps most misunderstood – case of the late-breaking voice.

'Until my 18th year', Haydn later wrote of his youth in Vienna, 'I sang soprano with great success, not only in St Stephen's but also at the Court.'[11]

---

[8] Michael Fuchs *et al.*, 'Predicting Mutational Change in the Speaking Voice of Boys', *Journal of Voice* 21(2) (2007), pp. 169–78.

[9] Martin Ashley, 'The English Choral Tradition and the Secular Trend in Boys' Pubertal Timing', *International Journal of Research in Choral Singing* 4(2) (2013), pp. 4–27.

[10] Finn, *Choral Technique*, p. 136.

[11] *The Collected Correspondence and London Notebooks of Joseph Haydn*, ed. H. C. Robbins Landon (London, 1959), p. 19.

This statement has often led to the bald assertion that Haydn's voice did not change until his late teens, but is it also possible that he simply sang on as his voice was changing? Or, indeed, that Haydn was bathing his youth in a nostalgic (but false) light? Georg Greisinger, a friend of Haydn's who wrote an early biography based on his conversations with the composer, suggests that this indeed was the case: 'From 1745 on [when Haydn was thirteen], things seemed to grow steadily worse. Slowly the voice of the boy approaching puberty began to deteriorate.' Eventually, Greisinger continues, 'Joseph was given no more solos after the Empress had complained about his "crowing like a cock"'.[12] Even if we disregard Greisinger and believe Haydn, we cannot unequivocally say when his voice changed. Rather, we are left with the (literally) equivocal knowledge that in his late teens Haydn retained the capacity to sing soprano.

During the process of mutation an adolescent male commonly has the capacity to sing in either an upper or lower register. The words 'upper' and 'lower', incidentally, are used here rather than 'falsetto' and 'modal', since at this stage of vocal development it is less an empirical observation and more a question of perspective as to when the higher voice of the maturing boy ceases to be his common – and therefore 'modal' – voice and becomes his 'falsetto'. This distinction is itself open to question, though, since an argument is made that even before mutation begins, the lower voice of a boy is his natural one, and the higher one less natural (if not 'false'). In the 1960s George Malcolm was director of Westminster Cathedral choir, where the boys were (and still are) encouraged to develop this lower resonance. Malcolm pointed to the football terraces for a demonstration of what constitutes a natural voice:

> Boys will be boys! – and in most parts of the world this applies to boy choristers too. When they sing [at Westminster Cathedral] they are expected to sound like boys and are not taught to produce an uncharacteristic quality of tone, remotely unlike that of the voices with which they talk, or laugh, or cheer at a football match.[13]

This is not the first time that the innocent sports fan has been dragged into this book, but whereas earlier we considered the adult male cheering in a natural high voice, in this case the cheering boy exhibits a natural low voice. Both, in different ways, ask questions of what we consider natural and – by implication – what we consider masculine.

In *The Boy's Voice*, the Victorian founder of the tonic sol-fa system, John Curwen, made a similar observation to that made by Malcolm, albeit with an alarmingly different conclusion. In a chapter on 'The special difficulties of agricultural districts', he addresses the issue of the 'country choir-boy, who perhaps in the day is shouting to scare birds':

---

[12] Cf. Karl Geiringer, *Haydn: A Creative Life in Music* (Berkeley, CA, 1968), p. 23.

[13] Cf. Ashley, *How High Should Boys Sing?*, p. 60.

The lower register of a country boy is, as a rule, coarse, so it is important to get him to use his higher register as soon as possible. Show him first of all that he has, as it were, *two voices*, and point out that he is required [...] to use that voice which is most like a girl's.[14]

Any choir director offering such advice today could expect to witness the proverbial revolving door, with alarmed boys exiting and irate parents entering. Yet the fact that Curwen was successful and influential suggests that things were very different in the Victorian era: evidently boys could actually be receptive to advice that they should sound like girls. The whole question of gender identity has an obvious significance for high male singing, and we will address it more fully later in this book. For the time being, all we need to note is that Curwen and Malcolm implicitly agree that the boy singer has a choice of registers. Choice, in turn, implies human agency. We now need to ask what factors shape this agency, and whether they have changed during the course of history. Again, we find ourselves with good evidence for the present, and a varied set of clues about the past.

Statistics of choral involvement suggest that the increasing participation of girls in choirs (particularly church choirs) has today made boys less willing choristers. Especially as they grow older, and the wish to appear masculine asserts itself, boys feel uncomfortable with doing something which is perceived (at least by their non-singing peer group) as a 'girly' activity. Before the mid-twentieth century, and the upsurge of girl sopranos, there could have been no such stigma. This helps to explain why Curwen's bird-scaring boys could be persuaded to use their 'girl's' voice: practically speaking, they were never in danger of actually being confused with girls.

The case of Ernest Lough and the 'Temple boys', star trebles from the early years of recording, illustrates perfectly how the issue of singing through adolescence has changed in the last hundred years. When Lough last recorded Mendelssohn's 'O for the Wings of a Dove', in November 1928, he had just turned sixteen. More than a year before that, George Thalben-Ball, the choirmaster at the Temple Church, had worriedly reported to HMV that there were definite signs that Lough's voice was already 'breaking'. In other words, the single most famous recording of a boy treble was made when the process of mutation was well advanced. Lough actually ceased singing treble when he was seventeen – more than two years after his voice had begun 'breaking'. Nor was Lough's longevity an exception at the Temple. There were a number of similarly magnificent boy trebles who sang on during vocal mutation. Denis Barthel was the same age as Lough when he was (literally) stood down:

I was conscious of the odd crack appearing, and unhappily the day came when Dr. Ball said to me "Denis, I think you had better come

---

[14] John Curwen, *The Boy's Voice* (London, 1891), p. 50.

down from the stalls and sit with the probationers". I knew then that my day had come, but I had had a good innings.

Many have wondered whether the secret of the 'Temple boys' long shelf-lives was the result of a particular vocal method which Thalben-Ball used. Whilst their vocal technique, on the evidence of their solo recordings, was remarkably easy and assured, the real reason for their longevity was less physiological and more psychological. Barthel remembers that 'Dr. Ball was extremely charismatic. All of us who were taught by him came to love him for his clear understanding of boys [...] They were wonderful years: I don't think I ever really left Temple, and my heart is still there.'[15] Ernest Lough's son George, who also sang in the Temple choir under Thalben-Ball, suggests that the boys there would explore whatever vocal possibilities they could to stay in the choir:

> It's possible that as the vocal range gets lower, trebles start to develop a form of falsetto. However there was the additional incentive to stay singing at The Temple as everyone enjoyed singing under George Thalben-Ball and the camaraderie of being in the choir meant more to us than being in any social group at school or at home.'[16]

Faced with changing voices, the Temple boys were not just permitted, but encouraged and inspired by their director to continue singing in their upper register. In different circumstances the same set of larynxes could easily have chosen to abandon their 'girl's' voices in favour of exploring their new 'manly' ones. The fascinating biographies and memories of the 'Temple boys' are the histories on which the early twentieth-century mutation age of fifteen to seventeen has largely been based; when scrutinised, the complexities of their tales warn against any simple statistical conclusions.

At exactly the same time as Lough and Barthel were singing on into adolescence in London, on the South Coast of England Alfred Deller was going one step further. At the point in the mutation process when Thalben-Ball had benignly silenced Barthel, Deller's choirmaster at Margate, Hector Shawcross, followed the conventional wisdom of retiring the boy when he reached the age of sixteen. But Deller felt that he could still sing, and when he was asked to take the top part in a minstrel quartet he accepted: hearing him in this context, Shawcross brought him back to the church choir to sing with the altos – in what would become his falsetto register. This underlines just how significant the choices and opinions of individuals are in the development of the changing male voice. Perhaps more than the boy himself, it is his choirmaster and parents who will determine with which voice, and for how long, he will sing. Neither does the element of human

---

[15] See the Denis Barthel page of 'The Better Land' website, at <http://www. thebetterland.org./bland008.html> [accessed 6 April 2014].

[16] Cf. Ashley, 'The English Choral Tradition, p. 7.

agency stop with these individuals, since they are only conduits of wider societal currents.

Although Lough and Barthel sang again as adults, they did so as basses. Deller, who was encouraged to sing through the break, became a falsettist. Tempting though it is to see Deller's high-profile example as proving William Finn's 'almost guaranteed' recipe for developing a lasting falsetto voice, countless unremarkable failures warn against such a reading. We should bear in mind the realistic caveat of the Cambrai authorities that their young falsettists should be employed 'as long as their voices shall last'. We should also remember that the changing male voice is an instrument – or two – the use of which is determined by people with mindsets of their own time and place, and not of ours.

CHAPTER 6

Baroque England

To what extent did England adopt Italian vocal practices? In Shakespeare's *Richard II*, when York speaks of 'Proud Italy / Whose manners still our tardy-apish nation / Limps after in base imitation' he seems simply to voice an observable trend in social history. From the Elizabethan period onwards, Italianate influences are evident in many aspects of high society, from the fabrics it wore to the madrigals it sang. Yet England's cultural relationship with Italy during the seventeenth century was actually a highly ambivalent one. When we read Shakespeare's lines with a more sceptical eye we can sense an artist both embarrassed by and dismissive of this 'base imitation'. Look at the music of Purcell and, for every Italian trait, one finds an obstinately English characteristic. Yet vocally, fashions in England seem to have been determined less by composers such as Purcell, and more by society, as reflected in the journals of amateur arbiters of taste such as the diarist John Evelyn. With the backing of a wealthy family, after graduating from Oxford Evelyn spent time in Italy. He was a typical Grand Tourist, and to read his later observations of music in fashionable London is to read the opinions of a man who can barely bring himself to commend a singer without remarking on his Italian pedigree.

Vocally, the performance practice of English Baroque can be seen as a whirlpool formed between currents – the backwater of English iconoclasm and the mainstream of Italian imitation. The implications of these conflicting currents, for falsetto singing, are significant. Italian singers began to appear in England from the Restoration onwards. Pietro Reggio, 'who sings Italian songs to the theorbo most neatly' according to Pepys, and who taught singing to the gentrified classes in London, was one of the first such 'masters'. His recently rediscovered 1677 treatise *The Art of Singing*, however, is concerned almost entirely with interpretation, and says little about the practical techniques he considered appropriate. The terms 'head' and 'chest' voice, let alone 'falsetto', are entirely absent. There is, though, one revealing passage, when he advises bass singers that 'the lower the Notes are the more he must strengthen his Voice: and on the contrary. The higher his Voice ascends, the softer he must Sing'.[1] Reggio's advice here tallies with almost every Italian method from the sixteenth to the early nineteenth century, suggesting that head voice, and by implication falsetto, were to be cultivated by all singers. Within a few years of Reggio's arrival, Tosi had begun the first of his two spells in London, teaching all comers the art of the falsetto extension.

It is worth stressing the fact that the Italian method was taught to singers

---

[1] Pietro Reggio, *The Art of Singing* (Oxford, 1677), p. 23.

of all types. Falsetto singing undeniably gained a foothold in Britain during the Baroque, but it can reasonably be argued that it concerned the counter-tenor voice no more than it did bass, baritone or tenor. There are numerous references, throughout the eighteenth century, to lower voices singing in falsetto. We will come to others in due course, but a particularly telling one concerns the singer and actor Robert Owenson. According to his daughter, around 1771 Thomas Arne told Owenson that he had 'one of the finest baritones he ever heard, and particularly susceptible to that quality of intonation then so much admired and now so out of fashion, the falsetto, then introduced from the Italian school.'[2] Arne's will be by no means the last voice we hear lamenting the vanishing 'Golden Age' of the modal-falsetto technique: in passing we might also note that, despite its nostalgic tint, this is one of the first instances in England of the term 'baritone' being used to describe an intermediate vocal type.

As the Italian influence took hold, and falsetto started to become a desirable feature of every aspiring singer's technique, we may ask whether there was a role for specialist falsettists in early Baroque England? Whereas falsettists had taken the top line in many Italian choirs during the Renaissance, in England the treble (and mean) parts had been the preserve of boys. There is a hint of change in the list of musicians who sang in the 1634 masque *The Triumph of Peace*, which was staged by the societies of the Inns of Court as a demonstration of loyalty to Charles I and his queen, Henrietta Maria of France. There, amongst the 'Queens musicians for the lutes and voices' (all with French names, and in a separate list from the boys), is listed a 'Monsieur Mari' as a soprano. There is no indication, in this source or elsewhere, as to whether Mathurin Mari was a falsettist or castrato, but we may assume the former, since even in Versailles the few castrati that the French tolerated were all Italian, and in any event did not appear there until the mid-seventeenth century. Even so, Mari is a curious case since, as we shall see in due course, during the Baroque the French displayed a limited taste (most often a singular distaste) for falsetto singing (this distaste could, of course, help explain why Mari was to be found plying his trade abroad). Elsewhere in the documents relating to this masque, we find that Mari was one of the highest-paid performers (£40). Although prominent as a soloist in the masque, Mari also sang soprano in the chorus, along with seven English boys.[3] The presence of Mari (about whom no other information has come to light) and his countrymen was obviously connected to the queen's own nationality. Mari appears to have been a fleeting visitor to England, yet his singing alongside boy trebles may have set a precedent for the Chapel Royal.

---

[2] Lady (Sydney) Morgan, *Lady Morgan's Memoirs* (London, 1863), vol. 1, p. 50.

[3] Murray Lefkowitz, 'The Longleat Papers of Bulstrode Whitelocke: New Light on Shirley's *The Triumph of Peace*', *Journal of the American Musicological Society* 18(1) (1965), pp. 42–60.

As a result of a choral malaise brought about by the British Civil Wars, for a short time afterwards the treble part in the Chapel Royal was reinforced by adult male voices. From 1642, when the Puritan Parliament decreed that all music in church was to be 'wholly forborn and omitted', until the Restoration of the monarchy in 1660, English choirs were effectively silenced. When music in services was resumed, Matthew Locke noted of the Chapel Royal that 'the superiour Parts of their Musick [were performed] with Cornets and Mens feigned Voices, there being not one Lad, for all that time, capable of Singing his Part readily.'[4] Although this was evidently no more than a temporary measure, it is noticeable throughout the English Baroque that when falsettists are referred to, they are associated with 'superiour' or 'treble' rather than counter-tenor parts.

The Purcellian Counter-Tenor

I N trying to assess what kind of voice the typical Restoration counter-tenor had, for the first time in this history we have a very particular kind of evidence. Not only do we have written descriptions of the voices, and a good idea of what pitch the music was performed at, but also theatre records and annotations in scores to provide us with evidence linking specific singers to specific solos. In the case of Purcell, the music historians Olive Baldwin and Thelma Wilson have compiled a wealth of evidence, which leads to this conclusion regarding counter-tenor parts:

> An analysis of the music we know Purcell gave to specific singers shows that he was writing for a range of tenor voices. His counter-tenors were tenors concentrating on the higher part of their voice, while his tenors were more like today's baritones'.[5]

Some of these links between individual singers and the parts they sang are now worth us exploring.

The actor Colley Cibber admitted that the song in *Sir Courtly Nice*, which William Mountfort had sung in a 'clear Countertenour [...] full and melodious', he himself could only manage 'under the Imperfection of a feign'd, and screaming Trebble', implying a clear distinction between 'Countertenour' and falsetto techniques.[6] For Mountfort, Purcell composed the song 'Say, cruel Amoret' in his incidental music to *The Wives' Excuse*. This song only goes up to *g'*, suggesting that Mountfort's 'clear

[4] Matthew Locke, *The Present Practice of Musick Vindicated* (London, 1673; repr. in facsimile 1974), p. 19.

[5] Olive Baldwin and Thelma Wilson, 'Henry Purcell's Countertenors and Tenors', in *Der Countertenor: die männliche Falsettstimme vom Mittelalter zur Gegenwart*, ed. Corinna Herr and Arnold Jacobshagen (Mainz, 2012), pp. 79–98, at p. 95.

[6] Colley Cibber, *An Apology for the Life of Mr. Colley Cibber, Comedian* [1740], ed. John Maurice Evans (London, 1987), p. 78.

Ex. 9 Henry Purcell, 'Be lively then and gay', from *Ye Tuneful Muses*, opening

Countertenour' was what we would call a tenor voice. As for 'trebble', this clearly indicates falsetto singing. But again, just because a man could sing in falsetto did not make him what we could term a falset*tist*, as the case of John Abell makes clear. In the diary of John Evelyn for 27 January 1682 we find the following entry:

> After supper, in came the famous Trebble *Mr. Abel* newly return'd from *Italy*, & indeede I never heard a more excellent voice, one would have sworne it had ben a Womans it was so high, and so well & skillfully manag'd: Being accompanied with Signor *Francesco* on the Harpsichord.[7]

The case of John Abell appears to present us with a problem because, for all that Evelyn describes him as a 'Trebble', this is evidently not a literal description. In public he was known as a counter-tenor – who sang parts by Purcell and John Blow mainly within the range *g–b'* (at something close to modern pitch). This is precisely the range of the solo 'Be lively then and gay', which Abell sang in the 1686 welcome song *Ye Tuneful Muses* (Ex. 9). It is difficult to see how this kind of range could have sounded remarkably 'high', as Evelyn commented, if Abell sang parts such as this in falsetto. An interesting suggestion that Abell was not primarily a falsettist is given by the German composer and theorist Johann Mattheson. Discussing the

---

[7] *The Diary of John Evelyn*, ed. de Beer (London, 1959), p. 505.

benefits of certain diets for singers, Matheson wrote that Abell 'possessed certain secrets for keeping his tender and natural high voice perfect until a late age. An extraordinary moderation and selection in eating and drinking helped very much.'[8] Abell had sung in Germany during Matheson's youth, so we should not simply dismiss his comment on Abell's 'natural' voice as distant hearsay.

A remark by another German composer, Jakob Greber, actually places Abell one rung lower on the musical ladder: according to Sigismund Kusser, Greber offered him the advice that 'If you don't give attention to Sr Abel, an English tenor, he will be jealous.'[9] So was Abell a tenor, counter-tenor or 'trebble'? Perhaps the clue to the riddle of Abell's voice lies in the context of his singing. When Evelyn heard him he was singing in an Italianate chamber style which, we might remember from the previous chapter, demanded the quiet fusion of registers as the voice ascended: this would explain Evelyn's otherwise curious comment that Abell's voice was 'skillfully manag'd'. In other words, whereas Abell's 'public' voice may well have been predominantly modal, his 'private' voice could accommodate higher notes by virtue of a falsetto extension.

Evelyn's non-literal use of the word 'trebble', incidentally, is confirmed by his remarks on:

> that celebrated voice of Mr. *Pordage* newly come from *Rome*; his singing was after the Venetian Recitative, as masterly as could be, & with an excellent voice both Treble & base.[10]

Here, 'Treble & base' seems to mean 'high and low'. This probably meant falsetto, but if so Pordage was using it in combination with his modal voice.

One noticeable (and potentially confusing) feature of Restoration London is the number of times we find a single singer operating under more than one vocal designation. In particular, the distinction between counter-tenor and tenor seems fluid. Richard Elford is a case in point. At Durham Cathedral, in 1695, he was admitted as a tenor. Moving down south, however, he held a variety of appointments, including one at the Chapel Royal, as a counter-tenor. In fact, as Donald Burrows has pointed out, the range of Elford's 'counter-tenor' and 'tenor' parts was not radically different.[11] At modern pitch Elford's range, to judge from the parts Burney tells us were 'expressly composed' for him, was about two octaves, up

---

[8] 'Derselbe befass einige Geheimnisse, seine zärtliche und natürliche Alt-Stimme auf das reinest bis in spate Alter zu bewahren, wozu die ungemeine Mässigkeit und wahl im Essen und Trincken sehr viel half.': Mattheson, *Der vollkommene Capellmeister*, ed. and trans. Harris, part 2, 1:9, p. 95. Translation adapted from *The Musical Magazine* 1 (1839), p. 129.

[9] Baldwin and Wilson, 'Henry Purcell's Countertenors and Tenors', p. 92.

[10] *The Diary of John Evelyn*, ed. de Beer, p. 786.

[11] Donald Burrows, *Handel and the English Chapel Royal* (Oxford, 2005), p. 539.

to *b'*: this represents a plausible pitch for a high modal voice at the time, but one far too low for a pure falsettist. Elford aside, even the two most famous 'counter-tenors' of the day, John Freeman and John Pate, are both known to have also sung tenor parts in performances of Purcell's music.[12] This practice of singers migrating between parts was to continue long after Purcell's time, as we shall see. One such 'migration', though, is probably spurious: Alexander Damascene, a counter-tenor who took up the place vacated by Purcell in the Chapel Royal in 1695, has also been cited as a bass soloist in the first performance of the *Song for St Cecilia's Day*, but this must be an error, since according to the autograph he only sang the counter-tenor solo 'The airy violin'. All other references to parts sung by Damascene confirm that he was solely a counter-tenor.[13]

Does the fact that a counter-tenor replaced Purcell in the Chapel Royal suggest that Purcell was himself a counter-tenor? If this situation happened today, in a professional chorus, we could certainly make that deduction, since replacements are made on a vocally like-for-like basis. In the Baroque, though, when vocal designations were a relative novelty, and much more fluid, this was not such an issue. In choir records there are many such cases of one type of singer being replaced by another type. Aside from the Chapel Royal register, the sole piece of evidence that Purcell sang counter-tenor himself is a single comma – or rather the absence of one. Peter Motteux, editor of *The Gentleman's Journal*, reported in the November 1692 issue that the *Song for St Cecilia's Day* had been:

> admirably set to Music by Mr. *Henry Purcell*, and perform'd twice with universal applause, particularly the second Stanza, which was sung with incredible Graces by Mr *Purcell* himself.

Lacking a comma after the word 'sung', this does indeed suggest that Purcell was the singer of the stanza ("Tis Nature's voice'). This meaning, though, would flatly contradict the autograph of the score, which tells us that in the 1692 first performance John Pate sang this solo. Bearing in mind the highly decorated writing in "Tis Nature's voice', it is far more likely that Motteux was noting that the graces had been written out by the composer, and not improvised by the singer as would usually be the case: to the seventeenth-century commentator this fact would have been remarkable. Although Pate's fame grew such that by 1698 Evelyn could describe him as 'reputed the most excellent singer, ever England had', 1692 actually marked his first recorded appearance in London. In other words, Pate was an inexperienced singer when Purcell gave him this solo – which may well explain why he had need to write out the 'incredible Graces' for him.

---

[12] Andrew Parrott, 'Performing Purcell', in *The Purcell Companion*, ed. Michael Burden (London, 1995) pp. 385–444, at pp. 423–4.

[13] Franklin B. Zimmerman, *Henry Purcell: His Life and Times* (London, 1967) p. 241.

Elsewhere in the manuscript of the 1692 *Song for St Cecilia's Day*, Purcell wrote beside the counter-tenor part of 'Hark each tree' the words 'High contratenor for Mr Howel'. Sure enough, since it ascends to a written *d"*, this part is high in relation to the majority of Purcell's counter-tenor parts. When the music historian John Hough first connected the singer to this part he added, in a tone of breathless reportage, that Howel 'takes the high D with agility'.[14] Although since then others have repeated this apparent observation verbatim, sadly there is no evidence for its authenticity. So can we surmise how one of Purcell's high counter-tenors did take such a note? At its likely sounding pitch, around a tone lower, this *d"* would certainly not be deemed 'high' by most modern solo falsettists, yet it would be uncomfortably high for today's tenors. And this brings modern performers to an apparent quandary. There is a distinction in Purcell's solo counter-tenor parts, which divide into low and (much more rarely) high ranges such as that of 'Hark each tree'. The higher of the parts, at modern pitch, would have sounded approximately *b–c"* or *d"*, with the lower sounding *g–a'*. But does this distinction indicate two specific voice-types? This is certainly the answer practically adopted by many modern performers, who find that the lower of the ranges is too low for their falsettists and the higher one too high for their tenors. Current practice, then, recognising that no single type of modern singer can cope with both ranges, tends towards using falsettists for the higher parts and tenors for the lower.

Yet how likely is it that Purcell and his contemporaries would have made such a fundamental distinction, without reflecting it in the names of the voice-parts? Indeed, would Purcell have even recognised the quandary we find? Probably not. For seventeenth-century high modal singers, generally smaller in stature than their modern equivalents, and thus with higher natural voices, there is no reason to believe that Purcell's lower counter-tenor range would have caused any problems. The higher counter-tenor range would probably have fallen within their modal ranges, too, but to imagine that this was deemed necessary is to misread the evidence we have already seen from the period. The regular yo-yoing of singers between England and Italy, and the adoption of Italian vocal methods such as Tosi's, suggests that the utilisation of a falsetto extension to the modal voice was standard. This higher part, then, would have been sung chiefly in modal voice, albeit with the possibility of falsetto top notes. So the distinction we are tempted to make between falsetto and modal counter-tenors was fundamentally not a distinction Purcell and his peers would have recognised. In fact, there is no reason to believe that they would have distinguished between falsetto and modal singers of any kind.

There is an undoubted resistance amongst modern performers to the notion that the highest notes in a part may have originally been taken in

[14] John Hough, 'The Historical Significance of the Counter-Tenor', *Proceedings of the Musical Association*, 64th session (1937–8), pp. 1–24, at p. 9.

falsetto. To those familiar with the modern operatic concept of the high point (the 'money note') of an aria also being its loudest point, the falsetto top is an anathema. A duet such as Purcell's 'Sound the trumpet', which has the distinct high and low counter-tenor ranges indicated above, might seem to mock the idea of singers taking their top notes in head voice or falsetto. Does not the presence of trumpets – in both the text and score – indicate a full-blown vocal technique from the soloists? Again, it is only an anachronism which suggests this: in fact, with its narrower bore, the Baroque trumpet was not a particularly loud instrument, and its best executants were often praised for the softness of their high playing. Take Altenburg's demand (a century later, but concerning the same basic instrument): 'thus should the clarino [trumpet] player try to imitate it [the human voice] as much as possible, and should seek to bring forth the so-called cantabile on his instrument.'[15] Bearing in mind the vocal culture of his time, when Altenburg wrote of imitating the human voice, he would have been imagining a style of playing which became quieter the higher it went. In other words, the synonymy of high pitch with low volume, which runs so contrary to our own aesthetic, was not confined to singing.

One further suggestion that in England the counter-tenor part was predominantly a modal voice is provided by the composer and organist Thomas Tudway. As late as 1717 Tudway was describing vocal scoring as he understood it:

> 'Base part, Tenor, Contratenor, & Treble, were all contriv'd for Church Music [...] according to the Naturall voices of men; some voices being fitted Naturally to sing the Base, or lowest part; others the Tenor; others, though very few, the Contratenor; the Treble, or highest part, is always sung by Boys, or women.'[16]

Tudway's repeated emphasis on the 'natural' voices of men is surely significant. So too is his observation – mirroring that of Charles Butler some eighty years earlier – that the counter-tenor voice was something of a rarity. Likewise, Burney later described the Restoration composer William Turner as 'a counter-tenor singer, his voice settling to that pitch: a circumstance which so seldom happens *naturally*, that if it be cultivated, the possessor is sure of employment'.[17] So, both Tudway and Burney tell us that the natural counter-tenor voice was rare. It follows that the voice they had in mind was

---

[15] 'Daher muß ihr auch der Clarinist so viel als möglich nachahmen, und das sogenannte Cantabilie auf seinem Instrumente herause zu bringen suchen.': Johann Ernst Altenburg, *Versuch einer Anleitung zur heroisch-musikalischen Trompeter-und Paukerkunst* (Halle 1795), p. 96: cf. *Essay on an Introduction to the Heroic and Musical Trumpeters' and Kettledrummers' Ar t...*, ed. and trans. Edward H. Tarr (Nashville, 1974), p. 80.

[16] Thomas Tudway, 'Services and Anthems', London, British Library, Harleian MSS 7337–42, vol. 4, preface.

[17] Burney, *A General History of Music*, ed. Mercer, p. 361.

one *not* available to every man – high modal singing – and not one which *is* – falsetto. The rarity of the counter-tenor voice in seventeenth-century England is also evidenced by the amount of music written for three vocal parts, in which a counter-tenor (or alto) part is absent.

As the evidence mounts up that the (primarily) modal counter-tenor voice in Baroque England was rare, so one question looms up alongside. How could there have been more famous counter-tenors than tenors and basses combined? This apparent paradox is easily resolved by considering singers in our own age. Since the closest modern equivalent of the seventeenth-century counter-tenor would be our tenor voice (albeit with different techniques at the top of their ranges) we are in a good position to appreciate precisely how rarity and fame complement rather than contradict each other. For Abell, Pate and Turner, we could read Alagna, Florez and Villazon. And as a final observation on this paradox, we should remember that Baroque counter-tenors were not actually the *most* famous singers of their day: those were the castrati, and they were even rarer.

Handel's Altos

BETWEEN the times of Purcell and Handel the range and tessitura of the counter-tenor part (or alto, as it was increasingly termed) rose, both in written and sounding pitch. Or, to be more precise, it came closely to resemble the higher of the two counter-tenor ranges Purcell had written for. Either way, in Handel's writing for alto there are few of the passages below *c'* which we frequently find in Purcell, and which modern falsettists find to be a problem.

What voice, or voices, did Handel hear on his alto parts? Even more so than with Bach, the alto voices Handel knew were many and varied. This much is obvious from a brief survey of some of the most famous Handelian altos – Susannah Cibber, Senesino, Gaetono Guadagni and William Savage.

Susannah Cibber (sister of Thomas Arne and daughter-in-law of Colley Cibber) was the alto soloist in the first performance of *Messiah*, in Dublin. Despite her notoriety in the public eye (largely resulting from her stage-acting and private life), Handel also engaged her for his subsequent London oratorio performances. In fact, Cibber was only one of a number of female altos who, for the first time in Britain, were gaining recognition. Her range was low, so that Handel had to transpose items down for her. Indeed, the aria 'He was despised' – in which Cibber's singing reportedly incited a clergyman to exclaim 'Woman, for this be all thy sins forgiven thee!' – is sufficiently low that after Handel's death (as we shall see) it became associated with tenors.

If Susannah Cibber sounded a drum roll for female altos who would take centre-stage in the next century, then Senesino was an echo of castrati in the previous one. Senesino was an Italian operatic superstar whom Handel recruited as *primo uomo* for his London season in 1720. However tempted we might be to assume that the high vocal pitch of the castrati was the chief cause of their popularity, evidently this was not so. Senesino, and the equally illustrious Guadagni, were not sopranists. Indeed, when Handel used Guadagni in arias originally designed for Mrs Cibber he tended to transpose material down, or rewrite it, to exploit the castrato's fine lower range. Although Burney's vocal designations can appear inconsistent to us, he described Guadagni as a 'full and well-toned countertenor'.[18] Both Guadagni and Senesino featured in Handel's English oratorios, where, of course, they would have shared the platform with English male altos in the chorus.

Of all Handelian altos, the most vocally intriguing is William Savage. Savage first sang for Handel in 1735 when, as a fourteen-year-old boy, he sang the treble part of Joad in *Athalia*. Three years later he was singing the small alto part of Childerico in *Faramondo* (although in the final ensemble Savage sang the tenor part). By the time he was nineteen, as a high bass, he was singing the title role in *Imeneo*: yet even in this instance there is evidence of Savage's vocal fluidity, since the earlier parts of the role (which took Handel two years to complete) are notated in the tenor clef, whilst the later parts are notated in the bass clef. What appears to be a classic case of a voice sliding gradually downwards as it broke, however, is confused by Savage's subsequent appearance at the age of twenty, probably as a counter-tenor, in performances of *Saul* and *Israel in Egypt*.[19] Later still Savage became a Chapel Royal bass, and indeed Burney refers to Savage's voice as being 'a powerful and not unpleasant bass'. What are we to make of a man who, as an adult, sang such a wide range of parts? To us, this is nothing short of remarkable. To Savage's contemporaries, however, it was almost *un*remarkable. Although there is the suggestion that some of these part attributions are dubious, and that perhaps he sang from some of these clefs in octave transpositions, the direct testimony of a pupil of Savage's confirms his vocal capacities.[20] This pupil, R. J. S. Stevens, calmly remarked of Savage that he had 'a pleasant voice of two octaves': no hyperbole there. But Stevens also wrote that 'To his friends he frequently sang songs in his falsetto voice, as an alto. These were generally songs of expression chiefly from Handel's oratorios.'[21] So the explanation for Savage's ability to sing counter-tenor parts seems to be that, by singing through puberty, his range gradually descended, but even as he acquired low bass notes, he did not

---

[18] Burney, *A General History of Music*, ed. Mercer, pp. 849 and 875.

[19] Robert Hugill, 'Handel's Singers', *Music and Vision*, 28 December 2003, online at <http://www.mvdaily.com/articles/2003/12/handel1.htm> [accessed 6 April 2014].

[20] Arnold Jacobshagen, 'Sängerinnen, Kastraten, Countertenöre. Besetzungsvarianten in Händels Vokalwerken', in *Der Countertenor: die männliche Falsettstimme vom Mittelalter zur Gegenwart*, ed. Corinna Herr and Arnold Jacobshagen (Mainz, 2012), pp. 113–36, at pp. 119–20.

[21] H. G. Farmer, 'A Forgotten Composer of Anthems: William Savage (1720–89)', *Music and Letters* 17(3) (1936), pp. 188–99, at p. 194.

abandon his falsetto register. Like Abell (and doubtless others) before him, Savage tended to reserve his falsetto for domestic contexts, focussing more on his modal voice in public.

Savage was not unique as an occasional singer in falsetto. In Samuel Arnold's 1790 *Cathedral Music* there is a mention of William Hine (1687–1730), which states that he 'sang elegantly in a feigned voice'. However, we should perhaps be wary of this, the only known reference to Hine's singing, since it was written sixty years after his death. (The nature of musical performance history in the age before recording is always a game of Chinese whispers, yet if we are the first or second receivers of the original message, a measure of faith seems justified. Standing so far down the line, though, it is difficult to rely on the evidence of a source such as that regarding Hine. Indeed, it is hard to avoid the conclusion that later receivers – be they Arnold or a modern commentator looking to establish a 'tradition' for his own counter-tenor voice – have often merely heard and passed on what best suited their assumptions.) In fact, Hine was primarily a composer and provincial cathedral organist, so whatever his attributes as a singer, they were practised only occasionally.[22] Thomas Bell, a Chapel Royal member, was described as 'an excellent base & yet Sings a high Counter-Tenor which is with all natural and not forced'.[23] Unless Bell had a truly freakish range in full voice, the only way we can make sense of this is by classifying him as a singer who had artfully joined his modal and falsetto voices. And when recalling singers of his youth, Michael Kelly (Mozart's first Don Curzio in Vienna) wrote of Anthony Webster that 'his voice was a fine baritone, with a sweet falsetto, of which, being a good musician, he made a judicious use.'[24] In an era when Tosi and others were advocating precisely this melding of registers, small wonder that Savage, Bell and Webster's wide-ranging voices did not astonish. All they had done was master the prevailing vocal technique.

Savage aside, Handelian counter-tenors seemed to use falsetto to a limited extent, if at all. Vocal strength is a recurrent feature in reports of these singers. The eighteenth-century music historian John Hawkins reported (albeit as hearsay) that 'Mr Francis Hughes, a gentleman of the Chapel Royal in the reign of king George I, who had a very strong counter-tenor voice, could with ease break a drinking glass.'[25] With a similarly mythologising tone, Edward Rimbault offers us glimpses of two other singers: of Walter Powell, a counter-tenor with 'the best voice in England',[26]

---

[22] Cf. Giles, *History and Technique of the Counter-Tenor*, p. 94.

[23] Burrows, *Handel and the English Chapel Royal*, p. 536.

[24] *Reminiscences of Michael Kelly*, vol. 1, p. 12.

[25] John Hawkins, *A General History of the Science and Practice of Music* (London, 1776), p. 839.

[26] Obituary, *The Gentleman's Magazine* 14 (1744) p. 619: cf. Hough, 'Historical Significance of the Counter-Tenor', p. 15.

Rimbault tells us that on his death-bed he reputedly 'sang an anthem, with the full powers of his voice'.[27] Of Thomas Barrow, another Chapel Royal counter-tenor from 1746, Rimbault says that 'his voice was a high, loud counter-tenor', and that Handel admired him 'for the strength of his voice and his steadiness'.[28] Whilst it is quite possible for a falsettist to have a 'high, loud' voice, even to be capable of shattering glass, it is less easy to equate this with the low to middling range of the counter-tenor parts Barrow sang for Handel. Although these posthumous reports may carry limited authority with regard to Handel's singers, they are suggestive of a continuity with the period that followed. In particular, they tell us that as late as 1847 there was nothing unusual in describing a low counter-tenor voice as powerful.

As with the singers of Purcell's time, there is evidence that Handel's altos also sang tenor parts. In a copy of the printed word-book for the Dublin *Messiah* performances, someone has written singers' names. 'Lamb' (William Lamb) is there named against the texts of two recitatives, 'Behold, a virgin shall conceive' (alto) and 'He that dwelleth in heaven' (tenor).[29] Similarly suggestive of fluidity on these inner lines, for parts sung by particular singers, the choice of alto or tenor clefs was far from regimented. Since modern altos and tenors sing with fundamentally different techniques, the interchangeability of these voices in the eighteenth century is something we might find difficult to comprehend. But in Handel's day they sang with similar techniques. Singing at Covent Garden in 1783, Jack Johnstone's voice was described as 'a clear melodious tenor with a very sweet, though somewhat disproportionate, falsetto'.[30]

There is evidence, then, that Handel associated women, boys and castrati with his alto parts, as well as men using their modal and falsetto ranges. Handel may have shown a preference for certain singers, but this is very different from suggesting that he had preferences for particular voice-types. Perhaps the best illustration of this is Susannah Cibber who, if reports are to be believed, had very little voice at all, but made up for this by her expressive powers. This quality, above timbre or method, seems to have been Handel's priority. There is no more evidence that Handel thought English counter-tenors 'equal to the Italians'[31] than that he 'does not seem to have liked the English male alto sound'.[32] If Handel's taste in

---

[27] Edward Rimbault (ed.), *Cathedral Music*, vol. 1 (London, 1847): cf. Giles, *History and Technique of the Counter-Tenor*, p. 74.

[28] Rimbault, *Cathedral Music*: cf. Giles, *History and Technique of the Counter-Tenor*, p. 74.

[29] I am grateful to Professor Donald Burrows for this information.

[30] James Boaden, *Memoirs of the Life of John Philip Kemble Esq., including a History of the Stage* (London, 1825), vol. 1, p. 70.

[31] Hodgson, 'The Contemporary Alto', p. 294.

[32] Peter le Huray, 'Handel's Messiah', in *Authenticity in Performance* (Cambridge, 1990), pp. 82–101, at p. 89.

singers was representative of his public's (and since he was commercially successful, by implication it must have been), then dogmatic assertions that the eighteenth-century alto was a particular type of voice carry little weight.

One particularly interesting piece of the jigsaw of the eighteenth-century high voice is the singer known as Leoni. Born in Frankfurt in 1750, Myer Lyon (to give him his real name) was a Jew whose fame as a boy singer took him to London, where he became a synagogue cantor. Introduced to Garrick, 'Leoni' became a noted theatre singer in London and, later, Dublin. And of his voice? One listener commented:

> When it is considered he sings in a feigned voice, admiration cannot be carried too high [...] He executed the divisions with a degree of neatness and articulation, that could not fail of giving delight to a cultivated ear'[33]

And an Irish commentator remarked:

> The truth is that Leoni has in reality, *no voice* at all – his tones being neither *vocal* nor *instrumental*. They have a peculiarity of sound in them that we have not heard before. When he stood before us on the Stage, the voice did not seem to proceed from his lips, but fell into our ears as if it had descended from the clouds. This rendered it a matter more of curiosity than delight.[34]

Neither critic suggests that Leoni's falsetto was allied to a modal voice. And, although their opinions diverge, one point on which they implicitly or explicitly concur is that this purely 'feigned' voice was in itself noteworthy. Leoni, then, seems to be an almost unique type of singer – an eighteenth-century English falsettist.

Beyond the luxuriant vocal scene of the Chapel Royal and London, we find a hint that altos were thin on the ground. In the mid-1770s John Crompton, a Suffolk church choirmaster, wrote that:

> Suitable voices for the middle, or counter part are rather difficult to find; but let no-one, for that reason, attempt it with a feigned voice, however there is but few wanted in comparison with the number who engage in other parts, and better quite omitted than not performed with a natural voice; therefore let a voice be chosen with great care, it should be soft, clear and very manageable, for this part may be compared to a thread run through the whole, and anything harsh, rough or grating, rends the music all to pieces.[35]

---

[33] Cf. T. J. Walsh, *Opera in Dublin, 1705–1797: The Social Scene* (Dublin, 1973), p. 231.

[34] Cf. Walsh, *Opera in Dublin*, p. 231.

[35] John Crompton, *The Psalm-Singer's Assistant* (London, 1778): cf. Hugh Keyte and Andrew Parrott (eds.), *The New Oxford Book of Carols* (Oxford, 1992), p. 672.

There is a certain resonance here with Charles Butler's description of the early seventeenth-century counter-tenor – the 'sweet shrill voice' which is 'too rare'. And Crompton's protestations about use of the 'feigned' voice serve only to prove that in however limited a way, falsetto was not unknown on the alto line. Yet falsetto singing was not the only option, should sufficient 'natural' voices not be found for the alto part: Crompton suggests that the part can be left out altogether. In any event, the tradition of music-making from the gallery of churches meant that instrumental doubling was commonplace. It was standard in these circumstances for a clarinet to play the alto line an octave higher than written.[36] This particular practice partly stemmed from the notational method, begun in the eighteenth century, of writing alto and tenor parts in the treble clef. Composers began doing this as a concession to the growing number of performers unacquainted with C clefs. Such use of the treble clef carried with it the understanding that performers would realise the part by transposing it down an octave – on both tenor *and* alto lines. As far back as 1673 John Playford had written that it was 'usual and common for Men to Sing those Songs which are prick'd in a *Treble* an Eighth lower'.[37] Evidently, though, this un-notated practice was not always understood. Sopranos, noting that the highest part in their music appeared to be the alto, opted to sing this line, but without transposing it. The results of this confusion offended purists: Thomas Billington wrote that it 'has produced the most horrid effect that can be conceived'.[38]

In all these cross-currents – between Italian and English traditions, amateur and professional practices, men singing occasional notes in falsetto and those who were pure falsettists – is it possible to summarise the English attitude to falsetto during the Baroque? Remembering its absence at the start of the Baroque, evidence of the widespread use of the falsetto extension by the time of Handel suggests that an aesthetic revolution had taken place during the period. This is probably something of an illusion, resulting from our natural desire to read history as one cogent narrative. When we look at reactions to the falsetto voice today we can find a variety of opinions, ranging from adulation to antipathy, with a broad swathe of indifference in between. Likewise, remembering the starring role played in 1634 by Monsieur Mari, we should bear in mind that even the falsetto voice was cultivated and admired early in the Baroque. Conversely, at its end we can find a critic of Leoni who seems to have had nothing but disdain for falsetto. Multiple narratives existed then, as now. But even so, perhaps it is safe to say that as the Baroque period developed, falsetto singing became better accepted and more firmly established in England.

[36] Nicholas Temperley, *The Music of the English Parish Church* (Cambridge, 1979), vol. 1, p. 199.

[37] Locke, *Musick Vindicated*, pp. 86–7.

[38] cf. Temperley, *Music of the English Parish Church*, p. 189.

A Musicological Red Herring:
The Etymology of the Counter-Tenor

> The fact that Elford [...] had a range as low as A at the bottom of the
> bass stave is a musicological red herring, for either Elford was a tenor
> [...] in which case he should not have called himself a counter tenor,
> or, more likely, this note was falsetto.
>
> G. M. Ardran and David Wulstan[1]

I MAGINE you are at some large governmental function, and are asked if
you would like to meet the 'secretary'. Armed only with that information,
as you are taken across the room perhaps you idly assume the person you
are about to meet will have certain office skills, and a relatively passive
working nature. You may even make an inappropriate assumption about the
secretary's gender. When you then learn that this same person is actually
Secretary of State, you may want to revise some of your assumptions.
You may also regret the imprecision of language – that one term can be
expected to cover such a broad remit: but would you hold the individual
responsible for the vagaries of his or her job title?

If a single term can mean two things at the same time and place, we
should hardly be surprised that historically it can cover an even broader
range of options. This self-evident (but easily forgotten) truth has already
been aired in this book. Now, though, we need to think about it with
reference to the 'counter-tenor' and its companion terms. In Chapter 5
we separated two entities more similar in appearance than reality – the
French *haute-contre* and the Italian contralto – and as we move on from
the Baroque we are about to encounter similar semantic tangles. Nowhere
are these knottier than in the European travelogues of the great musical
historian Charles Burney. These are a rich source of information on vocal
styles, but an equally rich source of potential frustration. Let us look, for
instance, at the references to contraltos in his writings. There should be
little cause for confusion here, since Burney defines the contralto in the
glossary to the account of his travels in Italy and France: '*Contralto*: a
counter-tenor, or a voice of higher pitch than a tenor, but lower than the
treble.'[2] Like all definitions, this makes certain assumptions of the reader –
most crucially, that we share Burney's understanding of what constitutes a
counter-tenor, a tenor and a treble. Burney and his contemporaries, unlike
us, made no gender distinction between counter-tenors and contraltos:
remembering Giuseppina Grassini, Michael Kelly wrote that 'she possessed

---

[1] Ardran and Wulstan, 'The Alto or Countertenor Voice', *Music and Letters*, p. 22.

[2] Burney, *Music, Men, and Manners in France and Italy*, p. 227.

a fine counter-tenor voice'.[3] Burney also omits to tell us how the contralto voice was produced – either because he assumes this to be understood, or because for some reason he did not consider it relevant.

In the actual text of the travelogues Burney encounters a wide variety of 'contraltos'. In Milan he hears a castrato contralto. Travelling south to Naples he hears 'a very fine contr'alto' alongside 'a young man with a soprano voice'. In Vienna, Gluck's daughter sings for Burney with 'a rich and powerful *contralto* voice'. So far, so dissectible. But whilst in Vienna Burney also reports that 'two of the poor scholars of this city sung [...] duets in *falset, soprano,* and *contralto.*' In Germany he remarks of Vittoria Tesi that she 'had by nature a masculine, strong *contralto* voice [...] she generally sung [...] such airs as are made for base voices.' And finally on the topic of the 'contralto', Burney relates a biographical anecdote told to him regarding the Czech composer Franz Benda, who had lost his treble voice at about the age of eleven, due to illness:

> At the Easter music he [Benda] was persuaded to attempt a *contralto* part in the church. At first, his voice was coarse, but it very soon grew so much better, that the same afternoon M. Benda found himself able to sing the counter-tenor, as well as he had formerly done the *soprano.* Having discovered his new voice, he went to Prague, where he was engaged [...] though there were already six counter-tenors in that service [...] He confessed to me, that the excellent singing which he then heard was the utmost use to him in his future studies, and particularly the performance of Gaetano Orsini [castrato], a *contralto* [...] Not long after this [still only in his mid-teens], he lost his counter-tenor voice, and was again obliged to return to his friends at Benatki.[4]

For Burney, then, 'contralto' could refer to a voice or a part, could be a singer of either gender, a youth or an adult, natural or castrated. Whilst synonymous with the counter-tenor, the contralto was evidently distinct from the falsettist. Reading his comments on the voice of Tesi literally, the contralto was also synonymous with the bass voice. Of course, the rather wide-ranging and fluid terminology Burney was using has now largely separated and set, so with deductions based on the context of his comments we can hazard a modern 'translation'. In Milan Burney heard a low-voiced castrato, and in Naples a high tenor. The lower-voiced scholar he heard in Vienna was also a tenor, and Benda was singing an alto part in a gradually changing voice. Miss Gluck and Vittoria Tesi were indeed what we would term contraltos.

Burney did not lack the vocabulary for greater precision. Rather, by our standards he seems to use terms arbitrarily and (if we assume his terminology to match ours) downright misleadingly. From our point of

[3] *Reminiscences of Michael Kelly*, vol. 1, p. 193.
[4] Burney, *The Present State of Music*, vol. 2, pp. 131–2.

view, it is easy to say that Burney could have been clearer, but just as clearly, as an explanation this will not do. The eighteenth century was an age of codification, and Burney, along with his friend Samuel Johnson, was one of its great champions. Along with an aim to facilitate understanding of the 'Science & the Mechanism of the Art', Burney also wished his writing to be 'divested of Pedantry and Jargon'.[5] Clarity, then, was paramount to Burney, so if his words can appear to us unclear, we really need to ask why.

Perhaps the easiest way to approach this is not to ask a question of Burney, but of ourselves. Why, in comparison to Burney, do we seem to have such a specific understanding of terms such as 'contralto' and 'counter-tenor'? If asked to define the modern counter-tenor to an average musical listener, with maximal clarity and brevity, *I* would say it is a male falsettist who sings the alto line in an all-male English church choir. And I would illustrate the type of singer by citing an individual: depending on the age of the listener this might be Deller, Bowman or Scholl. The point here is that each aspect of this definition relies on a point of reference which Burney and his readers did not share. Prior to the laryngoscope, definitions of 'falsetto' were to an extent subjective, and largely based on intuition rather than empirical observation. Similarly, because we now have a pitch standard and a received SATB vocal scoring, when the modern counter-tenor sings in a choir, we know he will be expected to sing the alto line. Lastly, and perhaps most crucially, unlike Burney, in the recorded age we can use aural examples as international standards: in our mind's ear we know what modern counters-tenors sound like.

If we doubt the significance of standardisation and homogeneity in modern musical life, we only need to read a letter written by Charles de Brosses – an educated and cosmopolitan near-contemporary of Burney: 'No one can hear a foreign song for the first time without wanting to laugh. Little by little one becomes accustomed to it and one has two kinds of pleasure instead of one. This is a real gain.'[6] De Brosses was writing back to France not from a distant corner of the globe, but from Italy. Burney, too, could find music he heard on his European travels decidedly strange. In Amsterdam, only two hundred miles from his London home, Burney encountered a trio of Jewish singers:

> One of these voices was a falset, more like the upper part of a bad *vox humana* stop in an organ, than a natural voice [...] This singer might boast his art, not of singing like a human creature, but of making his voice like a bad imitation of one [...] the tone of the falset was very

[5] *The Letters of Charles Burney*, ed. Ribeiro, p. 84.

[6] 'Il n'arrive à personne d'entendre pour la première fois un chant étranger, quel qu'il soit, sans avoir envie d'en rire; peu à peu on s'y accoutume et l'on acquiert deux espèces de plaisir du même genre, au lieu d'un; c'est un gain véritable.': De Brosses, *Lettres écrites d'Italie*, p. 348. Translation from MacClintock, *Readings*, p. 270.

disagreeable, and he forced his voice very frequently in an outrageous manner, yet this man had certainly heard good music and singing.[7]

If we want to find a modern equivalent to Burney's and de Brosses' reactions, we may need to look at our responses when we visit the more remote outposts of today's 'world' music. Our standard points of musical reference – and therefore vocabulary – will be of little use in describing an Aka Pygmie choir, or Tuvan overtone singers. If these sounds are unfamiliar to us (and perhaps even if they are familiar), descriptions of these voices by Western writers are unlikely to leave readers with a clear aural image. Asian 'overtone' technique, for instance, is most commonly described as 'throat singing', but as a way of technically distinguishing it from other vocal methods such a definition is patently useless. And attempts to be more specific can be just as problematic, as the following descriptions on a world music forum illustrate: 'One guy sings a bass line in something like karkhiraa and the other sings in normal voice and falsetto. Haven't heard any other sort of singing like it.' And, 'If you want to have something a little beyond using overtones to produce the melody of the song, there's some example of Uzbek or Kazakh bakshi singing using a khorekteer'.[8] What is 'bakshi' singing? And is 'khorekteer' a vocal technique, a mannerism, or an instrument? The vocabulary of world music – or at least our understanding of it – is very much work in progress. This is one way we should view Burney's 'contralto' references.

There is another feature of our own vocal scene that might help us to understand the relatively nebulous vocal terminology of eighteenth-century commentators, and that is non-classical Western music. Burney wrote of Handel's contralto soloist in the first *Messiah*, Susannah Cibber, that 'by a natural pathos, and perfect conception of the words, she often penetrated the heart, when others, with infinitely greater voice and skill, could only reach the ear.'[9] Burney, whose high opinion of Cibber was evidently shared by Handel, makes no mention here of her range or timbre. As we saw in the last chapter, even when a contemporary source described a singer as having a particular voice, this was often contradicted by other evidence: Guadagni, Savage and Mrs Cibber herself all fall into this category. Did their voice-types actually change or, more likely, is our concept of 'voice-type' something of an anachronism. Perhaps revealingly, today Mrs Cibber is described by Wikipedia as a 'singer and actress'. If we want to find similar descriptions of modern singers, we need to look to the world of music theatre: according to the same source Ute Lemper, for instance, is a 'chanteuse and actress', and American singer Kim Criswell is a 'musical

[7] Burney, *The Present State of Music*, vol. 2, p. 300.

[8] From <http://khoomei.com/forum/viewtopic.php?f=15&t=685> [accessed 4 April 2014].

[9] Charles Burney, 'Sketch of the Life of Handel', *An Account of the Musical Performances... in Commemoration of Handel* (London, 1785), p. 27.

entertainer and actress'. Yet Wikipedia is far more vocally specific about another modern American singer, describing Renée Fleming as a 'soprano specializing in opera and lieder', adding that she 'has a full lyric soprano voice' and 'has performed coloratura, lyric, and lighter spinto soprano repertoires'. This level of detail is a new phenomenon. Evidently Burney and Handel were, like non-classical audiences today, far more concerned about the communication of the message than the nature of the postman (or woman).

Now let us return to the early eighteenth-century singer referred to at the start of this chapter, Richard Elford. It is worth underlining that there is no evidence that Elford ever 'called himself a counter tenor', or even thought of himself as one. Rather, at one stage in his career he sang the counter-tenor part, just as, at another time, he sang the tenor part. In the age of Tosi and his acolytes, Elford probably thought of himself as nothing other than a singer, albeit an accomplished one who had melded his modal voice with a falsetto extension to give him a range that could encompass tenor or counter-tenor parts. Yet even if he had called himself a 'counter tenor', who would we be to disagree?

So, by the same token that we might now ask what *khorekteer* is (a style of overtone singing, incidentally), each time we come across a historical reference to the 'counter-tenor' we really need to ask not what is meant by the term, but what *was* meant. A line in a score, a vocal range, a technique, or a timbre? In various shades and combinations, the 'counter-tenor' has been all of the above – whatever it now *is*.

CHAPTER 7

The Nineteenth Century

ALTHOUGH the year 1791 saw the death of Mozart – and his final appearance singing as an alto – it is not for this reason that it makes a useful demarcation point in the history of the high male voice. A number of references from this year suggest that the old method of deploying modal and falsetto techniques, which we have traced from medieval times to the Renaissance world of Zacconi and then Tosi, was now on the wane. Not, of course, that 1791 represents any kind of sudden break. We should bear in mind that as far back as 1752 Quantz had written that at least in France the falsetto and modal voices were not commonly united by singers. And in due course we will read the astonishment of Rossini at hearing, in 1831, one of his tenor parts sung in this new, purely modal manner. The seismic rifting of old and new vocal styles rumbled on for decades, then, but we can place its epicentre at the end of the eighteenth century.

The Choral Alto in the Age of Haydn

CHANGES in performance practice are bound up in compositional developments, and they, in turn, tend to reflect changes in society. We should hardly be surprised, then, that around the time of the French Revolution we begin to sense a significant wind of change in the way that men sang high. The burgeoning egalitarian society, with its larger venues and performing ensembles, was less receptive to the intimate vocal style of Tosi and his acolytes. That older technique, which relied on a diminution of volume and a delicate shift into falsetto as the voice ascended, may have been perfect for a small aristocratic salon, or chapel and chancel, but was obviously ill-suited to the powerful projection of vocal lines in an opera house or large public hall. Not just in size, but in decoration too, the new venues proved unsympathetic to the old vocal technique. The acoustically live bare walls and floors of the older performance venues gave way to heavily upholstered spaces which encouraged richer voices with self-contained resonance. Even within the confines of salons and drawing rooms, composers were now writing music for the growing market of amateur singers. These amateurs had not necessarily studied (let alone mastered) the virtuoso technique of shifting seamlessly between registers. Instead, they relied on their basic modal ranges.

We might suppose that any such changes in singing methods were led by developments in vocal (as opposed to choral) music. It would seem almost axiomatic that choral singers, wittingly or unwittingly, are more likely to try to model their voices on their favourite solo singers, rather than the other way round. Yet in this case it seems to have been choral performance practice that provided the catalyst for change. In this sense, the years following the death of Handel were significant.

Early in the New Year of 1791 Haydn arrived in England for the first time. His notebook jottings about his London visits, and the comments of his contemporaries, offer us revealing glimpses into the changing aesthetics of the time. Haydn's reference to the Handel Commemoration Festival is cryptic but telling: 'Anno 1791 the last great concert, with 885 persons, was held in Westminster [Abbey]. Anno 1792 it was transferred to St Margaret's Chapel, with 200 performers. People criticised this.'[1] Handel had only been dead for just over thirty years, yet purely in terms of size, performances of his oratorios – particularly *Messiah* – would already have been unrecognisable to the composer. A relatively intimate venue, such as the Foundling Hospital, had been replaced by Westminster Abbey, and the number of performers had grown exponentially. Even the diminished 1792 *Messiah* (a minor blip on an upward trend) featured about four times the number of performers Handel would have known. Haydn's contemporary biographer, Giuseppe Carpani, wrote that when Haydn 'heard the music of Hendl in London, he [...] meditated on every note and drew from those most learned scores the essence of true musical grandeur'.[2] Although later reports would romantically embellish his presence in the Abbey with tears and exclamations, there is little doubt that Haydn was present, and that the sheer size of sound did impress him. It also directly influenced him. In 1798, when Haydn directed the public premiere his own oratorio *The Creation*, in Vienna, some 180 musicians took part – roughly three times the number Haydn would have heard at Viennese oratorio performances in the 1780s. This was also part of a more general trend – largely fuelled by reports circulating Europe of London's Handel Commemoration. In 1829, when Mendelssohn paid tribute to Bach by reviving the *St Matthew Passion*, his chorus numbered over 150 – compared to a likely eight in the original performance. In England, the Westminster Handel commemorations quickly spawned 'a mimic performance in almost every great town in the kingdom'.[3] The effect of this trend on singing in general, and the modal-falsetto technique in particular, can hardly be overstated.

Singing in a large chorus has an easily explained effect on the voice of an individual. Without being able to hear his or her own voice, a singer cannot easily gauge personal intonation or sound quality. Even more fundamentally, without being audible a singer will soon doubt (or should soon doubt) what possible value he or she has to any choral enterprise. Each singer, then,

[1] *Correspondence and London Notebooks of Haydn*, ed. Landon (London, 1959), p. 270.

[2] Giuseppe Carpani, *Le Haydine* (Milan, 1812), pp. 162–3. Translation from Nicholas Temperley, *The Creation* (Cambridge, 1991), p. 5.

[3] William Jackson, *Observations on the Present State of Music* (London, 1791), p. 24.

needs to be heard. Singing with one voice per part, or in a small choir, this rarely becomes an issue. In a chorus with perhaps tens of people singing the same line, though, the inevitable result is an inflation of each singer's general volume. Nowadays, a good choral director will harness this natural tendency by acting as the ears of the group, and curbing individual excesses. At the end of the eighteenth century, though, this role for the conductor did not yet exist. The cacophonic results, witnessed by countless commentators across Europe, were often excruciating. As Burney pithily observed, 'Sound can only be augmented to a certain degree, beyond that it is noise.'[4] In 1791 an anonymous journalist described choral singing in Berlin:

The outrageous botching of the finest four-part pieces, and the horrible screams and screeching, is so extreme that one can no longer endure it. Recently, at the Döhnhofschen Platz, on one of the coldest and harshest days, Schulz's brilliant chorus from *Athalia* 'Laut durch die Welten', which is in D major, was transposed a fifth higher into A major. Thus the poor sopranos shrieked and screeched up to *e'''* (it's unbelievable!), while the tenors and basses roared with dreadful screams of anguish.[5]

Friedrich August Weber commented on choral training that led singers to cough blood.[6] Perhaps surprisingly to us, accustomed as we are to large solo voices, Weber also remarks that 'Usually the choral voice has more fullness and strength than the solo voice, and the latter more delicacy and flexibility than the former.'[7] In other words, Tosi's artful gradations of tone, and the light falsetto extension, simply had no place in this larger choral texture. As vocal power became *de rigueur*, so the way that singers marshalled their strength also changed. Writing in 1791, William Jackson, the ageing

[4] Burney, *The Present State of Music*, pp. 203–4.
[5] 'Der Unfug, der in manchen derselben mit den Gesängen getrieben wird, das Sinn und Herz empörende Aufjauchzen, die Verhunzung der edelsten vierstimmigen Stücke und das entsetzliche Schreien und Quiken ohne Maas und Ziel geht so weit, dass man es nicht mehr damit aushahen kann. Unlängst wurde am Dohnhöfschen Platze, an einem Tage, der gerade einer der kältesten und rauhesten war, Schulzens brillantes Chor aus der Athalia: Laut durch die Welten tönt etc., das bekanntlich aus D dur geht, aus – A dur gesungen, und also kreischten und quikten die armen Diskantisten bis ins dreigestrichene e hinauf (es ist unglaublich!), während die Tenoristen und Bassisten mit entsetzlichem Angstgeschrei die Häuser anbrüllten.' *Studien für Tonkünstler und Musikfreunde: eine historisch-kritische Zeitschrift*, vol. 1: *Musikalisches Wochenblatt*, ed. F. A. Kunzen and J. F. Reichhardt (Berlin, 1792–3), pp. 173–4. Translation from Jerold, 'Choral Singing', p. 78.
[6] Friedrich August Weber, 'Von der Singstimme', *Allgemeine musikalische Zeitung*, 23 July 1800, p. 741: cf. Jerold, 'Choral Singing', p. 78.
[7] Friedrich August Weber, 'Von der Singstimme', *Allgemeine musikalische Zeitung*, 20 August 1800, pp. 809–10. Translation from Jerold, 'Choral Singing', p. 78.

choirmaster at Exeter Cathedral, complained of modern singers 'forcing the Voice in the upper part, where it ought ever to be soft; and singing the lower tones faint, which should always be full'.[8]

Haydn, however, found fault with some exponents of the older vocal style. During his first London visit, Haydn wrote of the English tenor Charles Incledon that he

> has a good voice and quite a good style, but he uses the falsetto to excess. He sang a trill on high C and ran up to G. The 2nd tenor tries to imitate him, but could not make the change from the falsetto to the natural voice, and apart from that he is most unmusical.[9]

What, we might ask, was Haydn's own vocal background? This is worth examining, because of the insights it affords on the kind of high male voices for which not just Haydn, but Mozart, Vanhal and their contemporaries, were writing. As we have already seen, Haydn was a chorister at St Stephen's in Vienna. When his unchanged voice began to wane, Greisinger records that a plan was mooted to have him castrated, noting that 'Quite a few castrati still had good positions in the imperial chapel.'[10] Nothing came of this, although once his voice had changed Haydn was taught by Nicolas Porpora, who years earlier had taught the most famous of all the castrati, Farinelli. Haydn's vocal upbringing, then, was very much old-school. His criticism of Incledon was bred not of ignorance, but knowledge.

Hearing mass at St Stephen's some thirty years after Haydn had left there, Burney simply remarked that 'the treble part was sung by the boys'. So boys, castrati and nascent falsettists sang soprano in the Viennese churches. What, though, of the alto part? Burney, again visiting the cathedral during the same visit, remarks that 'there was a girl, who sang a solo verse, in the *Credo*, extremely well, in a *mezzo-soprano* voice.'[11] It is not clear whether this 'girl' (presumably a young woman) was singing a soprano or alto solo. What is clear is that the alto part in the Viennese churches was sung on something of an *ad hoc* basis. Lower parts of Viennese church choirs had only one or two voices per part (little-changed from the practices Bach knew) and in tutti sections they were often doubled by instruments. Mozart perhaps alludes to this practice in a letter to his father, reporting of some domestic singing at the house of Baron van Swieten that 'he sings treble, I sing alto (and play at the same time), Starzer sings tenor and young Teiber from Italy sings bass.'[12] Mozart (if we are to believe the legend) made his

---

[8] Jackson, *Observations on the Present State of Music*, pp. 22–3.

[9] *Correspondence and London Notebooks of Haydn*, ed. Landon, p. 273.

[10] Cf. Geiringer, *Haydn*, p. 24.

[11] Burney, *The Present State of Music*, p. 326.

[12] '[...] daß ist alles nur, um es dem B van suiten hören zu lassen – er singt den Discant, ich den alt (und spielle zugleich) Starzer den Tenor – der Junge Teyber aus italien den Baß.': *Mozarts Briefe*, ed. Ludwig Nohl (Salzburg, 1865),

final appearance as an alto on his deathbed, as he and three friends tried out parts of the *Requiem*.[13] These private compositional workshops are the only references to Mozart as an alto, further suggesting that however clear the part may appear on paper, in practice it was often murkily filled in by whoever was game to make the attempt.

Mozart's experiences in Salzburg are similarly suggestive. In 1757 the Salzburg court, at which Leopold Mozart was deputy Kapellmeister, and for which Wolfgang Amadeus would later write most of his sacred music, counted among the ranks of its choir three adult male altos.[14] Of these, only two are listed as being falsettists, but no designation is given for the third. Assuming that he was not just another (for some reason unrecorded) falsettist, this omission leaves the vocal nature of this third man uncertain. He is unlikely to have been a castrato, since they were too expensive for mere choral roles: later, Mozart was to complain that in Salzburg 'we have no castrati, and we shall never have them, because they insist on being handsomely paid; and generosity is not one of our faults.'[15] Most likely, then, the third Salzburg alto was a modal (or chiefly modal) singer, or an indeterminate adolescent. Separate from the choir, the same 1757 court register lists soloists – primarily for court entertainments and sacred dramas: these soloists include two tenors and two basses – but no alto. Alto solo parts do occur in Mozart's masses, but much more in ensemble with other voices than alone. In Salzburg performance practice, then, the alto part had no firm identity, and evidently no great kudos.

Just how alienated the adult male alto (of whatever vocal type) was becoming from Germanic musical practice can be gauged by two contrasting examples. Firstly, on the largest scale, let us briefly return to the oratorios of Haydn. In so many respects the scoring of these works resembles the forces Haydn would have heard at the London Handel commemorations. However, one obvious difference (and one which chimes with practice in Salzburg) is the omission of an alto soloist – in both *The Creation* and *The Seasons*. One reading of this is that evidently the types of alto voices Haydn knew were simply not capable of competing with the size of orchestra he had in mind. Secondly, on the smallest scale, let us consider the repertoire of German social music for men's chorus, the *Liedertafel*, which began around this time and burgeoned during the nineteenth

pp. 401–2. Translation from *The Letters of Mozart and his Family ...*, ed. Emily Anderson (London, 1938), vol. 3, letter dated 12 March 1783.

[13] Cf. Albert Borowitz, 'Salieri and the Murder of Mozart', *Musical Quarterly* 59(2) (1973), pp. 263–84.

[14] Stanley Sadie, *Mozart: The Early Years, 1756–1781* (New York, 1983), p. 8.

[15] 'Non abbiamo Musici, e non gli averemo si facilmente, gia che vogliono esser ben pagati: e la generosità non è il nostro diffetto.': available onlline through <http://www.zeno.org/Musik> [accessed 4 April 2014]. Translation from, *The Letters of Mozart*, ed. Anderson, vol. 3, letter dated 4 September 1776.

century. This repertoire is commonly for two tenor and two bass parts, but
no alto, suggesting that for the first time we have a repertory in which the
alto (of whatever vocal type) is not commonly thought of as a male part.
These examples underline the point that, although in a mixed or church
chorus the alto part could be hidden as an inner line, when the part was
exposed as a solo line, or at the top of the texture, it was often thought
best to omit it. In the Germanic lands, developments in singing and society
were leaving the alto part as an old ship abandoned by its crew.

Rossini and the Passing of the Castrati

NOR was the situation much healthier elsewhere on the Continent.
Travelling across northern Europe in 1829, Vincent Novello made
a point of attending sung services in every major church he came to.
Comments on the outer voice-parts are frequent, and informative, but
tenors and particularly altos are only notable by their absence. Intriguingly,
in Antwerp Cathedral Novello notes that there are 'no *intermediate* altos
and tenors [...]' (his italics).[16] Did Novello mean by this that there were
simply no singers of the middle parts, or that there were, but they lacked
the modal-falsetto technique which, literally, mediates between the other
voices?

Only in Paris, at Notre Dame, did Novello notice an alto singer, and
his verdict (echoing Burney's experience in the same city a generation
earlier) was damning: 'a very disagreeable harsh and loud voice among the
Counter Tenors; it predominated over all the rest and *soured* every piece
in which it was heard.'[17] At first glance it seems as if little has changed
since the descriptions of forced *haute-contres* we met with at the end of
the Baroque period. Yet France had been through a minor vocal revolution
as well as a political one. Falsetto had never been greatly cultivated in
eighteenth-century France, and virtually disappeared with the Revolution.
Albeit temporarily, in 1790 the Chapelle Royale was closed down, and
with it almost the only forum for falsettists. The outdoor civic ceremonies
which sprang up in Paris on the Champ de Mars included massive, simple
music, but these offered no place for vocal subtleties. Neither, as the
nineteenth century progressed and grand opera took hold, did the theatres.
Yet between the times of Rameau and Meyerbeer, there was a time when
falsetto (if not falset*tists*) became more commonplace in France. Having
remained relatively insular throughout the Baroque, following the success
in Paris of Pergolesi's *La serva padrona* in 1752, the French suddenly
gained a taste for Italian opera. With Italian music and styles came Italian
musicians and styles of performing. Two singing teachers who arrived in

[16] Vincent Novello, *Mozart Pilgrimage: Travel Diaries of Vincent and Mary Novello in the Year 1829*, ed. Nerina Medici and Rosemary Hughes (London, 1955), p. 287.
[17] Novello, *Mozart Pilgrimage*, ed. Medici and Hughes, p. 319.

Paris from Italy in the 1780s, Tomeoni and Mengozzi, became particularly influential. The French *haute-contres* of the day now began to adopt the Italianate falsetto extension. In so doing, we should note, they sowed the seeds of future confusion about the 'true' nature of the *haute-contre*: what had until then been a single-register voice, now (briefly) became a dual-register one. Through the wistful remembrances of Rossini, this Tosiesque method would eventually become known as *bel canto*, a term which would no sooner be defined than it would metamorphose, appropriated by pedagogues to identify virtually any vocal technique which they personally viewed through a haze of nostalgia.

Composers in France exploited the potential of the 'new' falsetto extension further and further, with 'phrases constantly pushed not merely to the heights – but to the pinnacles, as it were – of the extreme falsetto'.[18] The French still drew the line at castrati in opera, so for the 1774 Paris performances of *Orfeo ed Euridice* Gluck adapted the protagonist's role. Originally written for the castrato Guadagni, Gluck transposed several items for the *haute-contre* Joseph Legros. If we are to believe Lalande, cited in the previous chapter, Legros perhaps would have taken the upper notes of this part in his modal voice. But Adolphe Nourrit, who became celebrated for playing *Orfeo* in Paris after Gluck's death, and was also a favourite tenor of Rossini's, used Tosi's modal-falsetto technique. Actually, Nourrit went on to become the most famous casualty of changing vocal taste, committing suicide when his modal-falsetto style fell out of favour. For all his early success at the Paris Opéra, Nourrit's 'clear and metallic voice – nasal in its falsetto' probably held in it the seeds of his insecurity, and ultimate demise.[19] Nourrit's near-contemporary in the Paris Opéra, Gilbert-Louis Duprez, began his career with a similar modal-falsetto voice and technique. Duprez, though, finding his ambition choked in Paris, moved to Italy, where he found inspiration in the singing of Domenico Donzelli, arguably the first of a new school of dramatic *tenore di forza*. Duprez adopted this technique, and most famously gained the adulation of the Italians with a high C in Rossini's *Guglielmo Tell*, sung in chest voice.

The *tenore di forza*, of course, represents a significant shift in the way that Italians viewed the top of the male voice. We find a hint of this change in the wind as far back as 1774, when Mancini stated:

> All that I have said concerning the defects of a veiled voice, refers only to sopranos and contraltos but never to a tenor or a bass, because these two voices being the foundation and support of harmony must

---

[18] Henry Chorley, *Music and Manners in France and Germany* (London, 1844), p. 148.

[19] Chorley, *Music and Manners*, p. 62.

therefore be robust and sonorous. Such voices cannot develop the tones that a veiled voice can render agreeable.[20]

From the end of the eighteenth century onwards, the falsetto extension was to play less and less of a part in the way Italians preferred their men to sing. Again, the Italian vocal influence was soon felt throughout Europe. Duprez returned from Italy in 1837, and first in Paris and then London achieved star billing: with each fêted high C he hammered another nail into the coffin of falsetto on the Continent. In later life Duprez became a celebrated Parisian teacher, further establishing the *tenore di forza* as a standard operatic voice. There is a certain irony here, in that having eventually persuaded the French to embrace falsetto, through Duprez the Italians now steered them back towards a purely modal technique.

The acclaim with which audiences met this vocal development was not always shared by critics and composers. Even sixty years later George Bernard Shaw was regretting the prominence given to any 'Italian ice-barrow costermonger who can shout a high C [...] roaring round the world to pass in every capital over the prostrate body of lyric drama like a steam roller with a powerful whistle'.[21] Nor, famously, did Rossini approve. After demonstrating this note to Rossini at a private audience, Duprez asked:

Well, then, Maitre, tell me sincerely, does my C please you?

Very sincerely, what pleases me most about your C is that it is over, and that I am no longer in danger of hearing it. I don't like unnatural effects. It strikes my Italian ear as having a strident timbre, like a capon squawking as its throat is slit. You are a very great artist [...] why in the devil abase your talent by using that humbug?'[22]

It is difficult to overstate the irony that, in our own time, Rossini's tenor roles should have become associated with modal-voice machismo, when the composer himself was so explicit in decrying this 'unnatural' approach.

Elsewhere Rossini was specific about how the voice should be developed:

[20] 'Quanto però dico di questo che ho nominato come difetto d'aver la voce appannata, intendasi solo esser ne' Soprano, o Contralti, e non mai in un Tenore, o Basso; poichè queste due ultime voci naturali, come sostegno e base dell'armonia, devono esser sonore, robuste e virili, nè possono agevolmente esprimere quella situazione, ed arrivar a quelle corde, dove una voce velata diviene aggradevole.': Mancini, *Pensieri, e riflessioni pratiche*, p. 46: cf. Mancini, *Practical Reflections*, ed. and trans. Buzzi, p. 66.

[21] Bernard Shaw, *Shaw's Music: The Complete Musical Criticism*, ed. Dan H. Laurence (London, 1981), vol. 1, p. 685.

[22] Edmond Michotte, *Richard Wagner's Visit to Rossini (Paris 1860) and an Evening at Rossini's in Beau-Séjour (Passy) 1858*, ed. and trans. Herbert Weinstock (Chicago, 1968), p. 98.

The contralto is the norm [...] One should concentrate on the central register in order to be always in tune; at the extreme ends, what you gain in force you often lose in grace, and by this abuse you paralyse the throat, resorting as a remedy to *canto declamato*, that is, out-of-tune shouting.[23]

(We might note, in passing, that here Rossini refers to the contralto not as a part, or a particular voice, but as a central part of every voice). Rossini's preferred style did not die out overnight. The 'King of the Tenors', Giovanni Battista Rubini, who did not retire until 1845, sang in this older style: those who might wonder what place the tenor voice has in a history such as this need look no further than the *f"* which Bellini wrote for Rubini in *I Puritani*. Manuel Garcia the Elder, another favourite tenor of Rossini's (and teacher of Nourrit), sang one aria of his own 1809 operatic monologue *El poeta calculista* as a duet between his modal and falsetto voices.[24] Yet it was his son, Manuel Garcia the Younger, who invented the laryngoscope, and as a teacher in Paris and London espoused the darkened *voix sombre* method of singing with a lowered larynx. This method, which in practice left no place for falsetto, has since become the bedrock of operatic technique.

The potential confusion of two Manuel Garcias, one a seminal figure in the old vocal method and the other in the new, is hardly resolved by the Russian novelist Turgenev in his 1872 novel *Spring Torrents*. In it, Turgenev has the ageing Italian baritone Pantaleone nostalgically recall the elder Garcia. Pantaleone

> began again talking of the classical period of singing, of the celebrated tenor Garcia, for whom he cherished a devout, unbounded veneration. 'He was a man!' he exclaimed. 'Never had the great Garcia (*il gran Garcia*) demeaned himself by singing falsetto like the paltry tenors of today – *tenoracci;* always from the chest, from the chest, *voce di petto, si!*' and the old man aimed a vigorous blow with his little shrivelled fist at his own shirtfront![25]

It is tempting to dismiss this fictional reference, which flatly contradicts all other evidence, without too much comment. After all, Turgenev himself never heard the elder Garcia sing, and his novel was written some forty years after the singer had died. But Garcia's daughter, Pauline Viardot, was Turgenev's muse and (perhaps) lover for the last forty years of his life, and so it seems likely that the novelist had at least an indirect knowledge of the great singer's voice. In fact, the Parisian music critic Paolo Scudo

[23] Leonella Grasso Caprioli, 'Singing Rossini', in *The Cambridge Companion to Rossini*, ed. Emanuele Senici (Cambridge, 2004), pp. 189–203, at p. 192.

[24] James Radomski, *Manuel García (1775–1832): Chronicle of the Life of a bel canto Tenor at the Dawn of Romanticism* (Oxford, 2000), p. 99.

[25] Ivan Turgenev, *Veshnie Vody* (1872); translated by Constance Garnett as *Torrents of Spring* (London, 1897), chap. 6.

wrote that it was not Duprez, but Garcia who first sang the high C in chest voice – though never on stage. Whatever the (ultimately unverifiable) specifics of Garcia's own singing, the wider implication of Turgenev's text remains – that older tenors sang always in chest voice, and that modern tenors 'demeaned' themselves with falsetto. At this point we need to take a step backwards, and recognise that this is not Turgenev speaking, but one of his characters. And the elderly Pantaleone, the narrator tells us later, is 'confused' – or as the character himself disarmingly puts it, 'off my head!'. Presumably, to those of his contemporary readers who were in the know, the comical nonsense in this passage would have alerted them to the unreliability of Pantaleone's mind. Pantaleone's comments on falsetto, then, should be taken as no more a reliable guide to contemporary vocal practices than should Chaucer's satirical observation that the Prioresse sang through her nose.[26]

By the end of his life Rossini was a man out of step with the way Garcia and Duprez had developed the art of singing. Perhaps the most eloquent testimony to the death of the chimerical *bel canto* style comes from an encounter between the ageing Rossini and Wagner (not, perhaps, a name one might have expected to find in this history). When Rossini was asked by Wagner to account for his abandonment of opera, the following conversation (as recalled by Wagner) took place:

> Rossini: 'The condition of the Italian theatres, which already during my career left much to be desired, then was in full decay; the art of singing had darkened. That was to be foreseen.'
>
> Wagner: 'To what do you attribute such an unexpected phenomenon in a country in which beautiful voices are superabundant?'
>
> Rossini: 'To the disappearance of the *castrati*. One can form no notion of the charm of voices and consummate virtuosity [...] those best of the best possessed. They were also incomparable teachers. The teaching of singing in the master schools attached to the churches and supported at the churches' expense generally was confided to them. Some of these schools were famous. But after a new political regime was installed throughout Italy by my restless contemporaries, the master schools were suppressed, being replaced by some *conservatories* in which, though some good traditions existed, absolutely nothing of *bel canto* was preserved. As to the *castrati* they vanished, and the usage disappeared in the creation of new customs. That was the cause of irretrievable decay in the art of singing.'[27]

We have observed throughout this history how symbiotic was the relationship between the castrato and falsetto voices: here the relationship

---

[26] Chaucer, 'General Prologue', in *Works*, ed. Robinson, p. 18, line 123.

[27] Michotte, *Richard Wagner's Visit to Rossini*, p. 72.

takes a final bow, as the dwindling voices go their separate ways – the falsetto to hibernation in the choir-stalls of the English cathedral, and the castrato to eventual extinction in the choir-loft of the Sistine Chapel. Some of the reasons for this marginalisation of hitherto mainstream voices have already been touched upon. Yet one of the key reasons is bound up in the ethos of 'Romanticism' itself. However illusory it may have been in practice, in theory the new generation of Romantics thought of their art as being fundamentally a natural and realistic one. Obviously the *artificial* castrato and the *falsetto* sat uneasily with this new ideology. In 1882 an anonymous correspondent to *The Musical Times* noted this: 'alto vocalists are never heard at ballad concerts, simply because there are no songs specially written for them. Let some of our song-writers try the experiment of composing for them and watch the result.'[28] To Romantic composers, such an exhortation would always fall on deaf ears.

For another, more straightforward reason, the Romantic period saw the withdrawal of the castrato and falsetto voices from centre stage. The changing nature of society itself, with the gradual emancipation of female singers, left fewer situations where men were actually required to sing upper parts. In opera, female heroines and modal-voiced tenors took the spotlight previously reserved for the castrati. Chorally, as early as 1737 Johann Adolph Scheibe in Leipzig (echoing Mattheson in Hamburg) had recommended women as the core sopranos and altos in a choir:

> A complete chorus, which is used the same way in the theatre as in the church and chamber, can consist of not fewer than eight persons: two sopranos, two altos, two tenors, a high bass (or so-called baritone), and a low bass [...] Because the chorus still needs to be filled out, one can train boys from the court's musical forces, or, in towns, some school boys. Among the eight principal singers, however, women should be selected for the soprano and alto parts, because their voices are more natural, and of better permanence and intonation.[29]

The minimally staffed Eisenstadt Castle Church Choir, for which Haydn wrote most of his sacred music, reflected this trend: both the soprano and alto were female.[30]

Historically, the Catholic church has had an ambivalent relationship with women singing in church. In I Corinthians 14:34, Paul writes 'let the women keep silence in the churches', and using these words as authority, for most of its history the church has not permitted women to sing (outside of convents). In reality the specific question of singing was something of

---

[28] 'The Scarcity of Alto Voices', *The Musical Times and Singing Class Circular*, 23/468 (1882), p. 100 [anonymous letter, signed 'An Alto'].

[29] Johann Adolph Scheibe, *Critischer Musikus*, 2nd edn (Leipzig, 1745), p. 156: cf. Jerold, 'Choral Singing', p. 81.

[30] H. C. Robbins Landon, *Haydn at Eszterhaza, 1766–1790* (London, 1978), pp. 82–5.

a side-issue. In church, singing was officially regarded as just another clerical function to be enacted in the sanctuary or chancel, and as such (again, largely due to the authority of Paul) it was effectively prohibited to women. As a way of bypassing prohibitions on female singers, though, from the Baroque period onwards women singing from outside the chancel have escaped from this ban on a technicality. And, of course, many Protestant denominations have long been open to the possibility of women singers. In more religiously conservative environments, though, the prohibition on women led to a continued role for the occasional falsettist. A tantalising anecdote in Grove's first *Dictionary*, around 1880, suggests that some southern European churches still harboured falsettists:

> A lady traveller in Spain and Portugal, writing some six or seven years ago, amusingly expresses her surprise, on discovering that certain high flute-like notes, which she believed to have been produced by some beautiful young girl, really emanated from the throat of burly individual *with a huge black beard* and *whiskers.*[31]

All-male choirs also remained the norm in some German churches, but here the upper two parts were increasingly taken by boys. Gender parity was a growing trend, though, and one which would have major ramifications for the high male voice on the Continent. As female altos became more accepted in the church (the only forum in which there was at least the pretence of an intellectual argument against their involvement) the theatre and concert-hall lost a major supply-line of male altos. Only in England, as we shall see in due course, was the situation subtly different.

Neither could the castrato and falsetto voices be comfortably reconciled with another social phenomenon – the nineteenth century's growing sense of gender identity. This trend (which we will explore in the next chapter) has been linked to the simultaneous upsurge in feelings of national identity. Nowhere, musically, is this link more obvious than in the Continental music for male chorus. The French *orphéon* movement, which at its mid-century height boasted some seven hundred provincial societies, mirrored the German *Liedertafel*, both in its alto-less vocal disposition, and in the patriotic nature of much of its repertoire. The largely working-class *orphéon* movement actually went further, with the uniforms, medals and banners of its competitive festivals overtly aping the trappings of military life.[32] In this context, it is easy to see why the falsetto, or even the modal-falsetto voice, could have no easy role to play. Nor, indeed, did the falsetto voice play a significant role in any other form of Continental musical activity until our own time.

---

[31] Grove, *Dictionary of Music and Musicians*, vol. 2, p. 521.

[32] Katherine Ellis, *Interpreting the Musical Past: Early Music in Nineteenth-Century France* (Oxford/New York, 2005), p. 224.

England and the First Counter-Tenor Falsettists

Y ET at the same time as we come to this significant hiatus abroad, in Britain falsetto was at least sowing the seeds for its growth in modern times – albeit on a very fallow field. We should again note, though, that the 'tradition' from which Deller eventually sprang was far from being an unchanging one, and certainly not one with links to antiquity. Rather, the 'tradition' gradually formulated itself during the nineteenth century. The English vocal scene which Handel left behind, let us also remind ourselves, was one which included tenors and altos utilising both their modal and falsetto voices. In this sense, the distinction between these voice-types was one of degree, rather than of fundamental technique. The notion that a tenor sang purely in modal voice, and the alto purely in falsetto, would not gain a firm footing in England for at least a hundred years after Handel's death. In the meantime, the demise of the dual-register voice became a vicious circle: the fewer singers who were trained to master the technique, the fewer teachers there were for the next generation of singers, and so on. Both in quantity and quality, there was a decline in singers using this technique as the nineteenth century progressed. Isolated instances aside, only in church choirs would falsetto (in any form) see the century out. We sense something of the decline of falsetto as a practical adjunct to the modal voice in a comment by Isaac Nathan:

> It is a species of ventriloquism, a soft and distant sound produced apparently in the chest, and chiefly in the back of the throat and head – an inward and suppressed quality of tone, that conveys the illusion of being heard at a distance: – It is as a sweet and soft melodious sound, wafted from afar, like unto the magic spell of an echo.[33]

There is little here to suggest that the falsetto Nathan knew in 1836 was a sound capable of focus and projection.

Returning to the end of the eighteenth century, this is perhaps the time briefly to clarify some of the Chinese whispers regarding singers from these 'halcyon days' of the counter-tenor.[34] Of John Dyne (d. 1788), John Hindle (1761–96), John Immyns (1700–64), Jonathan Battishill (1738–1801), John Jeremiah Goss (1770–1817), and Charles Smart Evans (1778–1849) – all of whom are repeatedly cited by modern authors as famous counter-tenors or altos – there is not one reliable contemporary reference to any of them using

---

[33] Isaac Nathan, *Musurgia vocalis: Essay on the Theory & History of Music* (London, 1836), p. 117.

[34] The expression 'halcyon days', and the information cited in this paragraph is taken from Giles, *The History and Technique of the Counter-Tenor*. Giles's assumptions have been used as an authoritative source by many subsequent writers.

falsetto, let alone to their being falsettists: doubtless some or all of them did use falsetto as an occasional adjunct to their modal voices, but they were not 'counter-tenors' in the way we use the term. Of John Saville (1735–1803) (to whom is devoted an excellent ten-page biography in *The History and Technique of the Counter-Tenor*) the one source which describes him as a counter-tenor was written over twenty years after the event described, and alarmingly, is actually a report of an occasion when Saville sang with his 'powerful' voice a tenor aria at a Gloucester Three Choirs meeting. Whatever part he sang, at whatever pitch, there is no evidence that Saville was a falsettist.

Perhaps just as misleadingly, the singing of Charles Bannister (1738–1804) has been addressed as if he was a professional musician.[35] Bannister, though, was an actor, and a closer look at the contexts in which his singing is described suggests that his singing was anything but sophisticated. In 1805 the *Thespian Dictionary* remarks of him that:

> His voice was a strong clear bass, with one of the most extensive falsettos ever heard; they were finely contrasted in a pantomime performed at the Haymarket several years ago, in which he was dressed one half like a huntsman and the other half like a beau; in which he sung a duet, one part in the rough tone of a sportsman, and the other with the most feminine shrillness.[36]

Charles Bannister's son John was also a comic actor, and his memoirs include the following recollection:

> Charles Bannister was one of the untaught class. His voice, uniting, in extraordinary perfection, the extremes of a deep bass and high-toned falsetto, and his ear, which was of great delicacy and perfection, enabled him not only to execute pieces of ordinary description, but to represent, with great humour, and without the grossness of burlesque or caricature, many leading performers of the day, both male and female.[37]

By the start of the nineteenth century modal-falsetto singing had evidently degenerated from being a mark of vocal sophistication to being a comic turn.

The case of another actor and singer, George Mattocks (1735–1804), appears intriguing. One modern author cites *The Theatrical Biographer* as reporting of Mattocks that 'We are often led to imagine, that we are listening to the notes of a *Castrato*, than to those of a British

---

[35] Cf. Roger Fiske, *English Theatre Music in the Eighteenth Century* (London, 1973), p. 271.

[36] J. Cundee, *The Thespian Dictionary ...*, 2nd edn (Oxford, 1805), *s.v.* 'Bannister (Charles)'.

[37] Adolphus John, *Memoirs of John Bannister, Comedian* (London, 1839), vol. 1, p. 5.

singer'.[38] Although this suggests that Mattocks sang falsetto, there is no confirming evidence of this. According to one contemporary ear-witness, Mattocks' voice was 'clear, soft, melodious and expressive', but there is nothing here to suggest that he was a falsettist.[39] Even if he was, there is no evidence that he was also regarded as a counter-tenor: for those wishing to make a connection between the falsettist and counter-tenor (or alto), in English musical history the two terms still stubbornly refuse to conjoin right up to the end of the eighteenth century.

At the start of the nineteenth, though, we at last find an individual with whom when those terms eventually became synonymous. Obviously this is a hugely significant point in this history, but a 'eureka' moment it is certainly not: as we shall see, for well over a hundred years following, the term 'counter-tenor' was (confusingly and – one suspects – confusedly) also used to refer to modal and dual-register singers. The individual in question is William Knyvett (1779–1856), and he is particularly interesting to us since he was not just written about, but wrote about himself and his voice-type. For *The Quarterly Musical Magazine and Review*, Knyvett wrote some 'Preliminary remarks on counter-tenor singing'.[40] This came about because of a rather luke-warm gesture of inclusiveness on the part of the journal's founder and editor-in-chief, Richard Mackenzie Bacon, who, having covered the tenor, soprano and bass voices in past issues, now invited Knyvett to 'complete the series of remarks on vocal art' with a 'professional memoir'. Knyvett's text, and the editorial commentary on it (anonymous, but presumably by Bacon), provide us with the fullest account of the nascent English counter-tenor falsettist. Knyvett begins with an interesting take on the recent history of the counter-tenor:

> From the introduction of the Italian opera [*c.* 1710] into this country till nearly the close of the last century [*c.* 1795], this part of a musical performance was sustained, as circumstances directed, by three different species of voice, though of the same general pitch – by Castrati, by females with low soprano voices, and by men using the falsette. The natural counter-tenor might also be enumerated, for we have heard those who could ascend to B in the natural voice, but the examples have of late become so rare as rather to afford exceptions, than to fall in with the rule.

---

[38] Fiske, *English Theatre Music*, p. 634. Frustratingly, this quote is not footnoted, and there is no evidence on the British Library database of any publication entitled '*The Theatrical Biographer*'.

[39] Cf. Philip H. Highfill, Kalman A. Burnim and Edward A. Langhans, *Biographical Dictionary of Actors, Actresses, Musicians, Dancers, Managers and Other Stage Personnel in London, 1660–1800* (Carbondale, IL, 1984), vol. 10, p. 145.

[40] Richard Mackenzie Bacon and William Knyvett, 'Preliminary Remarks on Counter-Tenor Singing', *The Quarterly Musical Magazine and Review* 2 (1820), pp. 468–76.

Read literally, Knyvett offers the same counter-tenor options we identified for the Handelian period, but with one significant departure: in place of one singer with a modal *and* falsetto technique, he suggests two counter-tenors with *either* modal *or* falsetto voices. At this point, some knowledge of Knyvett's own voice might help us see if this is actually what he means. Knyvett's 'falsette', the editor later tells us, stretched upwards for nine notes from middle C. In fact, Knyvett was a counter-tenor in the Chapel Royal and Westminster Abbey, the repertory of which would have required him regularly to descend below his falsetto range. In other words, when Knyvett refers too 'men using the falsette' he presumably means predominantly, but not exclusively.

As for the present, Knyvett tells us:

> The voice at present most in repute and most employed is the falsette, which is sweet and brilliant in its tones, but rarely powerful, and occasionally apt to go out of tune. The few natural counter-tenors we have heard have generally been coarse, and produced, as it appeared, by strong effort, impure and *throaty*, the expedient to which singers who wish to increase their volume have but too often recourse.

This seems a candid admission, by the best-known counter-tenor of his day, that the 'falsette' voice was by nature weak: and lest we assume false-modesty on the singer's part, Bacon subsequently informs us of Knyvett's voice that 'THE TONE is pure, sweet, and brilliant, but in point of volume it is so limited, that one never hears MR. K. in a song without lamenting its want of power.'

As for what he and his type were expected to sing, Knyvett tells us that the counter-tenor

> is by modern composers very much confined to glees. We presume the discontinuance [of the counter-tenor as a solo voice] arises from the thin and feeble effect which the falsette produces when contrasted with the power and fullness of soprano, tenor, or bass, in the large buildings, and to the very numerous audiences before whom signers are now a-days called upon to perform. Certain it is that we never experienced any of the grand effects described by the historians of music from the voices we hear.

Here we have the clearest admission that the nineteenth century's fascination with volume and sonority had made any form of falsetto virtually redundant on the main stage. Again, Bacon concurs: 'Certain we are that even the acknowledged science, taste, and polish or MR. W. KNYVETT are unequal to the task, [of singing solos in oratorios] and if he fails, where shall we be likely to find a successful substitute?' Bacon also agrees with Knyvett that the glee is the natural home of the falsettist:

> It is in this department [the English glee] that the brilliancy and sweetness of his voice, his intonation, and his chastity of manner, not

only are most visible, but the assimilation of tone – the exact light and shade – the distinct articulation, combined with such uncommon accuracy both of words and notes, are so finely shewn.

By profession Bacon was principally a political journalist. However, though only an amateur musician, he did not let any lack of knowledge bar him from opining on Knyvett and the current state of the counter-tenor voice:

> The natural voice of the object of our present notice [Knyvett] is, as we have understood, a base [bass], but distinguished by no superiority. Mr W. K. therefore preferred to avail himself of the falsette which usually accompanies the bass, and by indefatigable industry and sound science, he may be said almost to have created his counter-tenor. This species of voice has been extremely scarce for many years, but we question whether the rarity may not be very justly supposed to proceed from the greater delicacy which the more polished taste of our own age requires to satisfy delicate ears, than from any alteration in the dispositions of nature, or any change in the physical organisation of the throat. The fact, we conceive to be, that the natural counter-tenors whom PURCELL and CROFT employed (for in their days there appears to have been no scarcity), were coarse in proportion as they were powerful.[41]

Confusingly, Bacon suggests here that falsettists such as Knyvett's have been 'extremely scarce for many years', suggesting that they were once more common. But by then referring to 'the natural counter-tenors' of the early English Baroque, Bacon leaves us wondering when the falsettist could ever have existed in England. And there is an extra level of confusion here, because in using the 'delicate ears' of the present to account for the 'want of power' in Knyvett's voice, Bacon flatly contradicts the reality which the singer has already alluded to – 'the nineteenth century's fascination with volume and sonority'. In fact, a lower pitch, smaller venues and performing forces, and the dual-register technique, suggest a number of reasons why Purcell's 'natural counter-tenors' would never have had reason to sound 'coarse'. Bacon, though, carries with him the conceit that his own age represents the epitome of taste:

> There is, however, to be discerned in what belongs to the intellectual direction of art in MR. W. KNYVETT'S singing, all that is comprehended in the term, *fine taste* [...] though we are unable to specify any particular examples, in which he can be said deeply to have affected his hearers.[42]

---

[41] Bacon and Knyvett, 'Preliminary Remarks', p. 472.
[42] Bacon and Knyvett, 'Preliminary Remarks', p. 474.

The alarming caveat here is that Knyvett's voice can move men's minds, but evidently not their hearts.

Perhaps Bacon's most interesting piece of conjecture about the counter-tenor voice, though, comes when he coyly ventures into the field of physiology:

> The falsette is, we have reason to believe, affected by physical circumstances that operate upon the constitution, in a far greater degree and far more easily than upon any other kind of voice; perhaps to this extreme delicacy are owing its beauty and its defects, for what is very extraordinary, those accidents which injure the tone and lessen the power of the natural voice, are in a great many subjects found to heighten the quality and improve the flexibility of the falsette. This is a very curious subject, and seems to depend upon a *consent*, as physiologists term it, which might afford an interesting object of speculation to the philosophical anatomist.[43]

What, one wonders, are the 'physical circumstances' and 'accidents' which Bacon has in mind? Is he suggesting that some kind of chemical castration has taken place with Knyvett and those few of his ilk? His earlier reference to Knyvett's 'chastity of manner' does indeed suggest that Bacon has his suspicions.

One other piece of evidence that the falsettist counter-tenor was active in England in the early nineteenth century comes from a somewhat obscure source – press reports concerning William Penphraze, a London singer and actor who settled in the West Country in the 1820s.[44] Rival press notices document both Penphraze's voice and his reception at performances in Truro. At the same time the critics offer an insight into the differing ways in which a falsettist could be perceived at the time. In 1827 the critic of the *West Briton* notes a vocal novelty: 'A new voice in Mr Penphraze was introduced [...] we have not seen his equal on the Truro boards. His voice (a counter-tenor) is not very powerful, but possesses much flexibility and sweetness.' A 'new voice' could, of course, mean a new singer rather than a new vocal style, and it is true that in descriptions of Penphraze's singing from Truro falsetto is not specified; that said, falsetto would seem the most obvious explanation for the descriptions and strong reactions to his singing which appear in subsequent press notices. The same *West Briton* writer notes later in the same month – and here we catch the first whiff of enlightened condescension – that Penphraze 'continues to delight all who possess a taste for higher refinements of the vocal art – his talent places him far above many who make much *noise* in the musical world.'

---

[43] Bacon and Knyvett, 'Preliminary Remarks', p. 473.

[44] For the full account of William Penphraze, from which all these press notices are taken, readers are referred to the excellent discussion in Giles, *History and Technique of the Counter-Tenor*, pp. 99–101.

The object of this critic's irritation becomes clear when we look at Penphraze's reception by the *Royal Cornwall Gazette*. To this rival critic, the singer's 'strange tones and ludicrous gestures' produced a 'sensible effect on the risible muscles of the audience'. (In other words, they laughed.) In a duet, the *Gazette* critic regrets that the soprano was not supported by a 'manly English voice' instead of Penphraze's. The same critic noted, at a performance early in 1828, that Penphraze's lower notes 'scarcely reached the side boxes, and his upper notes defy description'. At this point, the *West Briton* critic responds by turning his ire on Penphraze's detractors:

> Respecting the treatment this excellent vocalist has received in Truro, we cannot refrain from saying a few words [...] what chance has a singer – a fine Counter Tenor (of astonishing compass) – has [*sic*] of becoming a favourite in a provincial theatre; especially where there be an orchestral leader who manifests on all occasions every possible hostility towards him. We recommend Mr Penphraze, notwithstanding the jeers to which he has been subjected [...] to cultivate his talent with assiduity.

This fascinating journalistic spat is highly revealing. It would be easy to characterise the *West Briton* critic's rather patronising tone as the voice of well-educated musical conservatism, and his rival critic as championing a more modern, 'manly' vocal style. In truth, it does not appear that either writer has heard quite this type of singing before. And why would they have? After all, Penphraze (to judge from the inaudibility of his lower notes) was evidently a pure falsettist, and not a modal-falsetto singer. In this sense, even though it would be over a century before his voice-type gained true recognition, William Penphraze was – like Knyvett – more a harbinger of the future than a relic of the past.

Although from the period before the mid-nineteenth century references to a counter-tenor singing purely in falsetto are rare, descriptions of falsetto as an adjunct to the modal voice (of all voice-types) remain plentiful. Indeed, contemporary descriptions of Englishmen singing in falsetto all seem to mine a similar vein. Haydn's description of the tenor Charles Incledon's falsetto we have already met. When the tenor John Braham, described by Kelly as 'the greatest vocalist of his day', made his London stage debut in 1796, the *Morning Chronicle* hoped that his success might 'induce us to *chace* from an English stage the degrading and disgusting form of the castrato'.[45] The irony here is that Braham had been taught by the castrato Rauzzini, and was evidently a master of the dual-register voice taught by the *musici*:

> Mr Braham can take his falsetto upon any note from D to A at pleasure and the juncture is so nicely managed that in an experiment

---

[45] Cf. Theodore Fenner, *Opera in London: Views of the Press, 1785–1830* (Carbondale, IL, 1994), p. 169.

to which this gentleman had the kindness to submit, of ascending and descending by semitones, it was impossible to distinguish at what point he substituted the falsetto for the natural note.[46]

From 1832, a reviewer in *The Harmonicon* confirms this, at the same time reminding us that this use of falsetto was as much the province of the tenor as the counter-tenor:

One accomplishment, in which Mr. Braham exceeds every other tenor singer of his own, or, as far as we know, any former time, is the skill with which he has assimilated his falsetto to his chest voice, so that although the difference of tone at the extremes of the passage is discernible, the exact point at which he passes from one to the other is beyond detection by the nicest ear [...][47]

By this time in history, however, not all of Braham's listeners were in sympathy with his modal-falsetto technique. Despite acknowledging that Braham's 'voice is of the finest quality', Richard Edgcumbe notes that 'it is therefore the more to be regretted that he should ever [...] quit the normal register of his voice by raising it to an unpleasant falsetto.'[48] One of Edgcumbe's most revealing observations is of a performance of *Messiah* in Westminster Abbey in 1834:

There being no good counter-tenor, the song 'He was despised', which is generally given to that voice, was assigned to a female contralto, a Miss Masson, who sung it correctly, but without feeling. As it is within the compass of a tenor, Harrison, Knyvett, and others, having sung it, Braham might have taken it, and would have given it all its deeply pathetic expression, which was totally lost.[49]

So by 1834 even such a prestigious event as this could not muster a 'good counter-tenor'. What this observation also tells us is that the tenor and counter-tenor voices could still be thought of as interchangeable – especially in the case of Braham, whose technique harked back to the previous century. In the case of Knyvett, the fact that he is referred to as a tenor suggests that his profile as a singer must by now have been waning. And sure enough, by this time in his career Knyvett was concentrating on composing and conducting. Evidently he, or the forces behind this 1834 *Messiah*, had taken the view that the 'thin and feeble effect' of his falsetto would be out of place in the Abbey amongst a huge throng of performers: there were 644 of them, and the very fact that such a precise number was

[46] *The Quarterly Musical Magazine and Review* 1 (1818), p. 89.

[47] *The Harmonicon*, 1832, part 1, p. 3.

[48] Richard Edgcumbe, *Musical Reminiscences of an Old Amateur ...* (London, 1831), p. 95.

[49] Edgcumbe, *Musical Reminiscences*, pp. 281–2: cf. John Potter, *Tenor: History of a Voice* (London, 2009), p. 41.

recorded tells its own tale about pride and priorities in the early nineteenth century.

The growing importance of vigour and strength is highlighted by the writing and singing of Michael Kelly. Perhaps ironically, Kelly's own voice gives us a small indication of changing tastes: writing in 1826, James Boaden remembered of Kelly's singing that 'In vigorous passages he never cheated the ear with the feeble wailings of falsetto, but sprung upon the ascending fifth with a sustaining energy, that often electrified an audience.'[50] It is difficult to imagine such an implied condemnation of the dual-register technique even fifty years previously. If we catch here the scent of a changing wind, Kelly's remembrance of his own teacher, Nicolò Peretti, also points in this new direction: 'He had a fine contre altro [*sic*] voice, and possessed the true portamento so little known in the present day.'[51] In the eighteenth and early nineteenth centuries, 'portamento' meant not a slide between pitches but, as Mancini puts it, something subtly different: 'the passing and blending of the voice from one tone to another, with perfect proportion and union, in ascending as well as descending.'[52] Earlier in the same book Mancini comments that 'a portamento cannot be acquired unless the student has first blended the registers of the voice which are in every one more or less separated.'[53] Kelly, then is praising the dual-register technique of his own teacher Peretti, whilst commenting that such a method is now rare.

Peretti is one of countless Italian names we encounter on the English vocal scene during this period. Many of these men had been singers themselves, and settled in England later in life. Not surprisingly, the views expressed in their treatises and manuals were (like Rossini's in his Parisian retirement) somewhat backward-looking. Of the time he spent in Edinburgh, Michael Kelly remembers 'Signor Urbani, a good professor, and, like his countryman, David Kizzio, very partial to Scotch melodies, some of which he sang very pleasingly, though in a falsetto voice.' Again, Kelly's use of that word 'though' smacks of changing tastes. Another Italian pedagogue working in Edinburgh at the time was the castrato Domenico Corri, a pupil of Farinelli's teacher Nicolò Porpora. About the importance of joining registers, Corri's treatise *The Singer's Preceptor* offered similar guidance

---

[50] Boaden, *Memoirs of the Life of John Philip Kemble*, vol. 1, p. 98.

[51] *Reminiscences of Michael Kelly*, vol. 1, p. 4.

[52] 'Per questo portamento non s'intende altro che un passare, legando la voce, da una nota all' altra con perfetta proporzione ed unione, tanto nel salire, quanto in discendere.': Mancini, *Pensieri, e riflessioni pratiche*, p. 137: cf. *Practical Reflections*, ed. and trans. Buzzi, p. 111.

[53] 'Premetto ora solamente, che un tal portamento non potrà mai acquistarsi da qualsivoglia scolare, se prima non avrà uniti I due divisati registri, I quail sono in gni persona separati, in chi più, in chi meno.': Mancini, *Pensieri, e riflessioni*, p. 133–4: cf. *Practical Reflections*, ed. and trans. Buzzi, p.108.

to the advice Tosi had been offering a century earlier. There is, though, a subtle change of emphasis:

> A great defect in most Singers is the imperfect Manner of joining the Natural to the Feigned Voice, the sudden transition of which, frequently gives a shock to the Ear, abrupt, as the squeek of a little Boy, which is unbecoming the dignity of manhood to utter.[54]

By recognising the lack of this skill in 'most singers' Corri now seems to accept that this is a dying art. Yet Isaac Nathan (a pupil of Corri) and Domenico Crivelli were still offering similar guidance in their London-published treatises (and presumably to their pupils) until the 1850s.[55]

In Britain, then, there was a glut of Italian vocalists repeating a mantra which was increasingly outdated on the Continent. This was hardly the first (or last) time that Britain would find itself musically out of step with mainstream Europe, but the reasons why it happened are worth briefly exploring. They are significant for us because it was only through the separate identity of its musical culture that Britain would later host the emergent counter-tenor falsettist. The long-standing argument about the extent to which Britain was a musical pauper during the nineteenth century need not concern us here: all we need to observe is that Britain was a net importer of music and musicians. And if this smacks of being a crude economic gloss on an aesthetic argument, it is fitting that it does. The language of imports and exports is apt, since it was only through its relative economic wealth that Britain acted as a magnet to foreign performers and composers. Britain's musical premier league did not need to rely on home-grown talent, but could buy in those who had already made their names abroad. By implication, then, musical life in Britain was destined to reflect what had previously happened in Europe. So it was that – albeit mostly as an adjunct to male modal voices – falsetto singing retained some currency in Britain at a time when it was being completely devalued on the Continent.

Even if we accept this line of argument, it still leaves us a long way from making a connection between the likes of William Knyvett and Alfred Deller. Every man from the early nineteenth century we have so far met singing with falsetto, we have met in a secular context – either on the boards or in the salon. Yet in these contexts falsetto – even in alliance with a modal voice – was to have virtually disappeared by the middle of the century. Observations by an American visitor to the Norwich Festival in 1852 suggest that any cultured falsetto extension to the male alto voice by then was unknown – at least in the context of this secular chorus:

> Again, the alto was composed mostly of men's voices. The effect was a harshness or roughness that has no mercy upon one's nervous

---

[54] Domenico Corri, *The Singer's Preceptor, or Corri's treatise on vocal music, etc.* (London, 1810), vol. 2, p. 66.

[55] Nathan, *Musurgia vocalis*; Domenico Crivelli, *The Art of Singing* (London, 1841).

system or musical sensibilities, and that, in the present instance, made one often curl or shrink away as if a severe blow had been inflicted; besides, in pressing up to the high tones, the men did not all quite reach the point; making altogether too much of that which the organ-tuners call 'wolf' – a name applicable as well to *quality of tone* (howling) in this case as to *intonation*.

The men's rough alto was like a sawmill, when the saw strikes a nail; how can this terrible grating be tolerated?[56]

Sung with 'harshness' and 'roughness', and sounding like a 'sawmill' – there can be little doubt that the Norwich altos were attempting (if not quite succeeding) to reach their upper notes with raw modal voices. In the secular chorus, where volume was valued over subtlety, this is quite believable.

Just how unfashionable falsetto singing had become by the mid-nineteenth century is clear from an 1889 music column by George Bernard Shaw. This is neither the first nor last appearance of Shaw's name in this history, and we need to be aware of his own vocal background. For all his love of Wagner, Shaw had been musically educated by his mother and her singing teacher, George Vandaleur Lee, who were proponents of the old *bel canto* style: throughout his life, this would be the style that Shaw would feel an affinity for, and have some knowledge of. Writing about the current state of the alto part in church music, Shaw digresses with a reference to an 1855 novel:

> Thackeray students will remember that when Colonel Newcome returned from India, and obliged a convivial circle by singing a ballad in a countertenor voice with florid ornaments in the taste of his own heyday, he was astonished to find everybody laughing at him.[57]

Except that Thackeray had not described Newcome's voice quite as Shaw remembered. What Thackeray actually wrote was:

> The Colonel sang, as we have said, with a very high voice, using freely the falsetto, after the manner of the tenor singers of his day.[58]

Shaw's faulty memory is itself revealing. Aside from his insertion of 'florid ornaments' (which Thackeray makes no mention of), why has Shaw transmuted the original 'tenor' to 'countertenor'? As we shall see in due course, by 1889 the tenor was an exclusively modal voice, and although the church alto part was by then sometimes taken (when it was taken at all) by men singing in falsetto, the term 'counter-tenor' was practically obsolete. Shaw, then, had unwittingly updated a practice that would have appeared quaint to Thackeray's readers in 1855, to one which would have appeared

[56] Lowell Mason, *Musical Letters from Abroad* (New York, 1854), pp. 261 and 284.

[57] Shaw, *Shaw's Music*, ed. Laurence, vol. 1, p. 831.

[58] William Makepeace Thackeray, *The Newcomes* (London, 1855), chap. 13.

quaint to his own readers in 1889. Shaw can tell us little about 1855 vocal practices, but about 1889 he tells us much.

Thackeray, on the other hand, tells us something about singing in mid-century England, and the continuation of his description is worth examining:

> The Colonel began his second verse: and here, as will often happen to amateur singers, his falsetto broke down. He was not in the least annoyed, for I saw him smile very good-naturedly; and he was going to try the verse again, when that unlucky Barnes first gave a sort of crowing imitation of the song, and then burst into a yell of laughter.

Thackeray's point here is that the aged Colonel's style of singing is an object of humour for his younger listeners. And whilst it might be striking to us that Thackeray describes the Colonel's falsetto being used after the style of the 'tenor' singers of his day, we need to remember that it was not the novelist's vocal label which caused his imagined listeners to laugh. No, what evidently amused the young men, now accustomed to virile modal singing, was simply the sound of a modal voice being rather clunkily joined to a falsetto. We might also note that, as an amateur, Newcome's technical mastery of the dual-register technique was found wanting.

On the stage, and even in the drawing room, falsetto was vanishing. If we want to trace a link between the likes of Knyvett and Deller, then, we need to look elsewhere. Deller's voice was to come to light in a sacred context, and it is in church that we next need to search for his forbears. And here, inevitably, the falsetto voice proves a much more difficult quarry to hunt down. The kind of press reports we have for the Norwich Festival, and the type of personal memoirs we have been reading of stage performances, are obviously lacking for church music. So too are the clues which we used to reveal voices in earlier church choirs – observations, audition notes and the like. There is a good reason that these clues are lacking, and that is because in the early nineteenth century church choirs themselves were lacking. Certainly they did not exist in any manner we would recognise from a modern English cathedral service. Choirs were often staffed not by singers, but by minor-canons. S. S. Wesley refers to them as a 'race of voiceless and incompetent priests'.[59] Similarly shocking reports are manifold, not just regarding numbers but also rehearsal (at Durham and York there was no such thing), and choice of repertoire (at Salisbury and St Paul's it was chosen by the Dean *during* the service).[60] When Wesley's *Blessed be the God and Father* was first sung, at Hereford Cathedral on Easter Day 1833, the choir included only one adult. This, we should note, was for the first

[59] Samuel Sebastian Wesley, *A Few Words on Cathedral Music* (London, 1849), p. 23.

[60] P. Barrett, 'English Cathedral Choirs in the Nineteenth Century', *Journal of Ecclesiastical History* 25 (1974), pp. 17–22.

performance of a major work on a prime feast day in a cathedral. Those wondering what form the alto part took in the nineteenth-century English church should initially assume no more than this: ink on paper.

This general laxity might remind us of Haydn's experience in Eisenstadt. There is at least one significant difference between the two, however, and this lies in the constitution and gender of the choirs. As we have seen, the admission of women in many European church choirs had, for them, removed the necessity of falsettists. Quite the reverse now began to apply in England. The reasons for this fundamental difference are complex, but significant for our search.

Since the Reformation the English Anglican church had always seen itself more as an adapted Catholic church than a radical Protestant one. As such, its innate conservatism led the Church of England to retain all-male choirs (even after the hiatus of the Civil War) with boys continuing to sing and (crucially) be educated as part of the fabric of the major churches. So, at a time when arguments were being successfully advanced for the introduction of women into European church choirs, in England there was neither the theological impetus nor the musical necessity for such a move. Boys, then, remained as sopranos in the all-male church choirs. At least at the start of the nineteenth century, the question of who sang alto in these choirs was largely academic: in most choirs, the answer was evidently anybody by any means. Or nobody. By about the 1870s, as the reforming zeal of the Oxford Movement (and individuals such as S. S. Wesley and Maria Hackett) led to a marked improvement in the standards of church music, the question becomes more meaningful.

After leaving Hereford, Wesley took up a series of appointments in which, as the leading church musician of his day, he was assured of relatively well-staffed choirs. There is no doubt that in the music Wesley wrote during this later period the altos who sang for him used their modal voices for much of the time. Choral recitatives in the baritone range are often marked 'altos, tenors and basses' (see Ex. 10). Even when the alto line is separate, it spends long periods camped below middle C, with exposed notes a fifth and more below. The top of Wesley's alto range is around an octave above middle C. With the pitch of most Victorian church organs being similar to our own, doubtless there were still men capable of taking this entire range in their modal voices. (Let us remind ourselves again that, at the time, the average Englishman is estimated to have stood at 166 cm (5'5½"), compared to 177.6 cm (5'10") in 2010 – the implication being that their modal voices would have been a good deal higher than ours.) Yet we have also seen enough evidence that, in Britain, the joining of modal and falsetto voices was still known, and (however roughly) presumably would have been the method used by many mid-nineteenth-century male altos. As this method continued its decline, in the latter decades of the century, it becomes clear that, for the first time, the majority of English male altos began to rely primarily on their falsetto production. In one sense, they had little option: composers, to satisfy the requirements of mixed choirs, were

Ex. 10 S. S. Wesley, *Ascribe unto the Lord*, opening

Ex. 11 Felix Mendelssohn, *Hear my Prayer,* first choral entry

increasingly writing alto parts with a much higher tessitura. The influence of Mendelssohn on English composers was particularly significant. Compare the alto part of Mendelssohn's 1844 *Hear my Prayer* (Ex. 11) with Wesley's alto ranges, and the difference is stark.

Mendelssohn's work was published simultaneously in London and Berlin, with a text in English and German. In other words, Mendelssohn was writing for the most plural market possible. Yet it is obvious that the 'default' alto he had in mind was a very different type of singer from the type Wesley knew. In Mendelssohn's opening choral unison, the alto is paired not with the lower voices, but with the soprano, taking the voice straight up to *e″* (a tenth above middle C). Even later in the work, when the alto has an independent part, it rarely descends below *c′*, and then only by a third at most. At this lower end of the range, male altos would have little if any need for their modal voice. At the upper end of the range, though, even their falsetto was evidently taxed: 'When foreign music with contralto parts is performed here, the man's alto fails at the higher notes; and in cathedrals in particular the 2nd part has to be sung by what is in practice a mixture of man's alto and weak boys' contralto.'[61]

The alto parts of the later Victorian church composers confirm that a major change has taken place. In his church works, Sir John Stainer mirrors Mendelssohn's practice in the lower extent of his alto parts. At the other end of the range (and probably to the relief of his altos at St Paul's Cathedral, where he was organist from 1872 to 1885) Stainer avoids Mendelssohn's upper third. The difference in tessitura between Wesley and Stainer's alto parts is vast. As far as English church music is concerned, it represents the most rapid upward shift in the history of the part. Those looking for a corresponding shift in the vocal production used by the majority of male altos – and coincidentally for the genesis of the modern counter-tenor – need look no further. Yet again, though, it is vital to stress that this shift to falsetto as the primary method was neither immediate nor universal in the English church: James Brown, in the choir of the Temple Church in London from 1882, was described by a contemporary as having 'an unusually fine alto voice with the timbre of a trumpet', which 'boomed out across the church'.[62] Until well after the Second World War we will find occasional descriptions which are similarly suggestive of modal voices on the alto line.

During the years when Stainer was at St Paul's, George Grove began the publication of his *Dictionary of Music and Musicians*. This leaves us in no doubt about the current nature of the English male alto, whilst making equally clear the editorial view of this. The composer and teacher John Hullah, who was the contributor for the entry on the alto voice, tried to trace the history of the part and voice:

ALTO.

called also counter-tenor, i.e. contra, or against the tenor. In the 16th and early part of the 17th centuries the compass of the alto voice was limited to the notes admissible on the stave which has the C clef on its third line; i.e. to the notes a sixth above and a sixth below middle C. Later however this compass was extended by bringing into use the third register of the voice, or falsetto, a register often strongest with those whose voices are naturally bass. The falsetto counter-tenor, or more properly counter-alto, still to be found in cathedral choirs, dates if musical history is to be read in music from the restoration of Charles II, who doubtless desired to reproduce

---

[61] A. H. D. Prendergast, 'The Man's Alto in English Music', *Zeitschrift der internationalen Musikgesellschaft* 1 (1900), pp. 331–4, at p. 334.

[62] David Lewer, *A Spiritual Song* (London, 1961), p. 188.

at home, approximately at least, a class of voice he had become accustomed to in continental chapels royal and ducal. The so-called counter-tenor parts of Pelham Humphreys [*sic*] his contemporaries and successors, habitually transcend those of their predecessors, from Tallis to Gibbons, by at least a third.[63]

Hullah, then, suggested that falsetto altos had existed in England since the period of the Restoration. By his own admission, he did this purely from the evidence of written ranges, but crucially, he assessed this evidence by not taking pitch variation into consideration – an omission which was noted by at least one of Hullah's contemporaries, the minor composer A. H. D. Prendergast.[64] In fact, the difference in sounding pitch between the counter-tenor ranges of Gibbons and Humphrey was probably a tone or less. Attempting to explain this apparent shift, though, Hullah had made his presumption about the musical experiences of Charles II in Europe. Of this, Prendergast noted that 'the idea of men alti suddenly developing and using a new register in order to please King Charles II can hardly be entertained with any seriousness'.[65] As we have seen, although falsetto probably was used in a limited fashion after the Restoration, the counter-tenor then was still primarily a modal voice. What we cannot reasonably doubt, however, is Hullah's comment on the present: that cathedral altos predominantly used falsetto.

In other entries, Grove's first *Dictionary* offers more detail on the current alto or counter-tenor. For instance, in the entry for 'Tenor' we read that 'The counter-tenor, or natural male alto, is a highly developed falsetto, whose so-called chest voice is, in most cases, a limited bass.'[66] Elsewhere, opinion claws its way over information, as in the entry for 'Falsetto', where we find this early description of what would become known as the 'Anglican hoot': 'The male counter-tenor, or alto voice, is almost entirely falsetto, and is generally accompanied by an imperfect pronunciation, the vowels usually partaking more or less of the quality of the Italian *u* or English *oo*, on which the falsetto seems to be most easily producible.'[67] From the entry on 'Voices', we learn about 'the peculiar form of Voice now called the Counter-Tenor; an unnatural register which still holds its ground in English Cathedrals, with a pertinacity which leads to the lamentable neglect, if not the absolute exclusion, of one of the most beautiful Voices in existence – the true Boy Contralto.'[68] In the same entry we find a similar lament for the way female contraltos are obstructed by male altos in some choirs: 'Happily

[63] Grove (ed.), *Dictionary of Music and Musicians*, vol. 1, pp. 57–8.

[64] Prendergast, 'The Man's Alto in English Music', p. 331.

[65] Prendergast, 'The Man's Alto in English Music', p. 332.

[66] Grove (ed.), *Dictionary of Music and Musicians*, vol. 4, p. 87.

[67] Grove (ed.), *Dictionary of Music and Musicians*, vol. 1, pp. 501–2.

[68] Grove (ed.), *Dictionary of Music and Musicians*, vol. 4 p. 334.

for Art, the value of the female Contralto is now no less freely recognised in England than in other countries; and it is only in Cathedral Choirs, and Choral Societies connected with them, that the Falsetto Counter-Tenor safely holds its ground.' The diminishing role of the male alto in nineteenth-century English secular music is well documented by Peter Giles in *The Counter Tenor*. A single letter to the *Musical Times* will suffice to highlight the trend:

> May I crave a space in your valuable paper to protest against the gradual disuse of the 'alto' voice in our leading Choral Societies? It is, I think, a very great mistake to do away with altos and substitute contraltos in oratorio music, at all events. Curiously enough, at one of our most celebrated choirs this is being gradually done, I am informed, through the conductor holding the opinion of ladies' superiority, while he himself is an alto, and has had several relatives in the profession with that voice.[69]

Aside for their championing of the female alto, the contributors to early editions of Grove's *Dictionary* showed a clear preference for the male modal voice. This betrays the influence of the younger Garcia (by this time living and teaching in London) and his school. This influence is never more obvious than when the *Dictionary* disagrees with Garcia about his idiosyncratic definition of falsetto: 'It is perhaps somewhat bold to combat the opinion of this eminent man, [Garcia] but falsetto (a word in general use in Italy as well as in England) seems very appropriate to that register which in the male seems to be scarcely natural, but to belong to another individual, and even to another sex.'[70]

Compared to the strenuous attempt at objectivity made in reference works of our own time (including *The New Grove*) the tone of these entries is disarmingly frank. Yet Hullah (one of the chief contributors of entries concerning the voice) was evidently tempering his true feelings when writing in the original Grove *Dictionary*. This much is clear from Hullah's memoirs, as published posthumously by his wife:

> By the limitation of church choirs to men and boys, one, and that perhaps the most beautiful, variety of the human voice is entirely excluded from them – the contralto, for which is substituted the male counter-tenor, which in most cases must be regarded rather as an anomalous, artificial mode of utterance than as a voice in the proper sense of the word. It is singular that the use of this mode of utterance or production, the very name of which, falsetto, is a reproach, and the result of which is a quality of sound which, if not exactly effeminate, is certainly epicene, should be confined to a people so

---

[69] William S. Anderson, 'The Alto Voice', *The Musical Times and Singing Class Circular* 25, no. 496 (1884), pp. 360–1.

[70] Grove (ed.), *Dictionary of Music and Musicians*, vol. 4 p. 337.

justly priding itself on manliness of character and simplicity as the English. The falsetto, or third register, is of course not unknown in Italy, France, and Germany, but it has been regarded always as an adjunct to, and an occasional resource from the first or second registers, even by singers – the late Rubini, for instance, who had it in the highest perfection and under the most perfect control. The very existence of the male counter-tenor is ignored by continental musicians [...][71]

Not since the Middle Ages, and the prohibitions of the exclusively male monastic communities, have we met quite such an overt, gender-based hostility to falsetto. Hullah is the only one to state it so explicitly, but running through these nineteenth-century descriptions is the persistent implication that falsetto was an affront to the manly character of the English. Not surprisingly, then, the low esteem in which the male alto was viewed by the musical establishment of the late nineteenth century is very much borne out by the withdrawal of the voice to the anonymity of the choir stalls. Even here, falsetto was hardly an object of pride. Neither John Bumpus nor Charles Abbot Stevens, in their histories of cathedral music, make any reference to the way the alto part was sung. At Peterborough Cathedral the choirmaster experimented with boy altos as a last resort, though he makes it clear that his preference was for adults.[72] A few miles away at Ely Cathedral the Precentor (reminding us that the grass is always greener on the other side) lamented that he had only male altos, asking:

Am I not right in maintaining that a perfect choir should consist of

FIRST TREBLES	TENORS
SECOND TREBLES	BASSES

well balanced as to numbers, and all singing with pure natural quality?[73]

Further down the musical ladder, in provincial parish churches, the situation was even more desperate. Mr. A. Isaac, choirmaster of a church in Liverpool, writes:

For the last twenty years I have been continuously engaged with male voice choirs [...] and, as you may readily guess, I have never yet had the good fortune to secure, for any length, the services of gentlemen who could sing falsetto effectively. I have had, therefore, to rely solely upon my boys for the alto part.

---

[71] Frances Hullah, *Life of John Hullah, LlD* (London, 1886), p. 71.

[72] Cf. Bernard G. Gilbert, *Voice Training Exercises for Boys* (London, *c.* 1900), pp. 102–3.

[73] Curwen, *The Boy's Voice*, p. 79.

From these examples, and the other opinions collated by John Curwen in *The Boy's Voice*, the message seems to be that the adult male alto (of whatever type) may be a nice idea, but is almost invariably an unpleasant reality. A rare positive endorsement of falsetto is voiced by J. Varley Roberts: 'nothing can replace the beautiful thin flute-like tone of the pure Alto, it brightens the entire quality of the tone of the choir.'[74]

For a view of the male alto away from the choir stall, we turn again to George Bernard Shaw. In 1889 a reader of Shaw's music column in *The Star* wrote to him in the hope that the eminent critic could settle a small wager. Shaw summarises the debate: 'The question at issue is whether alto parts are not frequently sung in our churches by men as well as by boys.' As an atheist, Shaw freely admits that he is 'hardly the man to settle such a point'. Not, of course, that he is actually deterred by his ignorance:

> Therefore, all I can say [...] is that adult male alto and countertenor singers, though no longer as common as they once were, are still to be heard in all directions singing the parts specially written for the kind of voice by the composers of the great English school: not the secondhand Handels and Mendelssohns of the past century and a half, but the writers of glees, madrigals, and motets and services which are the true English musical classics. Nowadays, however, since the opera and the concert platform offer golden opportunities to a tenor or a baritone, whereas an alto or countertenor is confined to the choir or the glee quartet all his life, a promising choir boy gets rid of his treble as soon as Nature permits him. The effect of this in diminishing the number of adult altos must be considerable.[75]

Shaw's reference to the 'glee quartet' offers a glimpse of another aspect of the falsettist's domain which, like the church choir, seldom gained public recognition. Unlike the Continental social music for men's voices, the glees of Sullivan and Hatton often have an alto line (going up to c'') as their highest part. As one writer commented at the time, the glee 'would be nothing without the man's alto [falsetto] voice'.[76] And Shaw offers a most unusual and touching testimony to the clandestine nature of the glee group. Shaw describes how:

> happening to be caught in a pelting shower in St Martin's Lane on a gloomy evening, I took refuge in the entry to a narrow court, where presently I was joined by three men [...] To my surprise, instead of beginning to talk horses, they began to talk music – pure vocal music [...] Finally one of them pulled out a pitchpipe; the three sang a chord; and away they went, *sotto voce*, but very prettily, into a three-part

[74] J. Varley Roberts, *A Treatise on a Practical Method of Training Choristers* (London, 1898), p. 12.

[75] Shaw, *Shaw's Music*, ed. Laurence, vol. 1, p. 830.

[76] Prendergast, 'The Man's Alto in English Music', pp. 331–4.

song, raising their voices a little when they found that the passers-by were too preoccupied by the deluge to notice them.[77]

Shaw's music criticism is full of uncannily prophetic observations. Despite being a passionate Wagnerian, he went out of his way to explore earlier music – sometimes quite literally, as in the case of the concerts held by Arnold Dolmetsch: it was at one of Dolmetsch's house-concerts in suburban Dulwich that Shaw heard a concert of sixteenth-century English music. Afterwards he wrote:

> The vocal music is still the main difficulty. The singers, with their heads full of modern 'effects', shew but a feeble sense of the accuracy of intonation and tenderness of expression required by the pure vocal harmonies of the old school [...] the only vocalist whom I felt inclined to congratulate was a countertenor, the peculiarity of whose voice had saved him from the lot of the drawing-room songster.[78]

Shaw realised that the falsetto voice was ill-suited to Romantic music. Further, he believed that the vocal style most appropriate for Romantic music was itself ill-suited to what (he suspected) were the wonders of early music. It would be forty years before Tippett and Deller began to convince the listening public of this, and in this sense, Dolmetsch's Dulwich counter-tenor was a significant herald of the modern counter-tenor revival. And yet, significantly perhaps, he has no name. Since Shaw was always particular in identifying his targets, we have to assume that this singer performed anonymously at the concert. Nor has his identity subsequently been uncovered. His anonymity, though, speaks volumes: whether in a lamp-lit choir stall, a darkened courtyard, or a suburban drawing room, the falsettist at the end of the nineteenth century is discernable, but only as a marginal, shadowy figure.

---

[77] Shaw, *Shaw's Music*, ed. Laurence, vol. 3, p. 102.

[78] Shaw, *Shaw's Music*, ed. Laurence, vol. 3, p. 128.

The Bearded Lady:
Gender Identity and Falsetto

I see we have the bearded lady with us tonight.
Orchestral leader overheard by Alfred Deller before a concert[1]

German lady: 'Meester Deller, you are absolute eunuch, ja?'
Alfred Deller: 'Umm ... I think you mean unique!'
German lady: 'Ja, ja. Eunuch.'
Audience member to Alfred Deller[2]

HOWEVER elegant the high male voice has sounded during its modern renaissance, it has often been heard in counterpoint with a quiet but discordant ground bass. The elements of this insidious lower part may vary – notes of homosexuality, effeminacy and castration can all be heard on occasion – but the repeated theme of sexual prejudice is always recognisable. In short, the accompaniment of grumbling voices avers that the male falsettist is not a true man.

In the early days of the falsetto revival the hostile undercurrent was at its strongest, and there is no doubt that Deller himself had more to contend with than his successors. As luck would have it, he was ideally placed to defy the contentious voices. Not only did Deller have a beard, and a speaking voice like any other man, but he was also happily married with children. Deller, then, had easy answers to the prejudice he met. But what of his successors? Although today there are no castrated counter-tenors there are, of course, openly gay ones, and some who might even be termed effeminate. There is, however, no evidence that the sexual makeup and orientation of counter-tenors is proportionally any different from that of the population as a whole. The sexual insinuations made against falsettists, then, are evidently a prejudice and nothing more.

Yet paradoxically, although no prejudice can ultimately be reasonable, neither is it likely to have been initiated without some cause. The reasons for tainting the falsettist's sexuality in modern times are worth us pausing to explore, chiefly because they are far from being historical constants.

[1] Cf. Hardwick and Hardwick, *Alfred Deller*.

[2] I am grateful to Mark Deller for his memory of this anecdote, and the following explanation: 'It has gone through various transformations in the telling of it over the years, but it did indeed originate with my Dad. It happened to him in the 60s in Germany (rather than France) which makes the verbal misunderstanding rather more relevant.'

In fact, for much of musical history there has been anything but a sexual prejudice against falsetto singing – and this casts an interesting light not just on the past, but on our own time too.

Bias against the 'womanly' singing of men is not, it should be said, an entirely new phenomenon. In Chapter 3 we examined the pronouncements of various clerics, and from St Ambrose in the fourth century, to Roger Bacon in the thirteenth, the charge of vocal effeminacy was a repeated one. This body of writers had an obvious (if unspoken) agenda: as celibate men in exclusively male communities, anything that smacked of a feminine ambience was considered potentially corrosive. When John of Salisbury remarks that womanly singing might 'arouse itching in the genitals' he reveals the ultimate concern of the monastic authorities.

Apart from isolated comments by men such as Lalande, these are the only examples of antipathy to effeminate singing by men we have encountered before the nineteenth century. The vast majority of commentators betray no prejudice whatsoever: to men such as Coryat and Tosi, effeminacy simply does not appear to be a concept they recognised. Why would it be? If men commonly sang in falsetto, what need was there to describe it with reference to the female voice – particularly when women's voices were heard so infrequently in public that they would have been a virtually meaningless point of reference? And in many other instances, from the eighth-century *mukhannath* of the Near East, to the castrati of the eighteenth century, we might observe not negative, but positive discrimination towards singers who were considered womanly or androgynous. Nowhere is this more apparent than the world of early opera, with its *en travesti* roles which, of course, utilised the castrato as the literal embodiment of sexual ambiguity. In a less extreme way, the tenor whose voice drifted upwards into a nebulous falsetto was appealing to similar sensibilities in his listeners.

Self-evidently, in order to display any sexual bias, one first needs a distinct sense of gender identity. To our post-Victorian age, gender identity might seem an inalienable truth, yet in many pre-nineteenth-century societies it was much less sharply etched. In Ancient Greece and Rome sexual identities and relations were blurred. Not surprisingly, Renaissance Italy followed this model. The scientific slant of post-Enlightenment Europe, though, took another view: Michel Foucault asserts that modern medicine, in particular, 'created an entire organic, functional, or mental pathology arising out of "incomplete" sexual practices [...] and undertook to manage them'.[3] The invention of the terms homosexual and heterosexual (which did not exist before 1870) can be seen as part of a movement towards defining one's self through gender and sexual orientation. Increasingly, whilst violations of matrimonial law were tacitly accepted (hence the continued prestige of the Don Juan character), violations of the natural function of

[3] Michel Foucault, *The History of Sexuality*, trans. Robert Hurley, vol. 1: *An Introduction* (New York, 1978), p. 41.

sex were not. Society increasingly required of both sexes that they conform more to distinct gender stereotypes. For men, this meant strength and vigour.

The significance of this development for vocal types was profound. In the previous chapter, for the first time since we read Cistercian edicts of the twelfth century, we encountered hostility to falsetto couched in terms of gender. In substance, the barbs that William Penphraze received from the critic of the *Royal Cornwall Gazette* differ little from those that Deller later withstood: sexual prejudice is common to both. Yet whereas Deller's detractors at least dressed their darts with a hint of humour, with the Truro critic, let alone John Hullah in the first *Grove*, the charge of effeminacy was no laughing matter. To them, falsetto was an affront. There is one other obvious difference between the cases of Penphraze and Deller. Not only did Penphraze fade into obscurity, but his voice type vanished – or at least withdrew to a closeted existence in the cathedral choir stall. Deller and his followers, however, triumphed. Why the difference in outcome? Deller may well have been a much greater singer, but there are also other likely reasons, primarily concerned with repertoire and changing aesthetics.

The staple fair of Penphraze would have been the music of his own time. The naturalistic and subjective nature of the Romantic aesthetic left little room for a voice which was, by definition, at one stage removed from the nature of the singer. Perhaps this explains why, of all the areas of 'old' music which have been appropriated or reappropriated by falsettists in recent years, the nineteenth-century art song has remained largely off-limits. In contrast to Penphraze, the core of Deller's solo repertoire was pre-nineteenth-century music. Whether or not specific types of music Deller sang had been composed with the falsetto voice in mind, their underlying aesthetics nonetheless allowed for a greater distance between object (the music and its text) and subject (the performer). The early music revival took root in the mid-twentieth century, at precisely the same time that the Modernist movement was flowering. The extent to which the two movements were entwined need not concern us here. All we need to note is that, as in early music, in Modernism there existed a similar distancing (in this case between the individual and previously sacrosanct authorities, such as religion and reason). Just as Stravinsky preferred cleaner-sounding wind instruments to indulgent violins during his Neo-Classical period, so Tippett was looking for an anti-Romantic vocal timbre. Deller himself may not have been an avowed Modernist, but he certainly owed much to the movement – in particular Tippett, who 'discovered' him, and Britten, who wrote for him.

Aside from their aesthetic points of reference, Tippett and Britten shared one other thing in common, in that they were both homosexual. We cannot gauge the extent to which this may have encouraged them to feel *simpatico* towards Deller's voice. What we can say, however, is that the falsetto voice was seen by the wider public to be part of a gradual breaking up of rigid gender identities. This sexual revolution was the other significant movement which coincided with the falsetto revival. In America, the high-profile research of Alfred Kinsey revealed that gender identity was not nearly as distinct as our received nineteenth-century values suggested. In particular, Kinsey 'reported' that nearly 50 percent of men had reacted sexually to members of both sexes in their adult lives. Kinsey's methodology may have been flawed (although subsequent, more scientifically sampled research produced similar results) but at the time this was not known, and his findings were seized upon by those who did not wish to conform to the straitened sexuality of the Victorians. Yet for every man who was emancipated by the notion that gender identity and sexual attraction were not matters of black and white, right and wrong, there were those who felt uncomfortable with (or threatened by) such a *laissez-faire* attitude. For whatever reasons, these conservatives preferred the proscriptions with which they had grown up. Amongst their number we may count the orchestral leader who sneeringly referred to Deller as 'the bearded lady'.

CHAPTER 8

The Early Twentieth Century

AT this point in our history, a very revealing light begins to search out our subject. Until now, in assessing how men sang high, we have been largely dependent on the pen (a notoriously subjective tool, as every writer must acknowledge). The way music was written, or the way music and its performers were written about, have been our staple. Now, in addition to the pen, we have a more objective tool of communication – the microphone. We should not fool ourselves that the microphone is absolutely objective, though: as we shall see, even its most accurate results still leave room for interpretation. Nevertheless, the start of the twentieth century marks an obvious break in any history of vocal performance practice. Not because there were any radical developments in the way that men sang, or the spirit in which they were heard, but because the tools of the history itself suddenly changed.

Moreschi and the Microphone

AS luck would have it, the dawn of the recorded age marginally preceded the twilight of the castrati. Much has already been written about Alessandro Moreschi, the one castrato whose voice was captured by the microphone.[1] It was Pope Pius X who was responsible for ending the practice of castrato singers in the Catholic church. In a 1903 *motu proprio* concerning sacred music, Pius made the following decree:

> On the same principle it follows that singers in church have a real liturgical office, and that therefore women, being incapable of exercising such office, cannot be admitted to form part of the choir. Whenever, then, it is desired to employ the high voices of sopranos and contraltos, these parts must be taken by boys, according to the most ancient usage of the Church.[2]

Though not banning them specifically, with the clause that 'these parts must be taken by boys' the castrati's days were effectively numbered. In practice, this decree applied only to the Cappella Sistina – the last remaining choir

---

[1] For those wanting his full story, see: Nicholas Clapton, *Moreschi: The Last Castrato* (London, 2004).

[2] 'Dal medesimo principio segue che i cantori hanno in chiesa vero officio liturgico e che però le donne, essendo incapaci di tale officio, non possono essere ammesse a far parte del Coro o della cappella musicale. Se dunque si vogliono adoperare le voci acute dei soprani e contralti, queste dovranno essere sostenute dai fanciulli, secondo l'uso antichissimo della Chiesa.': Pope Pius X, 'Motu proprio: Tra le Sollecitudini', 22 November 1903, chap. 5, para. 13.

to employ castrati. However, singers already in the choir, such as Moreschi, had life tenure.

It is perhaps unfortunate that Moreschi's voice alone represents the lost vocal skills of the castrati, because the late Romantic idiom in which he sang can only be distantly related to the art of Tosi and his acolytes. It is unfortunate for Moreschi, too, that his voice was captured by rudimentary equipment, in single takes, and in an unhelpful acoustic. Yet we should be careful not to patronise Moreschi by making too many allowances. He was not, as some have said, an old man at the time of the 1902 and 1904 recordings: although by then he had been a member of the Cappella Sistina for twenty years, Moreschi was only in his mid-forties – an age when many singers are in their prime. Nor was he a minor singer. When he joined the Cappella Sistina, 'L'Angelo di Roma' (as Moreschi was already known) was admitted as the leading soprano – ahead of five castrati who were already in post. In 1900 he sang as soloist at the funeral of Umberto I – at the express request of the Italian royal family. The esteem in which Moreschi was held can be directly gauged by the spontaneous 'bravos' with which his Sistine colleagues touchingly greet the end of his recording of *Ideale* by Tosi.

Moreschi's style is encapsulated in one contemporary listener's glowing tribute: 'He has a tear in each note and a sigh in each breath.'[3] As such, Moreschi's performing style is at one with contemporary recordings by other Italian singers such as Caruso. Yet, whilst today Caruso's mannerisms garner plaudits rather than stricture, Moreschi's are commonly ridiculed. Why should this be so? In part, it is because Caruso's repertoire and style are part of a living tradition: we hear an echo of Caruso in every modern Italianate tenor, and so remain comfortable when we hear the 'original'. As for Moreschi, he has no vocal progeny. Simply because they have appropriated much of the earlier castrato repertoire, modern counter-tenors are seen to be Moreschi's closest relatives, yet self-evidently this bond is more imagined than real. A recent compilation CD entitled *From Castrato to Countertenor* (which includes Moreschi) highlights this perceived relationship, at the same time suggesting that those who encounter Moreschi's singing often do so in the context of the modern counter-tenor voice. Since today's counter-tenors sing an entirely different repertoire from Moreschi, and with a radically different style, the poor castrato's voice is commonly viewed in an entirely misleading context. And when an esteemed modern critic dismisses Moreschi as 'making a noise which is frankly beyond nature' we are reminded that his sexual status hardly endears his singing to those with present-day sensibilities.[4] (The widespread derision of Moreschi amongst the early music community, incidentally,

[3] Anna Lillie de Hegermann-Lindencrone, *The Sunny Side of Diplomatic Life* (New York, 1914), pp. 118–19.

[4] Fiona Maddocks, *The Observer*, Sunday 25 January 2009.

lends ammunition to the argument that an interest in period performance is often a representation of Modernist taste rather than a product of genuine historical curiosity: even when presented with incontrovertible evidence of a historic performing style, there are those whose inclination is to dismiss it – if that style does not tally with the clean lines of our own times. Far from being natural embracers of distant aesthetics, as they imagine, such listeners may in truth be cultural absolutists. The cultural relativist, on the other hand, hearing Moreschi in the context of Caruso, is surely more likely to regard his portamenti and sobs as a stylistic commonplace, and not necessarily a mark of inferior singing.) Nicholas Clapton, in a detailed analysis of Moreschi's recordings, suggests that the singing (though not without blemish) is technically assured, and is always placed at the service of an expressive goal. When we stand Moreschi in an accurate historical context, he emerges as a serious artist: when we do not, he will always be found wanting. In short, Moreschi cannot be blamed for not being Farinelli or, indeed, Andreas Scholl.

The Counter-Tenor in America

MORESCHI was recorded in Rome by two Americans, Fred Gaisberg and W. Sinkler Darby. Since the microphone was an American invention, it is perhaps no coincidence that, as recorded sound enters this narrative, so too does the American counter-tenor. Although the term had little practical application in America beforehand, in the early decades of the twentieth century a number of recordings appeared of singers billed as counter-tenors. Yet these 'counter-tenors' bore no relation to English singers described in the same way at that time. Indeed, Shaw might have had the appellation 'counter-tenor' in mind when (anecdotally) he quipped that 'England and America are two nations divided by a common language', because for much of the twentieth century unnecessary confusion was caused by the dual meanings of this single term.

Before we come to the evidence provided by recordings of American counter-tenors, though, it is worth backtracking to look at some written definitions. These reveal that, although the theory of four-part harmony was adopted by early American composers, the practice of how these parts were to be realised (if they were to be sung at all) evidently presented a problem. This much is implied by the title page of Amos Bull's 1795 psalm collection *The Responsary* – 'a collection of church musick. Set with second trebles, instead of counters'. In Catholic Europe this would suggest that suitable men could not be found to sing the part, but to the Puritan Americans men were not the only possible answer. In Ananias Davisson's 1817 *Kentucky Harmony* we are told that 'The bass stave is assigned to the gravest voices of men, and the tenor to the highest. The counter to the lowest voices of the Ladies, and the treble to the highest of Ladies' voices.' Yet even women may not always have produced a satisfactory answer. Indeed, Nathaniel Gould's 1853 account of American church music, written late in life and as much autobiography as history, suggests that the alto part was an insurmountable problem:

> The alto – or counter, as it was then called – had a place on the third staff, and had a clef peculiar to that part, called the C clef, formed thus: this part was originally designed for boys, being written an octave higher on the staff than it is at the present day. It was rarely sung by female voices; and, when attempted, was usually sung at the top of their voices, just as written. It was therefore too shrill to be pleasant, and was soon abandoned. Boys could seldom be found who had skill enough to lead the part, and but few gentlemen could reach the high notes; so the consequence was that this part was seldom sung, although an important one in the harmony.[5]

The reasons that Gould offers may not bear close scrutiny, but his conclusion was probably based on practical experience. From the middle of the nineteenth century onwards, when the purely falsetto alto was starting to gain currency in England, a disparity arose between English and American church practices. In 1889 one commentator noted that 'The English alto, or counter tenor, as sung by men, if given with purity and taste, has a more dignified effect, and is especially suitable for ecclesiastical music. That, as yet, is a rare voice in America.'[6] For the next century, the situation would change little.

Of all the texts that tell us about the American counter-tenor before recordings, William Lines Hubbard's 1908 *American History and Encyclopedia of Music* is perhaps the most seminal. Like *Grove* in England, Hubbard and his fellow contributors regarded the unknown past less on its own terms than as a way of explaining the known present. There is a tendency, then, for writers to hypothesise, and one often senses that a historical observation is little more than a wishful projection back in time. In one other respect this history needs to be treated with some caution: Hubbard had spent a number of years in Europe before compiling his history, and his views occasionally reflect his wishes for, rather than the reality of, American music. Not surprisingly, then, Hubbard's work contains seemingly contradictory entries, and the references to the counter-tenor are no exception. At times entries imply that the counter-tenor is a falsetto voice, but closer scrutiny reveals that these references are either to a presumed historical practice, or to contemporary practice in England. When current American practice is being spoken of, in Hubbard's encyclopaedia a consensus emerges that the counter-tenor is more often primarily a modal rather than a falsetto voice:

---

[5] Nathaniel Gould, *Church Music in America* (Boston, 1853), p. 94.
[6] W. S. B. Mathews, *A Hundred Years of Music in America* (Chicago, 1889), p. 264.

> The high tenor, counter-tenor. This part between the tenor and the modern contralto was the original alto.[7]

> Alto at first signified the highest male part, sung by high tenor (counter-tenor) voices. Later boys took the part, and now for many years it has been sung by women with low voices (contraltos).[8]

> The most pronounced drawback [in American church choirs] has been the absence of suitable altos and the scarcity of competent choirmasters. In the English choirs the alto part usually is strengthened by men's voices trained to sing falsetto, and the result is most gratifying; but in this country we seem to have no such voices.[9]

Historically, it has always been common for American linguistic usages to preserve much earlier English meanings, and it appears that until quite recently the term counter-tenor was no exception. So, whilst Hubbard's American counter-tenor (or alto) might have little in common with his contemporaries singing the same part in England, he would have an obvious kinship with English (and European) counter-tenors of previous centuries.

A similarly disparate view of what constituted the American counter-tenor can be found in a monograph written by the choirmaster of an Episcopalian church in New York, G. Edward Stubbs.

> There are two varieties of the counter-tenor voice. First, there is a species of high, light tenor, ranging from *a* to *d"*. This voice has the following characteristics. The chest and falsetto tones are readily joined, and they are often so blended by nature that it is impossible to detect a difference of register in any part of the vocal range. The upper tones are easily reached, are entirely free from strain, and are full and rich. The lower tones, although less powerful and sonorous than in the ordinary tenor, are remarkably pure and free from coarseness. A distinguishing mark of this voice is that the conversational and the singing tones correspond, the former being pitched near the middle of the range.

> Second, there is the so-called 'falsetto alto,' in which the falsetto register is distinctly separated from the chest register; in which there is a break which can only be eradicated by careful training in early adult life; and in which the colloquial and the singing tones do not correspond. The first class of voice is the better of the two. But even when round and resonant, possessing all the attributes generally looked for in the well cultivated voice, it is often criticised as being 'unnatural,' especially if the range is of unusual extent. [...]

---

[7] William Lines Hubbard, *The American History and Encyclopedia of Music* (Toledo, OH, 1908), vol. 10, p. 28.

[8] Hubbard, *American History and Encyclopedia*, vol. 10, p. 27.

[9] Hubbard, *American History and Encyclopedia*, vol. 10, p. 70.

The comparative scarcity of the real counter-tenor, and the frequency with which the falsetto alto is met with, will always be considered a practical argument in favor of the latter. The chief characteristics of this second voice are the marked break between the registers, and the lack of correspondence between the speaking and the singing tones.

The first variety of counter-tenor may be called a one-register voice, and the second a two-register voice.[10]

For all that Stubbs states a clear preference for the 'high, light tenor' as representing the 'real counter-tenor', he goes on to offer pragmatic advice to fellow choirmasters about how they can identify and train the 'falsetto alto'. Throughout, Stubbs is unabashed in his debt to the European, and particularly the English Anglican tradition. Bearing in mind the context in which he is writing, Stubbs offers a clear analysis and sound practical advice. Yet had he cast his net beyond the choir stall, he would have found evidence of falsettists and modal counter-tenors (if not falsettist counter-tenors) in American music.

Perhaps confusingly, although the early twentieth-century American counter-tenor was primarily (or at least ideally) a modal singer, there was a long national tradition of falsettists appearing in public. In New Orleans during the 1830s a black singer known as 'Old Corn Meal' appeared in public. 'He sings in a manner as perfectly novel as it is inimitable', Sheridan wrote in his journal, 'beginning in a deep bass & at every other 3 or 4 words of his song, jumping into a falsetto of power'.[11] In 1854 an American naval lieutenant, travelling up the coast of Mexico to California, spent a happy hour relaxing ashore, 'While the negro minstrels charmed us with falsetto ballads or highly complicated jigs'.[12] From the 1860s onwards the Georgia Minstrels – a genuine negro group which spawned many imitators – toured America and played to vast audiences: their act incorporated the falsetto singing (partly as female impersonator) of T. Drewette.[13] This tradition of falsetto as part of minstrel acts was to continue in the twentieth century. However, although some of the early American counter-tenors sang in minstrel troupes, these particular singers were not falsettists.

Richard Jose, the earliest singer to be dubbed 'counter-tenor' on record, is a case in point. Jose was born in 1862 in Cornwall, England. He emigrated to Nevada as a teenager, first performing as a young man

[10] G. Edward Stubbs, *The Adult Male Alto or Counter-Tenor Voice* (New York, 1908), pp. 14–15 and 25.

[11] Francis C. Sheridan, *Galveston Island; or, a Few Months off the Coast of Texas: the Journal of Francis C. Sheridan, 1839–1840*, ed. Willis W. Pratt (Austin, 1954), pp. 93–4.

[12] Henry Augustus Wise, *Los Gringos* (New York, 1854), p. 316.

[13] Bernard L. Peterson, *Profiles of African American Stage Performers and Theatre People, 1816–1960* (Westport, CT, 2001), p. 293.

in saloons, and then across America in minstrel groups. Jose's growing fame helped popularise dozens of sentimental ballads, and between 1903 and 1906 he recorded for the Victor Talking Machine Company. His most famous recording, 'Silver Threads Among the Gold', reveals a modal voice, admittedly with a magnificent upper range, but never outside the orbit of a high tenor. Why, we might ask, did Jose bill himself as a counter-tenor and not a tenor? It is tempting to see Jose's adoption of 'counter-tenor' as being no more than an affectation: this was, after all, the same singer who later adopted the spelling José to hint at an exotic Hispanic heritage. But as we have seen, in American terminology of the time, the term 'counter-tenor' was used to describe the high tenor voice. Jose's use of the practically redundant term was, in this sense, no more an affectation than Tippett and Deller's appropriation of it forty years later. Following Jose's lead, a succession of American vocalists (whom we would simply think of as high lyric tenors) achieved fame as counter-tenors. Voice-type and voice-name aside, Richard Jose, Will Oakland, Manuel Romain and Frank Coombs also shared a repertoire of sentimental ballads, which gained them huge popularity.

At the same time that the modal 'counter-tenor' was gaining recognition in America, so too was the falsetto 'alto', albeit to a lesser extent. A Philadelphia choirmaster and composer, N. Lindsay Norden, commented in 1917 that 'In England, and generally in this country also, the alto part of a boy choir is sung by men who sing above the 'crack' in their voices.' (We need to note here that the term 'boy choir' here denotes not a choir of boys only, but one with boys on the top line and adult men below.) This seems to mark a change from the practices described by Mathews and Hubbard, quoted above. Yet Norden hardly greeted the development with any warmth:

> The sound produced is unnatural, atrocious, inhuman; it is but an unmusical hoot and often false in intonation [...] In other words, there is no alto part possible in a boy choir [...] It is a most exasperating experience to hear the awful squawk of the male altos in the boy choirs in our churches. The tone does not combine with the other three parts in producing a balanced ensemble, but – in all its horror – shines through the combined efforts of the other three parts of the choir. It seems as though it could not be subdued, for one male alto will well nigh ruin the work of a chorus of forty voices [...] Further, the difficulty of obtaining 'male altos' (who 'sing' falsetto), and the expense of remunerating such persons, results in a choir being able to possess only a very limited number of altos – perhaps only two or three.[14]

---

[14] N. Lindsay Norden, 'The Boy Choir Fad', *The Musical Quarterly* 3(2) (1917), pp. 189–97, at p. 195.

So the falsettists Norden knew in American churches, where all-male choirs were maintained, were evidently both rare and poor. Even so, the level of his vitriol suggests that more than just a musical agenda was in play. What this agenda might be is evident from a passage Norden quotes from a 'splendid book' by his compatriot Edmund Simon Lorenz. Writing of his European travels, probably around 1880, Lorenz comments:

> I remember well my admiration of the portly, heavy moustached, handsome man I saw in the singers' gallery of the Choir Chapel at St Peter's in Rome. I took it for granted that this was the basso-profundo of the choir. Later, a florid, semi-operatic solo, with a rumititum accompaniment was sung by a soprano voice of clear, but peculiar timbre, and looking up, I was amazed to see that the soprano soloist was my magnificent Adonis. Anything more incongruous it has never been my fortune to see and hear, unless it was the rendering of Root's 'Under the Palms' at the leading Methodist church of York, England, where all the alto solos were sung by men, who used the falsetto register. To one accustomed to the prominent part played in American church music by female voices, the whole arrangement was distressingly absurd, unnatural, and monstrous in spite of the knowledge of its theological and historical basis.[15]

These are intriguing words, which briefly draw us back to Europe. Who was Lorenz hearing in Rome? The mention of 'rumititum accompaniment' confirms that this was indeed the Cappella Giulia of St Peter's and not the Cappella Sistina (who still sang without instruments). Although the castrati in the Sistine Choir did occasionally 'guest' in the other Papal choirs, there is one obvious reason why the singer Lorenz heard was not one of them: the facial hair of the 'soprano voice of clear, but peculiar timbre' tells us that this could not have been a castrato at all. And this, in turn, points to the existence of falsetto sopranos in the Vatican for the first time in three hundred years. Whatever revival they enjoyed, though, was to be short lived: even in the Sistine choir, boys were set to take over the soprano line. Lorenz's reminiscence of what he heard in Europe tells us that, in contexts as far apart as Roman Catholic Italy and nonconformist England, the falsettist had a role to play. Lorenz and Norden together represent the progressive face of American church music in the early twentieth century.

Before telling us how 'absurd' he finds the falsetto voice, Norden states his agenda explicitly:

> The boy choir fad has grown so alarmingly that the choral ideals of the American church will degenerate unless a decisive check is firmly put upon this disastrous evil in church music [...] In

---

[15] Edmund Simon Lorenz, *Practical Church Music: A Discussion of Purposes, Methods and Plans* (New York, 1909), p. 247.

an age as rationalistic as ours, tradition should not have much consideration.[16]

Any envy of the English alto sound, which we might have sensed in the culturally apologetic comments of Mathews and Hubbard, has now been replaced by a rather superior disdain.

The all-male approach which Norden so despises is well represented by a choirmaster in Massachusetts, who describes his policy towards the 'difficulty of the alto part' as:

> (1) choosing suitable 'graduates' of the treble section; (2) training them in all honesty for what one wants; (3) releasing gladly those who show unusual tenor or bass possibilities; and (4) finally arriving at an adequate (and more) alto section.

Yet he too has a non-musical agenda – one rather less progressive than Norden's: 'This solution not only answers pictorially and ecclesiastically, but preserves for him the enjoyment of The Ladies (God bless them!) in the sphere they were meant to adorn, *i.e.* the social.'[17] With advocates like this, one might ask whether the American male falsettist of the time ever needed enemies.

Although in American usage the term 'counter-tenor' had always referred to a high modal voice, on the verge of the Second World War we find a fascinating signal of change. William J. Finn, a Boston priest and renowned choir-trainer, writes extensively about the counter-tenor and male alto voices. Whereas previous American writers had increasingly classified the former as modal and the latter as falsetto, Finn regards both as falsetto voices. Although Finn felt himself liturgically bound to do the best he could with these male falsettists, rather than introduce 'bob-haired mezzo cantatrices', he is no fan of them, as the following (unwittingly pertinent) comment makes plain:

> I have often thought, while rehearsing various personnels in the great music of the Polyphonic period, that if Palestrina, Vittoria, Tallis, Byrd, Aichinger, etc., had at their disposal only the contraband, spurious, anaemic intonations, by which even the utterances of the least undesirable male altos must be described, the marvellously balanced and perfectly co-ordinated independent lines of their rich polyphonies probably would not have been conceived.[18]

What perhaps Finn sensed (but could hardly have known) was that the great Renaissance composers – and Gregor Aichinger – *did not* conceive their music with 'anaemic' male altos in mind, but modal-voiced singers.

[16] Norden, 'The Boy Choir Fad', pp. 189 and 192.

[17] G. C. Phelps, 'The Problem of the Alto Part', *The Musical Times* 68, no. 1011 (1927), p. 450.

[18] Finn, *Choral Technique*, p. 147.

The real novelty of Finn's words on the alto part, though, is a distinction he makes between the '*made* falsetto alto' and the '*conserved* falsetto' of the counter-tenor.[19] Elsewhere he explains this distinction:

> Neither the male-alto nor the counter tenor is a natural voice: both are made, the former by introducing elements foreign to the natural estate of a man's settled voice, the latter by the preservation of certain soprano facilities during the changing period.[20]

Coincidentally, this process for becoming a 'counter-tenor' was exactly that being followed across the Atlantic by a young Alfred Deller. Whilst the basis of Finn's distinction never became widely accepted, at least his definition of the counter-tenor as a falsetto voice would become standard – even in America.

England in the Age before Deller

AMERICAN commentators often present their views on the falsetto alto with reference to the English model. Now, then, we need to examine the state of the English falsettist at the start of the recorded age. As we have seen, by the end of the nineteenth century the falsetto alto had retreated into a shell of virtual anonymity. It would be reasonable, looking forward to Tippett's 'discovery' of the voice forty years later, to assume that in the intervening years falsetto singing must have withdrawn even further. This is not quite the case. Fascinatingly, during those years at least one English falsetto 'counter-tenor' achieved a contemporary public recognition which even Deller would barely match.

John Hatherley Clarke was born in 1885, and as a young man was appointed first to an alto lay-clerkship at Westminster Abbey, and later the Chapel Royal. As a soloist on the classical stage, by the time of his retirement in 1957 he had sung the alto part in Bach's *St John Passion* more than a hundred times. Yet this was not Hatherley Clarke's real claim to fame. A Pathétone Weekly (cinemagazine) clip from 1937 shows Hatherley Clarke as part of what Tommy Handley, the presenter, refers to as the 'famous' Gresham Singers, performing a barbershop arrangement of the song *John Peel*.[21] As well as touring extensively, during the 1920s the Gresham Singers recorded for the prestigious label His Master's Voice. Their repertoire ranged from madrigals, through the glee repertoire, to folk-song arrangements. Yet before this Hatherley Clarke also made a number of records, on which we might note that he was termed 'counter-tenor', as a solo artist. Here the repertoire – of songs such as *Hills of Ben Lomond* and *Mollie Darling* – is even lighter. Though less Italianate, Hatherley Clarke's

[19] Finn, *Choral Technique*, p. 183.

[20] Finn, *Choral Technique*, p. 127.

[21] Avaliable online through <www.britishpathe.com> [accessed 6 April 2014].

style has more in common with Moreschi's than with that of a modern counter-tenor: his falsetto is rounded, with a gentle but constant vibrato and subtle portamento. On these recordings the singer is most often accompanied by orchestra, rather than just piano, and this is significant, because along with the prestige of the record labels and the worldwide sales of the discs, it tells us that these were far from being low-budget, curiosity items.[22]

Nor was Hatherley Clarke the only English falsettist to achieve fame in this repertory during the first half of the century. Charles Hawkins, a low falsettist with a contralto-like tone, was also billed on solo recordings as a 'counter-tenor'. Another London falsettist, Ben Millett, was referred to on recordings as an 'alto vocalist'. And in the first recording of Constant Lambert's *Rio Grande*, Albert Walter Whitehead sang the alto part under the composer's baton. Most intriguing, however, is the case of Frank Colman. Or is this Frank Ivallo? A singer called Frank Colman recorded for Decca in 1932, but no other information about him seems to exist. Yet in the same year a singer with an uncannily similar voice, called Frank Ivallo, appeared on Pathé Pictorial. Introduced as 'the man with a woman's voice', Ivallo sings *Still as the Night* by Carl Bohm, nonchalantly finishing on a soprano high *c'''*.

Historically, these pre-war singers are fascinating because they flatly contradict the traditionally held view that, prior to the discovery of Deller, the falsetto voice was lying in total obscurity. And, although there was a novelty element in the way the singers were presented (particularly Ivallo), this does not mean that they were treated as comedy items. Above all, their 'novelty' value should not blind us to their expressive and technical qualities. There is certainly nothing of the Anglican hoot to be found in them.

About 'Tiny' Winters, described in a *Gramophone* review as the 'five feet nothing bass player and falsetto vocalist of Lew Stone's band', a cautionary note needs to be added.[23] Five feet nothing he may have been, but falsetto vocalist he was not. Like so many singers of his stature, his highest notes were produced modally (although in fairness to the anonymous reviewer, the ease with which Winters reaches a tenor top *a'* is disconcerting).

What, though, of the English high male voice recorded in church? The evidence here is, inevitably, less clear, but church choirs were recorded in the early twentieth century, and these offer us some information. The two-dimensional nature of early recordings often means that in recordings of an SATB texture, just picking out the alto line becomes a taxing aural test in itself. Yet at least one recording, from 1927, with men's voices alone,

---

[22] Many of the singers mentioned here, English and American, can be heard on the CD *Chime Again, Beautiful Bells* (Opal 9848), which also contains excellent biographical notes by Peter Giles.

[23] *The Gramophone*, September 1936, p. 25.

offers a more revealing view of the male alto. In an anthem by Henry Loosemore, the altos of York Minster choir primarily sing in falsetto, but sound far from restrained. As with most of the recordings from this era which are discussed here, the altos sing in a way which simply would not be countenanced today – at least not in seventeenth-century music such as this. In particular, the portamento approach from beneath a note is used as an expressive gesture on certain key words. Whether we like them or not, these portamenti (along with a steady vibrato and a wide dynamic spectrum) are expressive gestures. And, according to the mythology that Tippett's discovery of Deller spawned, expressive gestures are precisely what early twentieth century English altos were incapable of producing.

There is certainly no shortage of written evidence that English altos of the pre-war period had their admirers. A correspondence in the *Musical Times* of 1919 begins with the query as to whether there is any 'legitimate reason' for the absence of altos in ballad concerts, 'since the alto voice can be just as capable of rendering certain kinds of songs with as much beauty and expression as other voices?'[24] In a subsequent issue there is a reply, which begins with an acknowledgement: 'That there is a prejudice against the male alto I will admit, and also must agree that in days gone by there has been ground for such prejudice.' Now, however, the writer claims that the demands of modern church music and ambitious cathedral organists have improved the quality of potential alto lay-clerks: 'the standard expected of the male alto has been considerably raised, with the consequence that there has been a great improvement both in range, beauty of tone, and musical ability in the type of man now coming forward.'[25] During the first half of the twentieth century the argument about the alto voice, and how best to staff the alto part in church, intermittently rumbles on in the pages of the *Musical Times*. It is clear that, outwith the cathedrals, good male altos were few and far between. Traditionalists clung to the hope of improving the quality and standing of male falsettists; others looked to boys or women as the answer. Sir Sidney Nicholson, whose passionate concern for the state of music in English parish churches led him to found the Royal Schools of Church Music in 1927, addressed the problem pragmatically:

> With regard to the alto part the case is somewhat different. It is often difficult to secure good men altos; boy altos need more training than can ordinarily be given them, and even at the best are not very satisfactory. But a good solution is often to be found in the employment of women for the alto part: if the voices chosen are not of the heavy contralto type, but are more in the nature of mezzo-soprano, a good blend can be secured which is very effective for chorus work. The main difficulty arises in 'Verses' with the alto at

[24] *The Musical Times* 60, no. 922 (1919), p. 697.
[25] *The Musical Times* 61, no. 924 (1920), p. 117.

the top, such as frequently occur in the older Services and anthems; these are all written for men altos or counter-tenors, and their effect is ruined if they are sung by women.[26]

The question of whether the alto and counter-tenor voices were one and the same thing, or different species, was one that would persist through much of the twentieth century. In 1905 W. H. Griffiths, a vocal pedagogue based in Liverpool, wrote:

> The counter tenor is from beginning to end a natural voice, possessing rich qualities and considerable power in the lower and upper thin registers. It is a rare voice, and consequently in great demand. Unlike the tenor voice, it possesses little or no value in the lower reaches, but has a peculiar silvery ring all its own from about *b* to *c"*.[27]

Later he adds that the 'natural counter-tenor [...] is not so brilliant as in the Falsetto-Alto voice'.[28]

The 'difficulty' associated with the alto part was addressed by John Hough in a 1937 paper delivered to the Musical Association in London.[29] Although the main thrust of Hough's paper was a historical survey of the counter-tenor and alto, for us the chief interest is perhaps the light it throws on how Hough and his audience viewed the contemporary situation. Like Griffiths thirty years earlier, Hough makes a clear distinction between counter-tenor and alto:

> In our time, by 'counter-tenor' is understood the rare *tenore altino* in Rimsky Korsakov's opera *The Golden Cockerel* – an unusually high voice whose worth is as inestimable as that of the *basso profondo*. A bass or baritone voice produces an alto falsetto whose working range corresponds to that of the counter-tenor.

In the discussion which followed his presentation, the chairman of the meeting, Sir Percy Buck, having clarified that Hough is making a distinction between counter-tenors (high tenors) and altos (falsettists), offered a personal observation:

> In all my experience, in Cathedral and Church Choirs, and elsewhere, I have only come across two singers who really had counter-tenor voices, *i.e.*, who had voices of tenor quality pitched exceptionally high. They could not sing anyhow else. All the other altos I have met (including myself) are really basses who have learnt an auxiliary form of production.

[26] Sidney Nicholson, *Quires and Places where they Sing* (London, 1932), p. 69.
[27] William Hargreaves Griffiths, *The Mixed Voice and the Registers ...* (London, 1904), p. 20.
[28] Griffiths, *The Mixed Voice*, p. 28.
[29] Hough, 'Historical Significance of the Counter-Tenor'.

Aside from being an organist (and evidently a make-do alto) Buck was an academic, and as the discussion proceeds he, and the young Purcell scholar Jack Westrup, started to circle in on two historical aspects of the counter-tenor part which they saw as problematic. Buck asked: 'why was so much of the vocal music of the sixteenth to the eighteenth centuries written in five parts with two altos? Any organist who has ever run a choir, especially a Cathedral organist, is always up against that.' And Westrup specifically brought up the problem of Purcell: 'One would not naturally assume from hearing modern counter-tenor voices that much of the music of Purcell's period was so virile in quality. Thoroughly manly songs were sung then by counter-tenors. What has happened to the voice in the meantime?' One senses that, for all the information which Hough had presented, fundamental questions remained unanswered. True, Hough had made reference to the likelihood of historically varying pitch in his paper, but neither he nor his audience yet had the detailed knowledge of this topic to understand its significance for the counter-tenor or alto. Other historical variables, such as human physiology and vocal technique, were not yet recognised as issues which may have helped answer Westrup's question. And within a decade, the appropriation of the term 'counter-tenor' by Tippett and Deller was to put Westrup's questions practically on hold until very recently.

For a first-hand comment on the voice before Deller, we can read the words of an executant 'alto singer or counter-tenor' (as he terms himself) in the 1920s. Frank Speakman, a highly esteemed lay-clerk at New College, Oxford, distanced himself from those who could merely sing the notes: 'Many men can so fix the larynx that it will produce a falsetto quality, but they cannot be classed as altos because of this.'[30] Speakman continues, with obvious reference to his own technique:

> The real alto voice is possessed by the man whose voice as a boy broke or changed at the age of adolescence, and settled down again at a pitch higher than is usually the case. This man speaks in the ordinary way and sings with a range of about two octaves: The break between upper and lower register is between C and F; in a well trained voice no change is noticeable.

Frustratingly, although we can assume that he means middle C, Speakman does not specify which 'F' he has in mind. Yet, since he describes the alto's 'settled' pitch as being higher than normal, and a dual-register voice, it seems probable that his break was in the fourth above middle C, not in the C–F an octave below. In other words, Speakman's 'well-trained' voice was a throw-back to an earlier technique, in which much of the range was taken modally, and between it and the falsetto, no break was perceptible.

---

[30] Frank Speakman, 'The Alto Voice', *The Musical Times*, 66, no. 986 (1925), p. 349.

A similar illustration comes from the north of England. When Brian Crosby became alto lay-clerk at Durham Cathedral in the late 1950s, he enquired of a colleague regarding the voice of his predecessor, James Cogan (who had been in post since 1914): 'He was a proper counter-tenor [...] It was not a 'big' voice, but he was like a tenor moved up a little – and at no point did he alter the method in which he produced his voice.'[31] Crosby also remembers Cogan as being a short man (which tallies with a memory Donald Hunt personally shared with me of the 'very small' altos (primarily modal-voice singers) in Leeds Parish Church Choir during the late 1950s). Crosby actually took lessons from Cogan, and sang alongside him when the older singer occasionally came back to sing with the Cathedral choir. Recalling this, Crosby now says that:

> James was a counter-tenor. Not of the type or timbre popularised by Alfred Deller after the war, but in the sense that his range was a 'translated upwards' version of a tenor's. He was proud of the fact that at the age of 70 he could still reach the F an 11th above middle C.[32]

The century which preceded them may have viewed James Cogan and Frank Speakman as representing a 'proper' counter-tenor voice. The following half-century, however, would take the counter-tenor in a quite different direction.

---

[31] Cf. Giles, *History and Technique of the Counter-Tenor*, p. 377.

[32] Personal correspondence with Brian Crosby.

The Angel's Voice:
Falsetto in Popular Music

> He had [an] extraordinary range that naturally included high notes, and then he had access to falsetto on top of that [...] This type of male singing voice is usually called counter tenor. Among counter tenors, Michael was the best in my opinion.
>
> angel_of_light[1]

A s we reach the mid-twentieth century in our history it has become increasingly clear that, far from having a fixed identity, over time the counter-tenor has taken on a number of different guises. Before we come to the present incarnation of the counter-tenor, we might pause to look outside our standard, Western classical context, into the world of popular music. Can we find relatives of the modern falsetto counter-tenor in other spheres and hemispheres, now and in the past?

Historically, this is virtually impossible. If the arguments for what constitutes a counter-tenor can be far from leak-proof in the history of Western classical music, in non-literate traditions they are often holed well below the water-line. For instance, the theory that Sir Francis Drake might have been a counter-tenor has been seriously floated on nothing more substantial than the evidence that he sang in his father's church, liked the sound of his own voice, and liked music.[2] Although not guilty of the original theory, as supportive evidence for Drake's being a counter-tenor Peter Giles cites a modern recording of an elderly sailor recalling a naval captain (around 1911) delivering orders in a high-pitched voice. So, Giles suggests that as a sailor Drake might have found that: 'The plangent carrying sound of the male high voice was useful in other ways. It seems that head voice was sometimes employed in the shouting of orders.'[3] But when we have finished diverting ourselves by imagining Drake in the foc'sle, chanting his orders in this way, we can perhaps reflect on the actual evidence that Drake was a counter-tenor (of any type), and conclude that the theory sinks like a stone.

It is one thing to look at a modern aural tradition and query its origins: Pakistani *qawwali*, South African *mbube*, Hawaiian *leo ki'eki'e* and Swiss yodelling might all pose questions about the historical

---

[1] 'Falsetto Question', discussion thread available online at <http://www.michaeljackson.com/us/node/471122> [accessed 6 April 2014].

[2] Fiske, *English Theatre Music*, p. 55; cf. Giles, *History and Technique of the Counter-Tenor*, p. 40.

[3] Giles, *History and Technique of the Counter-Tenor*, pp. 389–90.

and geographical use of falsetto. But, if we have no written music, no documented pitches, and no descriptions of vocal methods, at least before the recorded age our answers are unlikely to lead us to any confident conclusions.

In the last chapter we briefly met the 'black falsetto' of the American minstrels. Although the singing of Old Corn Meal is part of a non-literate tradition, his influence can be traced directly into the recorded age. In this respect, from the end of the nineteenth century onwards, enquiries into non-classical falsetto idioms become more fruitful. For instance, those looking for the origins of falsetto in American popular music often trace it through Jimmie Rodgers and his Blue Yodel songs of the 1920s and 30s. Earlier in his career Rodgers had also been associated with black minstrel singers, whose use of falsetto is commonly associated with African-American folk traditions.[4] Amish settlers, though, had brought to the American Mid-West a tradition of yodelling from Switzerland, and this might also have been an influence on the black minstrels. Jimmie Rodgers himself said (and it seems obvious when we listen to him sing a song such as *The Women Make a Fool Out of Me*) that it was the sound of a group of Swiss yodellers, on a tour of America, that persuaded him to try the effect in his songs. Yet the influences on Rodgers' yodelling may even not stop here. His wife later recalled that he 'bought phonograph records by the ton,' and 'toward the betterment of his own brand of music-making, he would play those records over and over.'[5] In other words, Rodgers was a musical magpie.

To an extent, every musician in history has been the sum of all they hear, but this is particularly significant now that we live in the recorded age. The fact that the microphone has been simultaneous with the musical shrinking of the globe means that the sum of all we hear is vast, compared to the parochial aural library which earlier generations had as reference. Tracing the myriad routes of falsetto singing through the twentieth century's popular music, then, becomes an absorbing maze. For example, the falsetto of the minstrels also took another route onwards from the one outlined above, to the early barbershop groups such as the Mills Brothers, the Ink Spots, and the Revellers. From America in the 1930s another thread passed to Europe and the Comedian Harmonists. Today, the King's Singers have the highest profile of a vast number of such groups. Not all of these feature falsetto singing constantly, but it is never far away. This is largely because the bottom-heavy nature of male barbershop, with its baritone lead and search for the mysterious overtones known as 'the angel's voice', mean that the lighter the highest part, the better.

---

[4] Lynn Abbott and Doug Seroff, 'America's Blue Yodel', *Musical Traditions* 11 (1993), pp. 2–11.

[5] Mrs Jimmie [Carrie] Rodgers, *My Husband Jimmie Rodgers* (Nashville, 1975), pp. 31 and 56–7.

Yet another route from the minstrel tradition led to the Soul Stirrers and the ecstatic falsetto of Rebert Harris, who 'introduced the soaring false soprano which was to become fundamental to gospel'.[6] From their gospel music developed soul, doo-wop and Motown, and with it the falsetto singing of Curtis Mayfield, Franki Valli and Michael Jackson. When we venture one move further down the path, into disco, pop and rock, the roster of singers who have used falsetto as part of their vocal style is vast. The best-known of these are worth listing, if only because it can be a shock to realise (so natural can it sound) that falsetto really is used by all of them: Eddie Kendricks (The Temptations), Russell Thompkins Jr. (Stylistics), Brian Wilson (The Beach Boys), Phillip Bailey (Earth, Wind, and Fire), Barry Gibb (The Bee-Gees), Sylvester, Lou Christie, Del Shannon, Roy Orbison, Jeff Lynne, Russell Mael (Sparks), Marvin Gaye, Mick Jagger (The Rolling Stones), Freddie Mercury and Roger Taylor (Queen), Morton Harkett (A-ha) Jimmy Somerville (Bronski Beat and The Communards), Don Henley (Eagles), Thom Yorke (Radiohead), Chris Martin (Coldplay).

Why has falsetto been so widespread in the recorded history of popular music? Cultural commentators, inevitably, focus on falsetto with regard to sexuality. With a nudge and a wink, people commonly refer to the (apparently) ironic use of falsetto in the Bee-Gees line *More than a Woman to me* from *Saturday Night Fever*. In this case, though, there is a far more prosaic reason. Arif Mardin, the producer of *Saturday Night Fever*, recalled that 'During the recording of the album I asked Barry to take his vocal up one octave. The poor man said, "If I take it up one octave I'm going to shout and it's going to be terrible." He softened up a little bit and that's how their falsetto was born.'[7] Freddie Mercury may have used falsetto as part of a deliberately androgynous musical persona, and an openly gay singer such as Jimmy Somerville might have been subconsciously drawn to the register because of its associations. This, though, hardly accounts for openly heterosexual singers whose hard-rock acts were anything but effete. In truth, though, popular singers probably find and use falsetto simply because it is there. Franki Valli, for instance, pointed out that: 'Falsetto was nothing new. Rhythm and blues music was doing it for years. I just developed my falsetto to make it fuller than anyone else's, and doing it on top, making it the lead, was what was different.'[8]

What none of these singers attest to, presumably because it is self-evident, is that the microphone and the recording process generally have

[6] Ian Hoare *et al.* (eds.), *The Soul Book* (London, 1975), p. 11; cf. Anne-Lise Francois, 'Fakin' It/Makin' It: Falsetto's Bid for Transcendance in 1970s Disco High', *Perspectives of New Music* 33(1/2) (1995), pp.442–57, at p. 452.

[7] Mehmet Dede, 'Jive Talkin' with Arif Mardin'; online at <http://www.lightmillennium.org/summer_fall_01/mdede_arifmardin.html> [accessed 6 April 2014].

[8] Stuart Miller, 'Biography: Francis Stephen Castelluccio, aka Frankie Valli'; online at <http://gilgweb.com/Bios/Valli_Bio.html> [accessed 6 April 2014].

been great facilitators of their falsetto. Crucially, with amplification being provided externally, their falsetto does not need to be projected with any great vocal power: this removes one obvious technical necessity – as resonant chapels and small chambers had for previous generations of singers. Similarly, because amplification can supply an artificially maintained volume, it allows a singer to reduce vocal pressure when negotiating a gear shift between their modal and falsetto voices: at one step, this bypasses the supreme technique which previous generations of singers had necessarily laboured to acquire. Finally, after the recording session, the mixing desk allows the voice to be synthetically altered.

If it does indeed come as a surprise to realise the extent of falsetto in modern popular music, perhaps this reflects on the way we listen to such music. Just as Handel (for instance) was concerned primarily with the emotional integrity of a singer, the listener to pop or rock tends to judge a singer more by their individuality of expression, than with the classical 'canary fancier's' marksheet of vocal attributes. Whilst Barry Gibb's falsetto was stratospherically saleable, we might note that the pop efforts of a classically trained falsettist such as Andreas Scholl have, in his own word, 'flopped'.

Often it is the alchemy of record production which masks how, vocally, singers achieve their effects. Freddie Mercury, for instance, is commonly cited as using falsetto in Queen's recordings (although, perhaps significantly, he hardly ever used this register in live performances). However, the eagle-eared have noticed that Roger Taylor's falsetto is often heard vocalising above Mercury's voice. Then we come to Michael Jackson. Following the 'Falsetto Master' article on michaeljackson.com, the thread of discussion contains some interesting observations:

D. E. L. B.:
I can't identify a Falsetto sometimes, because of how angelic and light and beautiful MJ's voice was.

DangerouslyBad:
I think the 'I don't knows' in 'Smooth Criminal' are falsetto ... are they? And at the back half of the 'Earth Song Demo' sounds like a falsetto to me ... but is it?

Planet Jackson:
'Human Nature' I would say is NOT falsetto. That is his regular voice singing in its higher ranges. I'm not sure about the 'I don't know' in 'Smooth Criminal'.

angel_watcher:
I agree – 'Human Nature' is not falsetto, but 'I don't know' in 'Smooth Criminal' is (maybe because he is trying to imitate a female answering the question, 'Annie, are you okay?') Also, when I saw TII, the chorus to 'Earth Song' (call and refrain 'What about ...?') he does not sing it the same way as the History recording. It sounded like falsetto to

me. I thought that was because, as he said, he was trying to conserve his voice. Normally he really goes at that chorus and I could hear the difference. I think the falsetto would be the easier way to rehearse that.

angel_watcher:
While many tenors need to use the falsetto to reach a very high note, Michael could sing the same note using either a falsetto or a natural voice, and at a very high pitch. He had the full use of his vocal instrument, top to bottom. As an artist, it was left to him to choose which he would use to color his music.[9]

And conclusive evidence for this last point can be found in a recording of Michael Jackson's vocal warm-up. Recorded in his hotel bedroom in 1994, he is guided through a standard series of octave-and-a-fifth arpeggios by his vocal coach Seth Riggs (heard on the other end of a telephone).[10] In his modal voice, Jackson goes up to the tenor's high c''. Then, starting just above middle C in his modal voice but moving seamlessly into falsetto, he is taken up to the soprano ab''. Whether or not we like Michael Jackson's voice, the point here is that the dual-register technique he is using strongly recalls the descriptions of so many of the singers mentioned earlier in this book. Likewise, the difficulty the listeners quoted above have in distinguishing his use of both registers could, simply by substituting a few song titles, be descriptions of Nourrit or Braham.

It might be tempting for us to think, having come to a consensus about what the counter-tenor now *is*, that this represents the final stage in the meaning of the term. However, a glance at the history of the counter-tenor, and a basic understanding of linguistics, suggests that this is a dangerous assumption. It is quite possible that to future generations the term 'counter-tenor' will be primarily associated with non-classical music – and that Michael Jackson may indeed be generally considered 'the best'.

[9] 'Falsetto Question', <http://www.michaeljackson.com/us/node/471122> [accessed 6 April 2014]

[10] 'Michael Jackson & Seth Riggs private rec.'; available on YouTube at <http://www.youtube.com/watch?v=I3IMEtsmau4> [uploaded 27 January 2011; accessed 6 April 2014].

CHAPTER 9

The Modern Counter-Tenor

W E have now reached the point at which we came in – 1943 and Tippett's discovery of Alfred Deller. By common consent this marks the birth of the modern era for the counter-tenor. Deller may not have been the first falsetto counter-tenor to achieve a level of fame, but as a revealer of great new musical vistas – early and modern – his influence and importance were profound. More than fifty years on, we still associate the counter-tenor with discoveries in non-mainstream music. In this sense it might appear that little has changed since Deller, and that he marks the real end of this history. In fact, the development of the counter-tenor voice has continued unabated. Most obviously, we can chart the exponential rise in numbers, geographical diffusion, and public recognition of the counter-tenor. Not so apparent, though, are the subtle ways in which the voice itself has developed, so that in terms of repertory, range and technique, today's best-known counter-tenors have less in common with Deller than we might at first think.

The Falsettist Counter-Tenor Enters the Limelight

D ELLER'S own story, well told in Michael and Mollie Hardwick's biography of the singer, needs only a brief summary here.[1] Championed by Tippett, Deller came to public notice in 1946 when he featured as a soloist in the BBC Third Programme's initial broadcast. Within five years Deller had moved to London, begun his recording career, and founded the Deller Consort. The Consort was conceived as an early music group, and initially this was the direction in which Deller's own inclinations took him. Prior to his meeting with Tippett, Deller remembered his first exposure to a seventeenth-century anthem by Loosemore: 'as I sang my part it suddenly felt as though a door had been opened in Heaven'.[2]

Although early music would remain the staple of Deller's repertoire, his singing also attracted the interest of contemporary composers – and not just Tippett. In particular, Benjamin Britten was attracted to the voice of Deller. In writing for his chief vocal inspiration, Peter Pears, Britten loved to exploit an unforced, supernatural quality which the singer could achieve in his upper range. This same aesthetic quality was an obvious feature of Deller's singing, and for him Britten wrote the part of Oberon in *A Midsummer Night's Dream*. This is one episode of Deller's career which is worth examining here, since it throws into relief most of the prevailing

[1] Hardwick and Hardwick, *Alfred Deller*.
[2] Hardwick and Hardwick, *Alfred Deller*, p. 29.

attitudes to the falsetto voice at the time. Having written to him to confirm his interest, and having received the singer's guidance on tessitura ('I like to live here ... [*g–c″*] a D [*d″*] is alright if taken in the phrase, but I don't like to sit on it for long!'), Britten wrote the part of Oberon with Deller's voice in mind.[3] The work was premiered at the Aldeburgh Festival in June 1960, and Deller's performance sharply divided not just the critics, but all those involved – composer and singer included. After the dress rehearsal, some adverse comments from the invited audience had reached Deller, who wrote a note to the composer saying that 'It now seems pretty clear that my inclusion in the Opera does much to prejudice its success with the Critics, and this must not be [...] so delete me when you think fit.' On the day of the premiere Britten wrote to reassure Deller that 'the realisation by you of my idea is really wonderful', and adding (doubtless with feeling) that 'Serious art has always had a difficult time – for one reason or another.' Not surprisingly, when Tippett heard the work, he too lauded Deller's singing. Others, though, were not so positive. Remembering the event later, Deller actually recalled that 'I sang in the first performance at Aldeburgh as well as I'm capable of singing, so it was depressing to receive such a panning from the critics.'[4]

The most common complaint amongst critics was that Deller's acting was wooden, but there were vocal complaints too – that 'his words, which carry most of the plot, are sometimes difficult to hear', and that his voice made 'sounds that came close to being inaudible'. Poor diction and inaudibility would ordinarily have cast aspersions on the singer alone, but so synonymous was Deller with the counter-tenor voice, that many openly questioned Britten's scoring. There was an element of protesting-too-much when the critic of *The Times* needed to state that 'A counter-tenor Oberon is no obstacle nowadays.' Certainly Ernest Bradbury, writing in *The Yorkshire Post*, did not see it that way: 'Britten is said to be thinking of rewriting the part for tenor; and the score suggests the use of a contralto voice.'[5] Although there is no documentary evidence that Britten had any such intention, it is true that when the work came to be staged at Covent Garden (as we shall soon see) Deller was replaced by a modal-voiced singer. And the composer did sanction the use of a contralto voice in the role. In the 1960s, then, the counter-tenor Oberon evidently still *was* something of an obstacle. Ironically, despite the role's seminal nature in the history of the modern falsettist, the low range requested by Deller (whose voice, we should remember, was honed as a cathedral alto) has made Oberon an ill-fitting glove for many of today's 'heldencountertenors'.

---

[3] Paul Kildea, *Selling Britten: Music and the Marketplace* (Oxford, 2002), p. 184.

[4] Hardwick and Hardwick, *Alfred Deller*, p. 148.

[5] *Letters from a Life: The Selected Letters of Benjamin Britten*, ed. Philip Reed and Mervyn Cooke, vol. 5: *1958–1965* (Woodbridge, 2010), pp. 228–34.

Although Deller was primarily known as a soloist in Britain, it was through touring and recording with the Consort that his voice became best known, and his influence most widespread. Significantly, the company with which Deller recorded most was the French label Harmonia Mundi. This meant that his voice did not remain isolated as an English phenomenon, but soon entered the mix of the burgeoning European early music scene. Not just through his performing, but through courses organised by Harmonia Mundi in the south of France, Deller's voice quickly gained acceptance amongst musicians who were not part of a surviving falsetto tradition. René Jacobs and Dominique Visse both studied with Deller in masterclasses, and subsequently pursued careers as counter-tenors. Directors such as Gustav Leonhardt, Sigiswald Kuijken, Frans Brüggen and René Clemencic also worked with Deller, and subsequently gave platforms for counter-tenors in their own performances.

A comparison between Jacobs (1946–) and the Swiss singer Hugues Cuénod (1902–2010) offers a revealing slant on the perceptions of different generations. Both men used fundamentally similar modal-falsetto techniques and sang pre-Classical music. But whereas Jacobs was known as a counter-tenor and commonly referred to as a falsettist, Cuénod was known as a tenor whose obvious falsetto was politely ignored by most critics. It was actually left to Cuénod himself, at the age of eighty, to admit that he was not really a tenor at all, but a baritone with 'a very easy falsetto'.[6]

In England the uptake from Deller's example was even stronger than on the Continent, partly because there was already a level of falsetto practice on which to build. (One revealing fact which is often ignored is that Deller's broadcast debut was in a counter-tenor duet, not a solo: his partner in 'Sound the Trumpet' from Purcell's *Come ye Sons of Art, Away* was John Whitworth, who himself was to become a significant influence on young counter-tenors.) In the late 1950s two contemporaries of each other, Paul Esswood and James Bowman, began careers as counter-tenors. In different ways, both men were to extend particular threads of Deller's career. Esswood, following Deller's example of working with Continental musicians, was to take the majority of alto solo parts in Leonhardt and Harnoncourt's complete series of Bach cantata recordings. Indeed, much of his career was to be pursued in Europe and America. But although his career may have had similarities with Deller's, his voice did not. Esswood once sang to Deller, with the possibility of taking lessons in mind. However, 'He didn't like my voice. He thought it sounded too much like a mezzo-soprano on the top and a contralto on the bottom and that if I studied with him, all that would have to change. I decided not to.'[7]

James Bowman built on the relationship Deller had established with Britten, taking over the role of Oberon at Sadler's Wells and later

---

[6] Giles, *History and Technique of the Counter-Tenor*, p. 240.

[7] Interview, *New York Times*, 24 January 1986.

Glyndebourne. (Deller's direct replacement at Covent Garden we shall encounter shortly). Bowman also appeared in the premiere of a Tippett opera, *The Ice Break*, in the role of Astron, 'a psychedelic messenger'. Self-deprecatingly, Bowman credits his operatic success with his tendency to 'show off', and on his ability 'to make a lot of noise'. Many a true word: Deller had been dropped from the Covent Garden production of *A Midsummer Night's Dream* because his acting was considered too stilted, and his voice too small. In both vocal strength and performing persona, Bowman's increased projection was a pointer for future generations of counter-tenors.

At the same time as Deller was making his mark in Europe, another counter-tenor was becoming well known in America. Russell Oberlin, though, was a very different singer from Deller. Whereas Deller was fundamentally a falsettist, Oberlin exclusively used his modal voice. Listening to Oberlin's recordings, this is not immediately obvious: his voice has a lightness and fragility that might suggest falsetto. Perhaps it was also confusing to listeners that he should term himself 'counter-tenor' at a time when Deller was establishing this as a falsetto voice. As we have seen, in regarding the counter-tenor as a modal voice, Oberlin was only following an accepted American usage. In a television interview dating from 1962, Oberlin stated that 'I have a falsetto voice although I don't sing in it.'[8] He then proceeds to demonstrate this by singing a vocal exercise once in falsetto and then (at the same pitch) in his modal voice. Sure enough, it is this latter sonority which is recognisable from his recordings. And elsewhere, Oberlin seemed to be irked by the misattribution of his vocal production: 'I have been described as a falsetto singer. This is not true. I have a naturally high tenor voice which enables me to sing the countertenor repertoire without resorting to the falsetto voice.'[9] Is there, in his use of the word 'resorting', an implied denigration of Deller and his ilk? Since Oberlin reputedly thought of himself as being the only 'true' counter-tenor, this may well be the case. And a comment Oberlin makes in his 1962 interview – that past pupils of Deller who had later come to him for lessons, had initially been taught to sing 'too quietly' – lends fuel to this fire. Perhaps the two men can be forgiven a level of rivalry with each other: on the one hand, Oberlin must have noted not just the success of Deller, but also the falsetto trend he was setting; Deller, on the other hand, regretted being replaced by Oberlin when Britten's *Dream* production was staged at Covent Garden. In fact, any lasting rivalry between the two men, and the vocal camps they represented, was cut short by Oberlin's ill-health and subsequent withdrawal from public performance in the mid-1960s. With

---

[8] Available on YouTube as 'Russell Oberlin explica o que é um contratenor', <http://www.youtube.com/watch?v=2YgrPBTRjMk> [uploaded 23 February 2008; accessed 6 April 2014].

[9] Interview, *House & Garden*, 111:30 (1957).

no modal counter-tenors remaining now before the wider public, we have no cause to prolong the long-running dispute about what the counter-tenor *is*, though the dispute about what counter-tenors *have been* (as this book must suggest) is still very much alive.

With Oberlin's retirement, a very significant note in the counter-tenor story reaches a conclusion. The fundamentally modal counter-tenor, known in England and Europe until the mid-nineteenth century, and subsequently in America, now falls virtually mute. How can we explain this silence? The theme of rising human height has been a leitmotif of this history, and here it must be sounded again. Although height has risen steadily throughout modern history, and the pitch of modal voices has consequently dropped, until the latter half of the twentieth century this trend was very slow. Since the Second World War, improved nutrition in the Western world has resulted in the trend rapidly accelerating. As a result, even fully modal tenors are becoming thinner on the ground. Into the territory vacated by high modal voices, the falsettists have marched in ever-increasing numbers.

Arguably, one can see the meeting between Deller and Tippett – and all that followed – as representing an inevitable collision between the physical development of the human frame and the aesthetic movement of Modernism. Whilst Deller reflected the reality that taller modern men could no longer sing the counter-tenor parts of Purcell *et al.* in a modal voice, Tippett represented the cutting edge of Modernism. The alacrity with which his fellow composers were drawn to the falsetto voice, as we shall see, underlines just how strongly the sound of the modern counter-tenor resonated with the *avant garde*. For our purposes, though, it may help to think of the Modernist movement as going beyond the front line of new music. In particular, recent commentators have pointed the finger at the formative early music movement, claiming that it was more an undercurrent of Modernism than (as its appearance and advocates suggested) historicism.[10] It is surely no coincidence that Tippett the Modernist was actually drawn to Deller's voice through early music. Above all, in noting the 'inviolable purity' of Deller's singing, Tippett implied that the voice attracted him because it appeared unsullied by the ego. Obviously, the objectivism that marked Modernist art also found an ideal mouthpiece in a voice which was not the normal speaking voice of an individual. Not that Deller (or his successors) necessarily sang in a detached way. Walter Bergmann, an early associate of Deller, tellingly remarked in his obituary of the singer that 'One had often the feeling that he personified the composer whose work he sang, so strong and complete was his involvement in every phrase, every word and every emotion.'[11] But of course, since the texts Deller was most often singing were relatively objective, even if he

---

[10] Most trenchantly argued in Richard Taruskin, *Text and Act: Essays on Music and Performance* (New York, 1995).

[11] Walter Bergmann, 'Alfred Deller', *Early Music* 8(1) (1980), pp. 43–6, at p. 41.

'personified the composer' this did not mean that his communication would seem subjective. Related to this, the unique quality of the counter-tenor voice can also be safely associated with one other aspect of Modernism: the Modernists' wish to break down gender stereotypes found a perfect voice in the androgynous sound of the falsettist.

New Counter-Tenors and Old Repertories

ONE decision which Deller made early in his career, acting on the advice of Walter Bergmann, was not to sing any music not composed for counter-tenor.[12] Aside from being an early harpsichord accompanist of Deller, Bergmann was a musicologist, who worked with Tippett on the staff of Morley College. Bearing in mind that later in life Deller was to voice serious misgivings about the advice of musicologists, there is a certain irony about his unreserved acceptance of Bergmann's advice. Yet this advice, and Deller's acquiescence, highlights one of the greatest problems for the modern counter-tenor: what to sing? It was certainly clear to Deller what he should *not* sing:

> As to the nineteenth century, I've been absolutely firm since I started to sing as a professional to keep clear of all the composers of the romantic period [...] They didn't conceive their music for anything like my type of voice, and it can never make their songs sound right.[13]

(Ironically, this belief excluded the first English works definitively written with the modern counter-tenor in mind – the music of the English glee school.) Initially, Bergmann's (and Tippett's) advice directed Deller to the English Restoration composers. Either side of that, historically, he was led to the songs of the English lutenist school, and the music of the later Baroque. In addition, his intermittent work as a lay-clerk (now at St Paul's Cathedral) had him singing the alto parts in Renaissance polyphony. Later, Deller would record the upper lines of French medieval polyphony, as well as English folk-songs. The irony here, of course, is that the consensus of modern musicology would not regard any of these musical parts and idioms as being composed specifically for Deller's type of counter-tenor voice.

Self-evidently, then, there is a discrepancy between Deller's intention of following a historical practice, and the outcome of his attempt. If there is a fault here (and it is a large 'if' which we will address shortly), where is the finger of blame to be pointed? Surely not at Deller. Any musician who is primarily a performer is bound to rely, to some extent, on the advice of musicologists – be they editors or advisors. Deller can hardly be faulted for taking heed of current thinking. Nor can we place much blame at the feet of any intellectually honest musicologist. Our knowledge of the factors

---

[12] Hardwick and Hardwick, *Alfred Deller*, p. 101.
[13] Hardwick and Hardwick, *Alfred Deller*, p. 182.

which surround historical voices has certainly increased in the last fifty years, but we would be guilty of the most ridiculous conceit if we did not accept that future musicologists are sure to uncover information which will challenge our current understandings. So any fault there is lies elsewhere in the musical chain. Fundamentally, solo singers have their hands tied by the requirements of the music industry – as dictated by impresarios and musical directors whose historical interest may be no more than a flag of convenience. If an aspiring counter-tenor is offered an engagement which will not compromise him vocally, it is simply unrealistic for him to do other than accept. This would certainly have applied to Deller, and has to many counter-tenors since. In this way are traditions fostered.

Yet traditions, in turn, may have had a part to play in the thought processes of influential men such as Tippett. Let us try to see, assuming Tippett's perspective, how he came to the 'clear' knowledge that Deller was the modern embodiment of the Purcellian counter-tenor. Firstly, Tippett saw Deller as part of an existing practice – of falsettists singing alto parts in English church choirs. Secondly, at the only pitch Tippett knew ($a' = 440$) Deller's voice fitted Purcell's counter-tenor parts like a glove. Thirdly, by assuming that the existing practice reflected an unbroken vocal tradition, he was able to project Deller's voice backwards in time, and so come to his 'clear' conclusion. Of these three steps, the first was irrefutable and the second would have seemed so too: the third was the most obvious way of reconciling the first two. Only with hindsight can we say that Tippett's second assumption was flawed: had he known this, it is unlikely that he would have progressed to the third step.

Perhaps, then, we cannot really fault Tippett, Bergmann or Deller for the historical misappropriation of the falsetto counter-tenor voice. Indeed, it seems axiomatic that individuals can only be answerable for their own beliefs, and in the 1940s the stances of those three men seemed perfectly reasonable. But if subsequent generations have chosen to perpetuate such beliefs in the face of new and contradictory evidence, we should perhaps be asking questions of them instead. After all, as early as 1969 Thelma Baldwin and Olive Wilson had convincingly argued that Purcell's counter-tenors were not falsettists, and subsequent estimates of lower Restoration pitch standards have only strengthened the argument that these parts were composed for fundamentally modal singers. Even in the twenty-first century, however, 'period-style' performances have presented Restoration counter-tenor solos with falsettists. When it was made, Tippett's theory that the Purcellian counter-tenor was a falsettist was a reasonable argument; more than half a century later, it should be rejected as a myth.

Similarly, the argument that the Renaissance counter-tenor, or alto, was a part composed for falsettists, has been compromised by tradition. In fact, it was the same existing practice we noted above – of falsetto altos in cathedral choirs – which was erroneously projected into the distant past to create a 'tradition'. In this case, the practice was cast chronologically backwards to make sense of the theory of Ouseley, Fellowes and Wulstan, that Tudor church music had originally been performed at a much higher pitch: by using a minor-third transposition, alto parts became more suitable for falsettists. As a convenient extension of this theory, Continental polyphony was similarly transposed to make its alto parts suit falsetto voices. The house of cards created by these theories could lead the *New Grove*, as late as its 2001 edition, to make the statement (as sweeping as it is erroneous) that 'Falsetto singing has been the most common source of alto voices in all-male choirs throughout the history of Western music.'[14] As the evidence in this book has indicated, with the exception of the English church since the late nineteenth century, altos singing exclusively in falsetto have had virtually no part to play in the history of the all-male choir.

For church choirs, pragmatic solutions to the problems of performing early music are not so much defensible as laudable, since otherwise they would be unable to perform the music. For today's choirs purporting to reflect original performance practice, though, with the high-pitch theory in English (let alone European) Renaissance music well and truly deflated, such solutions are less supportable. For most of today's professional counter-tenors, whose range is encouraged upwards in most of their other activities, singing these low-lying alto parts has become less and less appealing. Increasingly, particularly in European early music ensembles, falsettists in Renaissance music are now more likely to be heard singing soprano parts at low pitches, with tenors, baritones and basses taking the parts below. In Continental polyphony, if not English, this arrangement comes closest to historical practice.

Of course, simply by removing any pretence of performing in an 'authentic' manner, all these issues disappear. This, in a variety of strengths (or dilutions, depending on one's view), is precisely the stance that an increasing number of early musicians are adopting. In particular, replacing 'authenticity' with the term 'historically informed' (however clunky it may sound) implies a desire for knowledge tempered with an awareness of its limits and, implicitly, the inevitability of compromise. This pragmatic approach appears to be reasonable. Modern singers rarely possess the same attributes as their original counterparts: their physical stature, training and sensibilities are likely to be different, as will be their performing contexts. Even the way they are heard, be it through speakers or in modern concert halls, will bear little relation to the reception afforded the first performers. Given these current circumstances, it is improbable that any authentic recreation is an achievable goal. Once this is accepted, and the search for a single, absolute performance is deemed untenable, a number of options present themselves. Even amongst those with the best intentions of fidelity to a composer's intentions, honest compromises regarding a host of issues will need to be made. In this respect the early music movement yet again

---

[14] Sadie (ed.), *New Grove Dictionary of Music and Musicians*, s.v. 'Contratenor altus'.

finds itself in sympathy with broader cultural movements. Having shown Modernist sympathies in its earlier years, the movement's current plurality of approaches now carries the unmistakable whiff of Post-Modernism.

For the modern counter-tenor, the implications of this shift in thinking are striking. Were Deller's initial criteria still the order of the day, the earlier repertoire for the pure falsettist would now be minimal. Apart from Continental Renaissance soprano parts and English nineteenth-century glees, it is difficult to see what earlier music today's counter-tenor would have to sing. However, if an honest admission is made that Dowland and his peers, for example, were not writing for the modern counter-tenor voice, we can have no reasonable objection to today's falsettists performing an Elizabethan lute-song. The problem comes, perhaps, when counter-tenors neither confirm or deny that they are attempting to follow historical practice: by performing or recording lute-songs without comment, they are tacitly perpetuating the myth that Deller and his contemporaries had unwittingly created.

Most notably, a level of intellectual honesty about the limits of authenticity have opened up the repertoire of the castrati for modern counter-tenors, most of whom can manage the range in parts written for Senessino and Guadagni. The benefits of this casting would appear obvious. For opera audiences, it offers the possibility of hearing Handel's character Giulio Cesare, for example, sung by a man. For modern counter-tenors, it offers vastly expanded musical and dramatic possibilities. Following the lead of Bowman and Esswood, today's leading counter-tenors are more often found on the opera stage than in the choir stall. Inevitably, this has influenced the voice itself. Brian Asawa and David Daniels have been referred to as representing a new generation of 'heldencountertenors' – a term which could never have been applied to Deller.[15]

Sheer volume, though, is only part of the vocal difference between these two generations of singers. The move into the opera house, particularly in America, has encouraged falsettists to embrace a more constant vibrato, resulting in something of the timbre of the female mezzo-soprano. David Daniels proudly claims that 'My sound, until recently, was the only countertenor that appealed to mainstream opera-goers – the people who say, "Ugh, countertenors." [...] That word "countertenor" used to scare management away. Frankly, I have changed that.'[16] In truth, the real instigator of this change in taste predated Daniels: Paul Esswood, whose voice was often compared to Kathleen Ferrier's, had notable successes in American opera houses in the 1980s. In range, too, modern operatic counter-tenors have literally moved up the scale. In the early days of the

---

[15] Joel Kasow, 'An Interview with Brian Asawa', available online at <http://www.culturekiosque.com/opera/intervie/rheasawa.html> [accessed 6 April 2014].

[16] 'parterre box talks to David Daniels', available online at <http://parterre.com/daniels.htm> [accessed 6 April 2014].

revival, when counter-tenors were essentially altos by another name (and often singing that part in church choirs as a day job), it was necessary for them to retain good resonance around and below middle C. The part of Oberon, written for Deller, reflects this, since at least in range it could be sung by most cathedral altos. Later in life Deller admitted that he had no great love of high falsetto singing:

> An important thing for a countertenor to bear in mind always is that there's nothing remarkable about being able to sing high [...] There's a constant mistake on the part of young, enthusiastic countertenors to attempt things which are unnecessarily high.[17]

Does the 'mistake' lie wholly with the singers, though? Robin Blaze, whose range is about a third higher than Deller's, comments that 'more and more the way countertenors are pushed, or rather encouraged, these days is towards doing higher roles.'[18] The Svengalian impresario, one senses from the neat side-step in this remark, is only just out of earshot, lurking in the wings. And financial pressures even have a bearing on the way this higher range is negotiated. Most obviously, the 'money note' at the end of an operatic aria customarily marries high pitch and high volume, and modern operatic counter-tenors tend to adopt this practice. Not that falsettists necessarily have much option when pushing their ranges to this extreme. In fact one of the ironies of the counter-tenor's adoption of castrati roles is that, in order to sing in this range in large opera houses, they are forced to rely on a standard post-Garcia vocal technique. In the context they now find themselves, Tosi's method – in particular the artful *diminuendo* to the top of the voice – can have almost no practical application for the operatic counter-tenor. A good female mezzo-soprano, on the other hand, can still embrace something of Tosi's method since, unlike the falsettist, she still has a head voice above her normal working range.

Musically, then, the benefits of counter-tenors taking operatic castrati roles may be more apparent than real. And dramatically? Fundamentally, we need to ask whether the most obvious apparent gain – of seeing men playing the parts of men – actually brings us nearer to an understanding of Baroque drama. After all, the castrati were figures of sexual ambiguity *par excellence*, and nothing in our experience of these roles is likely to reflect this more accurately than a female with a relatively straight voice and an assumed 'masculine' stage persona. René Jacobs, now wearing two hats – as conductor and counter-tenor – prefers this latter option: 'In recent times, our voice has been misunderstood [...] No, we are not a contemporary replacement for the castrato.' Jacobs (who despite teaching

[17] Hardwick and Hardwick, *Alfred Deller*, p. 188.
[18] Roderic Dunnett, 'A Countertenor Virtuoso', *Music and Vision*, 26 December 2001, online at <http://www.mvdaily.com/articles/2001/12/blaze1.htm> [accessed 6 April 2014].

Andreas Scholl and others tends to cast female mezzos in castrato roles) concludes with a surprising lack of solidarity that 'there are not very many good countertenors around today.'[19] It should perhaps be left to others in a more objective position to compare the relative merits of Jacobs and his peers, with the qualities of Scholl and his generation.

Curiously, there are at least two singers in the world today who can claim exemption from charges laid against counter-tenors singing castrato roles. Michael Maniaci and Radu Marian both experienced health issues in adolescence which left them with the vocal attributes of the castrati. Listening to the high-pitched voices of these men when they talk, it is clear that when they sing they are using the same voice: they are not falsettists. Maniaci and Marian are able to sing the same repertory as the soprano castrati, including works such as Mozart's *Exsultate Jubilate*, with its original soprano high *a"* (and an adapted final cadence taking them a third above this). Listening to these men offers modern listeners a fascinating experience, though we should not delude ourselves about its level of 'authenticity': both men owe at least as much to Garcia as to Tosi. After listening to Maniaci, René Jacobs declined to cast him, considering his style to be too 'American'.[20]

With modern opera directors now having a choice of genders when casting, one inevitable result has been the casting of 'trouser' parts – male roles composed for female singers – by men. Jochen Kowalski (who shares something of the medical background and vocal disposition of Maniaci and Marian) has specialised in such roles as Prince Orlofsky in *Die Fledermaus*. More generally, the way that the modern operatic world has embraced the counter-tenor voice has tempted some of these singers towards other mainstream genres, such as the nineteenth-century *lied*. For Kowalski this might mean Schubert's *Winterreise*, and for French counter-tenor Philippe Jaroussky the *chansons* of Reynaldo Hahn are a central part of his recital repertory. In short, by luring singers with the promise of wider acceptance, the music industry has encouraged the voice of the modern counter-tenor towards a new repertoire and vocal style. In fairness to the industry, the promise has been duly delivered, for the obvious reason that mainstream music and performance require a smaller cultural leap on the part of listeners. Whether the counter-tenor voice has been betrayed or liberated by this development will depend entirely on the stance of each listener.

[19] Interview with Rene Jacobs, available online through <http://music.barnesandnoble.com/features/browseInterviews.asp#j> [accessed 6 April 2014].

[20] Robert Dawson Scott, 'The Man with the 300-Year-Old Voice', *The Times*, 12 October 2007.

New Music for a Developing Voice

B EARING in mind its roots in the early music movement, one peculiar irony of the modern counter-tenor revival is that the largest repertoire the singers can now undisputedly claim as their own did not even exist in 1943. The corpus of contemporary music written for the counter-tenor voice is already vast, and ever increasing.[21] Not surprisingly, the first composers to write for counter-tenors were English. Aside from Tippett and Britten, a number of less well-known composers, such as Alan Ridout, Geoffrey Burgon and John Tavener were particularly drawn to the voice. Few composers since Tippett have been more explicit than Tavener in recognising the super-personal qualities of the counter-tenor voice. In his note to *The Hidden Face*, Tavener describes the work as 'a prayer, for solo counter-tenor, oboe, and a distant group of muted violins and violas. It tries to hold within it a whole tradition with nothing personal or idiosyncratic.'

As the sound of the counter-tenor gained recognition beyond Britain, a more eclectic mix of composers began to write with it in mind. In the case of Leonard Bernstein's 1965 *Chichester Psalms* we have to say 'with it in mind' rather than 'for it', because although the work has since become associated with the counter-tenor voice, the composer only stipulated that 'the long male-alto solo in the second movement must not be sung by a woman, but either by a boy or a counter-tenor.' As an American Jew, it is unlikely that Bernstein had any first-hand knowledge of the falsetto counter-tenor voice, and certainly at the first performance, and in the recording Bernstein himself later conducted, this solo was taken by boy altos. Bernstein's chief concern here was evidently not the particular timbre of the counter-tenor voice, but simply the gender of the soloist who, in the text of this movement, represents the psalmist David. However, the intended and actual destinations of a piece of music (as we have seen throughout this history) are rarely quite the same, and the *Chichester Psalms* were gratefully appropriated by counter-tenors. The work did, of course, already have one foot in the English choral tradition by virtue of its commission. With the choir of King's College Cambridge, James Bowman recorded the solo before Bernstein's own studio recording was made, and this helped to establish the work as a part of the counter-tenor repertory. An indication of the strength of this appropriation can be gauged by the Wikipedia reference to a later recording, which tells us that 'With Bernstein's approval, the countertenor part was sung by Aled Jones, then a treble'. Partly because of that recording with a famous boy treble, the *Chichester Psalms* solo has again become a site of shared occupancy.

Even the next generation of American composers, writing more specifically for the counter-tenor, had to contend with a lack of first-hand

---

[21] The fullest listing of the repertoire can be found in Steven L. Rickards, *Twentieth-Century Countertenor Repertoire: A Guide* (Lanham, MD, 2008).

knowledge of the voice. The title role in Philip Glass's 1983 opera *Akhnaten*, for instance, was first performed, and subsequently recorded, by Paul Esswood. Glass wrote of his composing the opera that

> I had no special problem writing the music, except for the counter-tenor part itself. Here I was working with a voice that was unfamiliar to me. What I knew of the sound I had learned from recordings and a very few live performances. Until then, I had never met anyone who actually possessed such a voice. Eventually I did meet with Paul Esswood [...] [who] carefully looked over his part, making comments and suggesting changes to make my musical ideas singable for his voice. Moments like these are invaluable for a composer.[22]

Although he introduces Akhnaten to the action early in the opera, Glass deliberately delays his first utterance, so that when the falsetto voice is eventually heard it has maximum dramatic effect:

> The attraction for me in using a countertenor for Akhnaten must, by now, be obvious. The effect of hearing a high, beautiful voice coming from the lips of a full-grown man can at first be very startling. In one stroke, Akhnaten would be separated from everyone around him.[23]

Glass's motivation for using the falsetto voice, then, was actually similar to Britten's in *A Midsummer Night's Dream*, and Tippett's in *The Ice Break*: to represent, in a word, 'otherness'. Glass went one step further, however, when he explicitly likened his use of the falsetto voice to the use of castrati by earlier composers.[24] To Glass and his audience in 1980s America, the sound of the counter-tenor was as novel as it had been to English listeners in the 1960s and 70s. But the currency of novelty is by definition ever changing, and as the sound of the falsetto counter-tenor has become more familiar, the voice's value in 'startling' listeners has inevitably been diminished.

Our growing familiarity with the counter-tenor voice on stage is underlined by the inspiration behind, and reaction to, the trio of counter-tenors in John Adams's 2000 opera-oratorio *El Niño*. Like Britten and his successors, Adams used the sound of the counter-tenor to represent distanced (in this case Biblical) voices. In a stroke of compositional genius Adams further diminishes the egotistical trappings of the human voice by using three counter-tenors singing homophonically – an effect at once novel and archaic. Perhaps significantly, though, in the many interviews with the composer which accompanied the first performances of the work, none of his inquisitors probed the reasons behind his use of the counter-tenor voice: evidently it was, to them, literally unremarkable. Simply because

[22] Philip Glass, *Opera on the Beach* (London, 1988), pp. 159–60.

[23] John Richardson, *Singing Archaeology: Philip Glass's Akhnaten* (Hanover, 1999), p. 138.

[24] Richardson, *Singing Archaeology*, p. 138.

of its method of production, the falsetto voice will always raise eyebrows: the extent to which it can represent the shock of the new is another matter. And if we need reminding about how our perceptions of vocal normality and abnormality change with time, we might note that whereas in the 1970s the sound of the falsettist was startling at a time when that of the female soprano was standard, for listeners in Renaissance Europe precisely the opposite was the case.

For the first generation of modern European composers to write for the counter-tenor, it was perhaps the idea of the voice, rather than its reality, which appealed. When Aribert Reimann composed his 1978 opera *Lear*, for instance, he conceived the role of Edgar to be sung by a tenor or counter-tenor. With virtually no European falsettists active at the time, unsurprisingly it was a tenor who took the role in its first performances.

The continued enthusiasm for the voice shown by a younger generation of composers, such as Michael Nyman, Thomas Adès, Jonathan Dove, James MacMillan, Judith Weir, Arvo Pärt and Olga Neuwirth, suggests that the contemporary counter-tenor repertoire is far from waning. Of these composers, perhaps the most interesting departures have been taken by the Austrian Olga Neuwirth. Together with her near-contemporary Andreas Scholl, Neuwirth illustrates just how firmly established the counter-tenor has become in Europe. Aside from the obvious difference between the two – that one is a composer and the other predominantly a performer – there is a marked difference between their approaches to the counter-tenor voice. Scholl's performing career has largely been in the musical mainstream, and whilst he acknowledges the potential androgyny of the falsetto voice, there is nothing to encourage such associations in his own vocal style or persona. Neuwirth, on the other hand, has unashamedly explored the androgynous edges of the counter-tenor voice. Other modern composers may have politely deferred to their counter-tenors by exclusively writing for their falsetto register, but in her 1994 *Five Daily Miniatures* Neuwirth also lays bare the uncomfortable underside of the voice. Here, there is no room for semantic quibbles to distinguish between modal and speaking voices, since the singer is required to speak (or at least *sprechstimme*) modally. As an experimental work, though, the *Miniatures* pale beside Neuwirth's *Hommage à Klaus Nomi* (Ex. 12), a theatrical tribute to the kitsch icon who

Ex. 12 Olga Neuwirth, *Hommage à Klaus Nomi*, excerpt

was her teenage idol. With references from Purcell to Marlene Dietrich, this is a high-camp celebration of the counter-tenor as androgyne.

In *Bählamms Fest* (1997–2000) Neuwirth raises further questions in the ear of the listener, by subjecting the voice to various electronic enhancements. Stefan Drees, who has written extensively about Neuwirth, comments that 'since the 1990s the specific vocal quality of the countertenor has, in Neuwirth's thinking, become interwoven with the concept of artificiality – the voice's capacity to act as a sound cipher in representing the "other".'[25] Olga Neuwirth, then, makes explicit a theme which has sporadically been murmured in the background of this history since the *mukhannath* of the early Islamic world.

In the Post-Modern age of multiple narratives, it should come as no surprise to find other composers taking the counter-tenor voice on a radically different kind of journey from the one offered by Olga Neuwirth. To an extent, the music of the Estonian Arvo Pärt belongs to the aesthetic of 'no emotional irrelevancies', which Tippett saw as the time-honoured way for the falsetto voice. And David James, the counter-tenor in Pärt's long-standing musical advocates the Hilliard Ensemble, confirms this:

> Everything is written into the music, and you mustn't try to put your own personality into it, because the music will just die. I believe that it requires a lot of courage to do this, because you really are exposed: I've described it as being naked, performing naked. You've got nowhere to hide.[26]

We can gauge the fearsome extent of this exposure in a section from Pärt's *Passio*. At the word 'crucifigeretur', against a quiet and static accompaniment, the composer takes the alto soloist up to high f'' (Ex. 13). On one level, the simplicity of Pärt's writing here takes us back to the appearance of Dufay's music, and the first works written with the falsetto voice in mind. On another level, though, we are aware that Pärt is writing for a new breed of virtuoso falsettist. In this sense, the aesthetics of Pärt and Neuwirth have something in common: both, in different ways, require their performers to bare all.

In the creation of this growing body of contemporary music for counter-tenor, much credit should go to the singers themselves. Unlike many performers in the traditional musical mainstreams, counter-tenors have shown themselves to be not just receptive to new works, but proactive in instigating them. Beyond that, they have often been happy to involve

---

[25] A fuller introduction to the music of Olga Neuwirth for counter-tenor can be found in 'Musikalische Repräsentation des "Anderen": Der Countertenor als Klangchiffre für Androgynie und Artifizialität bei Olga Neuwirth', in *Der Countertenor: die männliche Falsettstimme vom Mittelalter zur Gegenwart*, ed. Corinna Herr and Arnold Jacobshagen (Mainz, 2012), pp. 251–68.

[26] 'As Purely, Cleanly and Simply as Possible' [interview], available online through <http://www.arvopart.ee> [accessed 6 April 2014].

Ex. 13 Arvo Pärt, *Passio*, excerpt

themselves in the whole creative process. Returning to Olga Neuwirth, the counter-tenors Jochen Kowalski, Andrew Watts and Kai Wessel have had symbiotic relationships with the composer in realising her potentially improbable sound images.

The contemporary composers listed above have very evidently had no problem in acknowledging the qualities of the voice itself, and of specific singers. Neither have listeners around the world had a problem with accepting the falsetto counter-tenor. Far from it. Despite the hostility that Deller first encountered, the sound of the counter-tenor is increasingly commonplace to musical listeners. But love of the voice is not universal. When Kowalski approached Elisabeth Schwarzkopf for lessons, he relates that she simply said, 'I cannot stand countertenors.'[27] And this comment probably has a wider significance: the falsetto voice is always likely to be more of an acquired taste for those (like Schwarzkopf) brought up on a diet of large modal voices. But if not universal, the appreciation of the falsetto voice is certainly global: the counter-tenor league of nations now includes persuasive singers from virtually every country in Europe, from North America, Japan, and many points between and beyond. The man who claimed, after hearing one of Deller's radio broadcasts, that the counter-tenor was 'just a gimmick thought up by the BBC' certainly had an opinion, but there is no evidence yet that he had the gift of prophecy.[28]

WHEN our predictions are based on aesthetic hunches, prophesying the future for any aspect of music is futile. Just as no one looked forward from the complexities of the Second Viennese School and foretold minimalism, neither did anyone in the early twentieth century foresee that the falsetto counter-tenor would, within fifty years, be at the cutting edge of musical explorations. Artists can see the future, of course, but the moment they begin to realise this vision it has already become the present.

---

[27] Interview with Jochen Kowalski, online at <http://www.oakweb.ca/harmony/kowalski/spe.html> [accessed 6 April 2014]; originally printed (in German) in *Der Spiegel* 52 (1994).

[28] Cf. Giles, *History and Technique of the Counter-Tenor*, p. 378.

Foretelling a plot for the modern counter-tenor voice, though, is perhaps not entirely a matter of gazing into a crystal ball. Let us first take one step backward in time. As we have seen, with the benefit of hindsight it is possible to read the rapid flowering of the modern counter-tenor voice as a historical inevitability – the collision of aesthetics and physical developments. And whilst we cannot foresee the future of aesthetics, our physical course is more easily plotted: the ongoing rise in human height means that we can predict the further lowering of men's modal voices, and with it the likelihood that falsetto singing will have an ever-increasing role to play.

This prediction, though, comes with numerous caveats. Firstly, there is always a chance that genetic or environmental factors will arrest, or even reverse the rise in human height. If average height decreases, and modal voice pitch rises, then in future decades certain parts – seventeenth-century counter-tenor and French *haute-contre* lines being examples – would gradually edge back towards the comfort zone of high modal singers. This, though, leads to a second caveat, because it assumes that we will remain interested in performing the music of the past within the pitch band of the last two hundred years. We may take this as a given, but unaccompanied early vocal groups often decide to perform at pitches well below those suggested by historical evidence, simply to retain what is known of the original disposition of modal and falsetto vocal parts. Future generations may not feel bound by modern or historical pitches. Neither, by the same token, will they necessarily feel any need to replicate the kind of voices, or the gender of singers, which earlier composers envisaged. Most obviously, if the desire to maintain single-sex choirs wanes, and likewise the public's current preference for male singers playing male roles in early opera, there will be little practical need for the falsettist in his most familiar present-day guise.

However, for as long as something of our present tastes prevails, we can predict with some confidence that the male falsetto voice will remain with us. Singing what, though? For the first fifty years of the modern revival, the terms 'falsetto', 'male alto' and 'counter-tenor' were virtually synonymous. There is, though, nothing sacrosanct about this linkage: four hundred years ago a 'counter-tenor' had a modal voice, and a falsettist was most likely to think of himself as a 'soprano'. And at least on one level, today it seems as if this last link is reasserting itself: outwith the English cathedral choir stall, one is now as likely to encounter the male falsettist on soprano as on alto parts. If this suggests that the falsettist is heading upwards in the vocal texture, though, there is an important distinction we need to make – between professional and amateur practice. True, if we hear Renaissance polyphony sung at a prestigious early music festival, we are likely to hear falsettist sopranos, alongside modal altos, counter-tenors and *haute-contres*. When we see a local choral society performing Handel's *Messiah* at modern pitch, however, increasingly we are as likely to hear falsetto singing on the chorus tenor line as elsewhere. The reason for this is that (as the relatively small numbers of choral society tenors now testify) untrained men capable of singing a tenor's top a', in full voice at modern pitch are few and far between. Of necessity, then, in such choirs there is an increasing acceptance not just of low female singers, but of high baritones who will sing the majority of the tenor range in a full voice but 'fake' the highest notes. If this is an issue now, for the generation of boys whose voices are currently changing (and whose greater height and lower adult voices we can already predict) the dual-register technique is only likely to become more prevalent: without it, amateur choirs may well struggle to recruit tenors.

This, of course, sounds like a call to arms for Tosi's method, but for a number of reasons we should be wary of assuming that the old dual-register system can easily be replicated in the modern musical world. Tosi's technique was fundamentally aimed at professionals, and with good reason: the fluid joining of vocal registers was (and is) one of the most difficult feats for the human larynx to accomplish. With little or no training, amateurs who can manage the technique will be very rare creatures. Paradoxically, though, it may prove easier for an amateur choral tenor to adopt (if not master) the dual-register technique, if only because any audible break between his modal and falsetto voices will always be masked by other singers. The professional soloist is afforded no such cover. Nor will the distant rear walls of large modern concert halls and opera houses encourage the solo singer to ease over the break by reducing air pressure and dynamic volume. One thing would appear clear: whether amateur or professional, current singers are unlikely to find much encouragement or assistance from their teachers. The vast majority of classical vocal teachers have themselves been taught a post-Garcia technique, and understandably it is this that they pass on to students.

There appears, then, to be a gulf between the likely demand for such a hybrid voice, and the methods by which it might be produced and supplied. This, though, should not concern us unduly. The next chapter will write itself in due course. And after all, if the real history of high male singing is not quite the one we had been led to believe in, we should hardly be surprised if its future story follows an unpredictable and deceptive plot.

Bibliography

Abbott, Lynn, and Doug Seroff, 'America's Blue Yodel', *Musical Traditions* 11 (1993), pp. 2–11

Agricola, Johann Friedrich, *Anleitung zur Singkunst* (Berlin, 1757)

—— *Introduction to the Art of Singing*, ed. and trans. Julianne C. Baird (Cambridge/New York, 1995)

Anderson, William S., 'The Alto Voice', *The Musical Times and Singing Class Circular* 25, no. 496 (1884), pp. 360–1

Anon., *Instituta patrum de modo psallendi sive cantandi*, available online at <http://www.chmtl.indiana.edu/tml/13th/PATPSAL_TEXT.html> [accessed 4 April 2014]

Ardran, G. M., and David Wulstan, 'The Alto or Countertenor Voice', *Music and Letters* 48(1) (1967), pp. 17–22

Aristotle, *Problema/Problems*, trans. W. S. Hett, Aristotle in Twenty-Three Volumes 15 (London, 1970)

Arlt, Wulf (ed.), *Ein Festoffizuium des Mittelalters aus Beauvais in seiner liturgischen und musikalischen Bedeutung*, 2 vols. (Cologne, 1970)

Arnold, Denis, 'Music at the Scuola de San Rocco', *Music and Letters* 40(3) (1959) pp. 229–41

Arnold, Denis, and Nigel Fortune (eds.), *The Monteverdi Companion* (New York, 1968)

Aron, Pietro, *Libri tres de institutione harmonica* (Bologna, 1516)

Asher-Greve, Julia M., 'The Essential Body: Mesopotamian Conceptions of the Gendered Body', in *Gender and the Body in the Ancient Mediterranean*, ed. Maria Wyke (Oxford, 1998), pp. 8–37

Ashley, Martin, *How High Should Boys Sing?: Gender, Authenticity and Credibility in the Young Male Voice* (Farnham, 2009)

—— 'The English Choral Tradition and the Secular Trend in Boys' Pubertal Timing', *International Journal of Research in Choral Singing* 4(2) (2013), pp. 4–27

Ashley, Martin, and Ann-Christine Mecke, '"Boyes are apt to change their voice at about fourteene yeeres of age": An Historical Background to the Debate about Longevity in Boy Treble Singers', *Reviews of Research in Human Learning and Music* 1 (2013)

Bacon, Richard Mackenzie, and William Knyvett, 'Preliminary Remarks on Counter-Tenor Singing', *The Quarterly Musical Magazine and Review* 2 (1820), pp. 468–76

Bacon, Roger, *Opera quaedam hactenus inedita*, ed. J. S. Brewer (London, 1859)

Bailleux, Antoine, *Solfege pour apprendre facilement la musique vocale, etc.*, 3rd edn (Paris, 1760)

Baldwin, Olive, and Thelma Wilson, 'Alfred Deller, John Freeman, and Mr. Pate', *Music and Letters* 50(1) (1969), pp. 103–10

Barbier, Patrick, *The World of the Castrati* (London, 1998)

Barrett, P., 'English Cathedral Choirs in the Nineteenth Century', *Journal of Ecclesiastical History* 25 (1974), pp. 17–22

Beer, Johann, *Musikalische discurse ...* (Nuremberg, 1719)

Beet, Stephen, *The Better Land: In Search of the Lost Boy Sopranos* (Portlaw, Co. Waterford, 2005)

Bennett, Peter, 'Collaborations between the Musique de la Chambre and the Musique de la Chapelle at the Court of Louis XIII: Nicolas Formé's *Missa Æternae Henrici Magni* (1638) and the Origins of the Grand Motet', *Early Music* 38(3) (2010), pp. 369–86

Bergmann, Walter, 'Alfred Deller', *Early Music* 8(1) (1980), pp. 43–6

Bernard of Clairvaux, 'Ordo Cluniacensis per Bernardo', in *Vetus disciplina monastica*, ed. Marquardus Herrgott (Paris, 1726)

—— 'Statuta Ordinis Cisterciensis, 1134', in *Statuta Capitulorum Generalium Ordinis Cisterciensis*, ed. Joseph Canivez (Louvain, 1933), vol. 1

Bernstein, F., and P. Schläper, 'Über die Tonlage der menschlichen Singstimme', *Sitzungsberichte der Preussichen Akademie der Wissenschaftern* (Berlin, 1922)

Boaden, James, *Memoirs of the Life of John Philip Kemble Esq., including a History of the Stage*, 2 vols. (London, 1825)

Borowitz, Albert, 'Salieri and the Murder of Mozart', *Musical Quarterly* 59(2) (1973), pp. 263–84

Bouquet, Marie-Therese, 'La cappella musicale dei duchi di Savoia dal 1450 al 1500', *Rivista italiana di musicologia* 3 (1968), pp. 233–85

Bowers, Roger, 'The Performing Pitch of English 15th-Century Church Polyphony', *Early Music* 8(1) (1980), pp. 21–8

—— 'The Vocal Scoring, Choral Balance and Performing Pitch of Latin Church Polyphony in England, c. 1500–58', *Journal of the Royal Musical Association* 112 (1987), pp. 38–76

—— 'To Chorus from Quartet', in *English Choral Practice, 1400–1650*, ed. John Morehen (Cambridge, 1995), pp. 1–47

Bremner, Robert, *Compleat Tutor for the Violin* (London, c. 1760)

Britten, Benjamin, *Letters from a Life: The Selected Letters of Benjamin Britten*, ed. Philip Reed and Mervyn Cooke, vol. 5: *1958–1965* (Woodbridge, 2010)

Burgh, T. W., '"Who's the man?" – Sex and Gender in Iron Age Musical Performance', *Near Eastern Archaeology* 67(3) (September 2004), pp. 128–36

Burney, Charles, *Music, Men, and Manners in France and Italy ...* [1770], ed. H. Edmund Poole (London, 1974)

—— *The Present State of Music in Germany, the Netherlands and United Provinces*, 2 vols. (London, 1773)

——*An Account of the Musical Performances … in Commemoration of Handel* (London, 1785)

——*A General History of Music from the Earliest Ages to the Present*, ed. Frank Mercer, vol. 2 (London, 1935)

——*The Letters of Charles Burney*, ed. Alvarro Ribeiro (Oxford, 1991)

Burrows, Donald, *Handel and the English Chapel Royal* (Oxford, 2005)

Butler, Charles, *The Principles of Musik* (London, 1636)

Butt, John, *Music Education and the Art of Performance in the German Baroque* (Cambridge, 1994)

Caffi, Francesco, *Storia della musica sacra nella già Cappella ducale di San Marco in Venezia dal 1318 al 1797* (Venice, 1854)

Campion, Thomas, *A Relation of the Late Royall Entertainment …* (London, 1613)

Caprioli, Leonella Grasso, 'Singing Rossini', in *The Cambridge Companion to Rossini*, ed. Emanuele Senici (Cambridge, 2004), pp. 189–203

Carpani, Giuseppe, *Le Haydine* (Milan, 1812)

Castiglione, Baldassare, *Il libro del cortegiano* (Venice, 1528)

Chadd, David, 'Liturgy and Liturgical Music', in *Cistercian Art and Architecture in the British Isles*, ed. C. Norton and D. Park (Cambridge, 1986), pp. 299–314

Channon, Sir Henry, *Chips: The Diaries of Sir Henry Channon*, ed. Robert Rhodes James (London, 1993)

Chartier, Jean, *L'Ancien Chapitre de Notre-Dame de Paris et sa maîtrise, d'après les documents capitulaires (1326–1790)* (Paris, 1897)

Chaucer, Geoffrey, *The Canterbury Tales*, ed. and trans. Nevill Coghill (London, 1951)

——*Works of Geoffrey Chaucer*, ed. F. N. Robinson, 2nd edn (Oxford, 1957)

Chorley, Henry, *Music and Manners in France and Germany* (London, 1844)

Cibber, Colley, *An Apology for the Life of Mr. Colley Cibber, Comedian* [1740], ed. John Maurice Evans (London, 1987)

Clapton, Nicholas, *Moreschi: The Last Castrato* (London, 2004)

Coclico, Adrian Petit, *Compendium musices descriptum ab Adrian Petit Coclico discipulo Josquini de Pres* (Nuremburg, 1552)

Collectionis Bullarium, brevium, aliorumque diplomatum sacro sanctae Basilicae Vaticanae, vol. 3 (Rome, 1752)

Comberiati, Carmello Peter, *Late Renaissance Music at the Habsburg Court* (New York, 1987)

Comstock, Gary David, and Susan E. Henking (eds.), *Que(e)rying Religion: A Critical Anthology* (New York, 1996)

Corri, Domenico, *The Singer's Preceptor, or Corri's treatise on vocal music, etc.*, 2 vols. (London, 1810)

Cortese, Paolo, *De Cardinalatu* (Rome, 1510)

Coryat, Thomas, *Coryat's Crudities; Hastily Gobled up in Five Moneths Travells in France, Savoy, Italy …* (London, 1611; repr. 1905)

Crivelli, Domenico, *The Art of Singing* (London, 1841)

Crompton, John, *The Psalm-Singer's Assistant* (London, 1778)

Cundee, J., *The Thespian Dictionary* ..., 2nd edn (Oxford, 1805)

Curwen, John, *The Boy's Voice* (London, 1891)

Cyr, Mary, 'On Performing 18th-Century Haute-Contre Roles', *Musical Times* 118, no. 1610 (1977), pp. 291–5

David, Hans, Arthur Mendel and Christoph Wolff (eds. and trans.), *The New Bach Reader: A Life of Johann Sebastian Bach in Letters and Documents* (New York, 1998)

Dawson Scott, Robert, 'The Man with the 300-Year-Old Voice', *The Times*, 12 October 2007

De Brosses, Charles, *Lettres écrites d'Italie à quelques amis* ... (Paris, 1858)

Dede, Mehmet, 'Jive Talkin' with Arif Mardin'; online at <http://www.lightmillennium.org/summer_fall_01/mdede_arifmardin.html> [accessed 6 April 2014]

Defaye, P., and J. P. Sauvage, 'Les Castrats: hypothèses phoniatriques', *Les Cahiers d'O.R.L.* 19(10) (1984), pp. 925–30

De Hegermann-Lindencrone, Anna Lillie, *The Sunny Side of Diplomatic Life* (New York, 1914)

Dunnett, Roderic, 'A Countertenor Virtuoso', *Music and Vision*, 26 December 2001, available online through <www.mvdaily.com> [accessed 3 April 2014]

Dyer, Joseph, 'A Thirteenth-Century Choirmaster: The *Scientia Artis Musicae* of Elias Salomon', *The Musical Quarterly* 66(1) (1980), pp. 83–111

Edgcumbe, Richard, *Musical Reminiscences of an Old Amateur* ... (London, 1831)

Ellis, Katherine, *Interpreting the Musical Past: Early Music in Nineteenth-Century France* (Oxford/New York, 2005)

Evelyn, John, *The Diary of John Evelyn*, ed. Austin Dobson, 3 vols. (New York, 1906)

—— *The Diary of John Evelyn*, ed. Edmond S. de Beer (London, 1959)

Fallows, David, 'Specific Information on the Ensembles for Composed Polyphony, 1400–1474', in *Studies in the Performance of Late Medieval Music*, ed. Stanley Boorman (Cambridge, 1983), pp. 145–59

Farmer, H. G., 'A Forgotten Composer of Anthems: William Savage (1720–89)', *Music and Letters* 17(3) (1936), pp. 188–99

Fellowes, Edmund, *English Madrigal Composers* (Oxford, 1921)

Fenner, Theodore, *Opera in London: Views of the Press, 1785–1830* (Carbondale, IL, 1994)

Finck, Hermann, *Practica musica* (Wittenberg, 1556)

Finn, William J., *The Art of the Choral Conductor*, vol. 1: *Choral Technique* (Boston, 1939)

Fiske, Roger, *English Theatre Music in the Eighteenth Century* (London, 1973)

Foucault, Michel, *The History of Sexuality*, trans. Robert Hurley, vol. 1: *An Introduction* (New York, 1978)

Francois, Anne-Lise, 'Fakin' It/Makin' It: Falsetto's Bid for Transcendence in 1970s Disco High', *Perspectives of New Music* 33(1/2) (1995), pp. 442–57

Friderici, Daniel, *Musica figuralis* (Rostock, 1618)

Fuchs, Michael, *et al.*, 'Predicting Mutational Change in the Speaking Voice of Boys', *Journal of Voice* 21(2) (2007), pp. 169–78

Fuss, Diana (ed.), *Inside/Out: Lesbian Theories, Gay Theories* (New York, 1991)

Gaumy, Christian, 'Le Chant des castrats', *Opera International*, December 1984, pp. 26–9

Geck, Martin, 'Bach's Art of Church Music and his Leipzig Performance Forces: Contradictions in the System', *Early Music* 31(4) (2003), pp. 559–71

—— 'Bach's Sopranos', *American Choral Review* 46(2) (2004), pp. 1–8

Geiringer, Karl, *Haydn: A Creative Life in Music* (Berkeley, CA, 1968)

Gerbino, Giuseppe, 'The Quest for the Soprano Voice: Castrati in Sixteenth-Century Italy', *Studi Musicali* 32(2) (2004), pp. 303–57

Gilbert, Bernard G., *Voice Training Exercises for Boys* (London, *c.* 1900)

Gilbert of Sempringham, 'Regulae Ordinis Sempringensis sive Gilbertinorum Canonicorum', in *Lucæ Holstenii […] Codex regularum monasticarum et canonicarum: quas ss. patres monachis, canonicis & virginibus sanctimonialibus servandas præscripserunt* (Augsburg, 1759; repr. Graz. 1957), vol. 2, pp. 467–536

Giles, Peter, *The History and Technique of the Counter-Tenor* (Aldershot, 1994)

Glass, Philip, *Opera on the Beach* (London, 1988)

Gould, Nathaniel, *Church Music in America* (Boston, 1853)

Griffiths, William Hargreaves, *The Mixed Voice and the Registers …* (London, 1904)

Grossi da Viadana, Lodovico, *Cento concerti ecclesiatici* (Venice, 1602)

Grove, Sir George (ed.), *A Dictionary of Music and Musicians (a. d. 1450–1880)* (London, 1878–99)

Guempel, Karl-Werner, *Die Musiktrakte Conrads von Zabern* (Wiesbaden, 1956)

Haberl, Franz Xaver, *Wilhelm du Fay* (Leipzig, 1885)

—— 'Die romische Schola Cantorum und die papstlichen Kapellsanger bis zur Mitte des 16. Jarhunderts', *Baustein fur Musikgeschicte* 3 (1888)

Hardwick, Michael and Mollie, *Alfred Deller: A Singularity of Voice* (London, 1980)

Hawkins, John, *A General History of the Science and Practice of Music* (London, 1776)

Hayburn, Robert, *Papal Legislation on Sacred Music* (Collegeville, MN, 1979)

Haydn, Joseph, *The Collected Correspondence and London Notebooks of Joseph Haydn*, ed. H. C. Robbins Landon (London, 1959)

Haynes, Bruce, *A History of Performing Pitch: The Story of "A"* (Oxford, 2002)

Herbst, Johann Andreas, *Musica practica sive instruction pro symphoniacis* (Nuremburg, 1642)

Herr, Corinna, *Kastraten und Falsettisten in der Musikgeschichte* (Kassel, 2013)

Herr, Corinna, Arnold Jacobshagen and Kai Wessel (eds.), *Der Countertenor: die männliche Falsettstimme vom Mittelalter zur Gegenwart* (Mainz, 2012)

Highfill, Philip H., Kalman A. Burnim and Edward A. Langhans, *Biographical Dictionary of Actors, Actresses, Musicians, Dancers, Managers and Other Stage Personnel in London, 1660–1800*, vol. 10 (Carbondale, IL, 1984)

Hoare, Ian, *et al.* (eds.), *The Soul Book* (London, 1975)

Hodgson, Frederic, 'The Contemporary Alto', *The Musical Times* 106, no. 1466 (1965), pp. 293–4

Holland, Arthur Keith, *Henry Purcell: The English Musical Tradition* (London, 1932)

Hough, John, 'The Historical Significance of the Counter-Tenor', *Proceedings of the Musical Association*, 64th session (1937–8), pp. 1–24

Hubbard, William Lines, *The American History and Encyclopedia of Music* (Toledo, OH, 1908)

Hugill, Robert, 'Handel's Singers', *Music and Vision*, 28 December 2003, available online through <www.mvdaily.com> [accessed 4 April 2014]

Hullah, Frances, *Life of John Hullah, LlD* (London, 1886)

Idung of Prüfening, 'Dialogus inter Cluniacensem et Cisterciensem monachum', in *Thesaurus novus anecdotorum*, ed. Edmond Martène and Ursin Durand (Paris, 1717), vol. 5

Jackson, William, *Observations on the Present State of Music* (London, 1791)

Jerome of Moravia, *Tractatus de musica*, ed. S. M. Cserba, Freiburger Studien zur Musikwissenschaft 2(2) (Regensburg: Pustet, 1935)

John, Adolphus, *Memoirs of John Bannister, Comedian*, 2 vols. (London, 1839)

John of Salisbury, *Frivolities of Courtiers and Footprints of Philosophers* [...] *the Policraticus of John of Salisbury*, ed. Joseph B. Pike (Minneapolis, 1938)

—— *Ioannis Saresberiensis episcopi Carnotensis Policratici*, ed. Clemens C. I. Webb, 2 vols. (New York, 1979)

—— *Policraticus*, ed. Cary Nederman (Cambridge, 1990)

Johnstone, Andrew, '"As it was in the beginning": Organ and Choir Pitch in Early Anglican Church Music', *Early Music* 31(4) (2003), pp. 506–24

Juul, A., *et al.*, 'Age at Voice Break in Danish Boys: Effects of Pre-Pubertal Body Mass Index and Secular Trend', *International Journal of Andrology* 30(6) (2007), pp. 537–42

Kasow, Joel, 'An Interview with Brian Asawa', available online through <www.culturekiosque.com> [accessed 4 April 2014]

Kelly, Michael, *Reminiscences of Michael Kelly*, 2 vols. (London, 1826)

Keyte, Hugh, and Andrew Parrott (eds.), *The New Oxford Book of Carols* (Oxford, 1992)

Kildea, Paul, *Selling Britten: Music and the Marketplace* (Oxford, 2002)

Kunzen, F. A., and J. F. Reichhardt (eds.), *Studien für Tonkünstler und Musikfreunde: eine historisch-kritische Zeitschrift*, vol. 1: *Musikalisches Wochenblatt* (Berlin, 1792–3)

Laborde, Jean-Benjamin de, *Essai sur la musique ancienne et moderne* (Paris, 1780)

Lalande, Joseph de, *Voyage en Italie* (Paris, 1796)

Lane, Edward William, *Arabic–English Lexicon*, 2 vols. (London, 1865)

Lefkowitz, Murray, 'The Longleat Papers of Bulstrode Whitelocke: New Light on Shirley's *The Triumph of Peace*', *Journal of the American Musicological Society* 18(1) (1965), pp. 42–60

Le Huray, Peter, *Music and the Reformation in England, 1549–1660* (London, 1967)

—— 'Handel's Messiah', in *Authenticity in Performance* (Cambridge, 1990), pp. 82–101

Lewer, David, *A Spiritual Song* (London, 1961)

Locke, Matthew, *The Present Practice of Musick Vindicated* (London, 1673; repr. in facsimile, 1974)

Lockwood, Lewis, *Music in Renaissance Ferrara, 1400–1505* (Oxford, 1984)

Lorenz, Edmund Simon, *Practical Church Music: A Discussion of Purposes, Methods and Plans* (New York, 1909)

MacClintock, Carol, *Readings in the History of Music in Performance* (Bloomington, IN, 1979)

MacCulloch, Diarmaid, *Thomas Cranmer: A Life* (London, 1996)

Maekawa, Kazuya, 'Female Weavers and their Children in Lagash: Presargonic and Ur III', *Acta Sumerologica* 2 (1980), pp. 81–125

Maffei, Giovanni Camillo, *La lettera sul canto ... libro primo* (Naples, 1562)

Mancini, Giambattista, *Pensieri, e riflessioni pratiche sopra il canto figurato* (Vienna, 1774)

—— *Practical Reflections on the Figurative Art of Singing*, ed. and trans. Pietro Buzzi (Boston, 1912)

—— *Practical Reflections on Figured Singing ...*, ed. and trans. Edward Foreman (Minneapolis, 1967)

Marchetto of Padua, *Lucidarium of Marchetto of Padua: A Critical Edition, Translation, and Commentary*, ed. Jan W. Herlinger (Chicago, 1985)

Martin, Gregory, *Roma Sancta*, ed. George Bruner Parks (Rome, 1969)

Mason, Lowell, *Musical Letters from Abroad* (New York, 1854)

Mathews, W. S. B., *A Hundred Years of Music in America* (Chicago, 1889)

Mattheson, Johann, *Der vollkommene Capellmeister* (Hamburg, 1739)

—— *Der vollkommene Capellmeister*, ed. and trans. Ernest C. Harriss (Ann Arbor, MI, 1981)

Maugars, André, *Lettre à un curieux* (Rome, 1639)

McGee, Timothy J., *The Sound of Medieval Song: Ornamentation and Vocal Style According to the Treatises* (Oxford, 1998)

Mecke, Ann-Christine, *Mutantenstadl: der Stimmwechsel und die deutsche Chorpraxis im 18. und 19. Jahrhundert* (Berlin, 2007)

Novello, Vincent, *Mozart Pilgrimage: Travel Diaries of Vincent and Mary Novello in the Year 1829*, ed. Nerina Medici and Rosemary Hughes (London, 1955)

Medina, Angel, *Los atributos del capon* (Madrid, 2001)

Michotte, Edmond, *Richard Wagner's Visit to Rossini (Paris 1860) and an Evening at Rossini's in Beau-Séjour (Passy) 1858*, ed. and trans. Herbert Weinstock (Chicago, 1968)

Migne, J.-P. (ed.), *Patrologiae cursus completus, series graeca* 137 (Paris, *c*. 1857)

Miller, Stuart, 'Biography: Francis Stephen Castelluccio, aka Frankie Valli'; online at <http://gilgweb.com/Bios/Valli_Bio.html> [accessed 6 April 2014]

Monteverdi, Claudio, *Correspondance, préfaces et épîtres dédicatoires*, ed. and trans. Jean-Philippe Navarre and Annonciade Russo (Mardaga, 2001)

Moran, Neil K., *Singers in Late Byzantine and Slavonic Painting* (London, 1986)

Moran, Neil K., 'Byzantine Castrati', *Journal of the Plainsong and Medieval Music Society* 11 (2002), pp. 99–112

Morgan, Lady (Sydney), *Lady Morgan's Memoirs*, 2 vols. (London, 1863)

Mörner, M., F. Fransson and G. Fant, 'Voice Register Terminology and Standard Pitch', *Speech Transmission Laboratory, Quarterly Progress and Status Report (STL-QPSR)*, 4(4) (1963), pp. 17–23

Mozart, Wolfgang Amadeus, *et al.*, *The Letters of Mozart and his Family* ed. Emily Anderson, 3 vols. (London, 1938)

Nathan, Isaac, *Musurgia vocalis: Essay on the Theory & History of Music* (London, 1836)

Newcomb, Anthony, 'Carlo Gesualdo and a Musical Correspondence of 1594', *The Musical Quarterly* 104(4) (1968), pp. 409–36

Nicholson, Sidney, *Quires and Places where they Sing* (London, 1932)

Norden, N. Lindsay, 'The Boy Choir Fad', *The Musical Quarterly* 3(2) (1917), pp. 189–97

Odo de Deogilo, *De profectione Ludovici VII in orientem*, ed. and trans. Virginia Gingerick Berry (New York, 1948)

Orton, J. Louis, *Voice Culture Made Easy* (London, 1900)

Ouseley, Frederick A. Gore (ed.), *A Collection of the Sacred Compositions of Orlando Gibbons* (London, 1873)

Page, Christopher, and Andrew Parrott, 'False Voices', *Early Music* 9(1) (1981), pp. 71–5

Parrott, Andrew, 'Performing Purcell', in *The Purcell Companion*, ed. Michael Burden (London, 1995) pp. 385–444

—— *The Essential Bach Choir* (Woodbridge, 2000)

—— 'Falsetto and the French', *Basler Jahrbuch für historische Musikpraxis* 26 (2002), pp. 129–48

—— 'A Brief Anatomy of Choirs, c. 1470–1770', in *The Cambridge Companion to Choral Music*, ed. André de Quadros (Cambridge, 2012), pp. 7–26

Peterson, Bernard L., *Profiles of African American Stage Performers and Theatre People, 1816–1960* (Westport, CT, 2001)

Petri, Johann Samuel, *Anleitung zur practischen Musik* (Lauban, 1767)

Phelps, G. C., 'The Problem of the Alto Part', *The Musical Times* 68, no. 1011 (1927), p. 450

Phillips, Peter 'Performance Practice in Sixteenth-Century English Choral Music', *Early Music* 6(2) (1978), pp. 195–9

Planchart, Alejandro Enrique, 'Choirboys in Cambrai in the Fifteenth Century', in *Young Choristers, 650–1700*, ed. Susan Boynton and Eric N. Rice (Woodbridge, 2008), pp. 123–45

Platter, Thomas, *Beschreibung der Reisen durch Frankreich, Spanien, England und die Niederlande ...* (Basel, 1968)

Potter, John, 'The Tenor-Castrato Connection, 1760–1860', *Early Music* 35(1) (2007), pp. 97–110

—— *Tenor: History of a Voice* (London, 2009)

Pougin, Arthur, *Un Ténor de l'Opéra au XVIIIe siècle* (Paris, 1905)

Praetorius, Michael, *Syntagma musicum*, 3 vols. (Wolfenbüttel, 1614–18)

Prendergast, A. H. D., 'The Man's Alto in English Music', *Zeitschrift der internationalen Musikgesellschaft* 1 (1900), pp. 331–4

Quantz, Johann, *Versuch einer Anweisung Flöte traversière zu spielen* (Berlin, 1752)

Radomski, James, *Manuel García (1775–1832): Chronicle of the Life of a bel canto Tenor at the Dawn of Romanticism* (Oxford, 2000)

Ravens, Simon '"A sweet shrill voice": The Countertenor and Vocal Scoring in Tudor England', *Early Music* 26(1) (1998), pp. 123–36

—— 'Countertenor Counterblast', *Early Music* 28(3) (2000), pp. 507–8

Reeves, Sims, *On the Art of Singing* (London, 1901)

Reggio, Pietro, *The Art of Singing* (Oxford, 1677)

Remondino, Peter Charles, *History of Circumcision from the Earliest Times to the Present* (Philadelphia, 1891)

Ribera, Julian, *Music in Ancient Arabia and Spain* (London, 1929)

Richardson, John, *Singing Archaeology: Philip Glass's Akhnaten* (Hanover, 1999)

Rickards, Steven L., *Twentieth-Century Countertenor Repertoire: A Guide* (Lanham, MD, 2008)

Rifkin, Joshua, 'Bassoons, Violins and Voices: A Response to Ton Koopman', *Early Music* 25(2) (1997), pp. 302–8

Rimbault, Edward (ed.), *Cathedral Music*, vol. 1 (London, 1847)

Robbins Landon, H. C., *Haydn at Eszterhaza, 1766–1790* (London, 1978)

Robinson, Hastings (ed. and trans.), *The Zurich Letters: Comprising the Correspondence of Several English Bishops and Others ...* (Cambridge, 1842–5)

Rodgers, Mrs Jimmie [Carrie], *My Husband Jimmie Rodgers* (Nashville, 1975)

Rousseau, Jean-Jacques, 'Voix', *Dictionnaire de musique* (Paris, 1768), p. 545

Rowson, Everett K., 'The Effeminates of Early Medina', *Journal of the American Oriental Society* 111(4) (1991), pp. 671–93

Sadie, Stanley (ed.), *The New Grove Dictionary of Music & Musicians* (London, 1980)

—— *Mozart: The Early Years, 1756–1781* (New York, 1983)

Sataloff, Robert T., 'Genetics of the Voice', *Journal of Voice* 9(1) (1995), pp. 16–19

Sawa, George Dimitri, *Music Performance Practice in the Early Abbasid Era, 130–320 ah/750–932 ad* (Toronto, 1989)

Sawkins, Lionel, 'The Brothers Bêche: An Anecdotal History of Court Music', *Recherches sur la musique française classique* 24 (1986), pp. 192–221

—— 'For and Against the Order of Nature', *Early Music* 15 (1987), pp. 315–24

Sayer, Gregory, *Clavis regia sacerdotum, casuum conscientiae* (Venice, 1615)

Selwood, Trevor, 'Counteraguments', *Early Music* 27(2) (1999), pp. 349–50

Shakespeare, William, *Plain Words on Singing* (London, 1924)

Shaw, Bernard, *Shaw's Music: The Complete Musical Criticism*, ed. Dan H. Laurence, 3 vols. (London, 1981)

Sheridan, Francis C., *Galveston Island; or, a Few Months off the Coast of Texas: the Journal of Francis C. Sheridan, 1839–1840*, ed. Willis W. Pratt (Austin, 1954)

Sherr, Richard, 'Gugliemo Gonzaga and the Castrati', *Renaissance Quarterly* 33(1) (1980), pp. 33–56

Shiloah, Amnon, 'Muslim and Jewish Musical Traditions of the Middle Ages', in *Music as Concept and Practice in the Late Middle Ages*, ed. Reinhard Strohm and Bonnie J. Blackburn (Oxford: Oxford University Press, 2001), pp. 1–15

Smith, Bruce R., *The Acoustic World of Early Modern England: Attending to the O-Factor* (Chicago, 1999)

Snyder, Kerala J., *Dieterich Buxtehude* (New York, 2007)

Socrates Scolasticus, *The Ecclesiastical History of Socrates Scholasticus*, ed. and trans. Rev. A. C. Zenos (New York, 1891)

Speakman, Frank, 'The Alto Voice', *The Musical Times* 66, no. 986 (1925), p. 349

Stark, James, *Bel Canto* (Toronto, 2003)

Steckel, Richard H., 'New Light on the "Dark Ages": The Remarkably Tall Stature of Northern European Men during the Medieval Era', *Social Science History* 28(2) (2004), pp. 211–28

Stewart, Rebecca, 'Voice Types in Josquin's Music', *Proceedings of the Josquin Symposium* (Cologne, 1985), pp. 97–193

Strohm, Reinhard, *The Rise of European Music, 1380–1500* (Cambridge, 1993)

Stubbs, G. Edward, *The Adult Male Alto or Counter-Tenor Voice* (New York, 1908)

Sulzer, Johann Georg, *Allgemeine Theorie der schönen Künste*, 2nd edn (Leipzig, 1793; repr. 1967)

Sykes, Katherine, *Inventing Sempringham: Gilbert of Sempringham and the Origins of the Role of the Master,* Vita Regularis 46 (Munster, 2011)

Johann Ernst Altenburg, *Essay on an Introduction to the Heroic and Musical Trumpeters' and Kettledrummers' Art ...*, ed. and trans. Edward H. Tarr (Nashville, 1974)

Taruskin, Richard, *Text and Act: Essays on Music and Performance* (New York, 1995)

—— *Oxford History of Western Music*, 6 vols. (New York, 2005)

Taylor, Gary, *Castration: An Abbreviated History of Western Manhood* (New York, 2000)

Telemann, Georg Philipp, *Briefwechsel*, ed. Hans Grosse and Hans Rudolf Jung (Leipzig, 1972)

Temperley, Nicholas *The Music of the English Parish Church*, vol. 1 (Cambridge, 1979)

—— *The Creation* (Cambridge, 1991)

Terry, Charles Sanford, *Bach: A Biography* (London, 1928)

Thackeray, William Makepeace, *The Newcomes* (London, 1855)

'The Scarcity of Alto Voices', *The Musical Times and Singing Class Circular*, 23/468 (1882), p. 100 [anonymous letter, signed 'An Alto']

Thoinan, E., [A. E. Roquet]: *Maugars: célèbre joueur de viole ...* (Paris, 1865)

Tilmouth, Michael, 'Music and British Travellers Abroad, 1600–1730', in *Source Materials and the Interpretation of Music: A Memorial Volume to Thurston Dart*, ed. Ian Bent (London, 1981) pp. 358–69

Tinctoris, Johnannes, *Expositio manus* (Naples, c. 1475)

—— *Liber de arte contrapuncti* [1477], in *Opera theoretica*, ed. Albert Seay, Corpus scriptorum de musica 22 ([Rome]: American Institute of Musicology, 1975), vol. 2, pp. 90–145

—— *Diffinitorium musicae*, in *Scriptorum de musica medii aevi nova series a Gerbertina altera*, ed. Edmond de Coussemaker, repr. edn (Hildesheim: Olms, 1963), vol. 4, pp. 177–91

Tippett, Michael, 'Alfred Deller', *Early Music* 8(1) (1980), p. 43

Tosi, Pier Francesco, *Opinioni de' cantori antichi* (Bologna, 1723)

—— *Observations on the Florid Song*, ed. Michael Pilkington, trans. J. E. Galliard (London, 1987)

Tudway, Thomas, 'Services and Anthems', London, British Library, Harleian MSS 7337–42

Turgenev, Ivan, *Torrents of Spring* [*Veshnie Vody* (1872)], trans. Constance Garnett (London, 1897)

Uberti, Mauro, 'Vocal Techniques in Italy in the Second Half of the 16th Century', *Early Music* 9(4) (1981), pp. 486–98

Varley Roberts, J., *A Treatise on a Practical Method of Training Choristers* (London, 1898)

Vicentino, Nicola, *L'antica musica ridotta alla moderna prattica* (Rome, 1555)

Villetard, Henri (ed.), *Office de Pierre de Corbeil ...*, vol. 4 (Paris, 1907)

Walsh, T. J., *Opera in Dublin, 1705–1797: The Social Scene* (Dublin, 1973)

Wegman, Rob C., *The Crisis of Music in Early Modern Europe, 1470–1530* (New York, 2005)

Wesley, Samuel Sebastian, *A Few Words on Cathedral Music* (London, 1849)

Williams, R. G., 'The Human Voice in Health and Disease', unpublished MPhil thesis (University of Wales, 1990)

Williams, R. G., and R. Eccles, 'A New Clinical Measure of External Laryngeal Size which Predicts the Fundamental Frequency of the Larynx', *Acta Otolaryngologica* 110 (1990), pp. 141–8

Wise, Henry Augustus, *Los Gringos* (New York, 1854)

Wistreich, Richard, 'Reconstructing Pre-Romantic Singing Technique', in *The Cambridge Companion to Singing*, ed. John Potter (Cambridge, 2000), pp. 178–91

—— *Warrior, Courtier, Singer: Giulio Cesare Brancaccio and the Performance of Identity in the Late Renaissance* (Aldershot, 2007)

Wright, Craig, 'Dufay at Cambrai: Discoveries and Revisions', *Journal of the American Musicological Society* 28 (1975), pp. 175–229

—— 'Performance Practices at the Cathedral of Cambrai, 1475–1550', *The Musical Quarterly* 64(3) (1978), pp. 295–328

—— *Music and Ceremony at Notre Dame of Paris, 500–1550* (Cambridge, 1989)

Wulstan, David, *Tudor Music* (London, 1985)

Yoshioka, Masataka, 'Singing the Republic: Polychoral Culture at San Marco in Venice (1550–1615)', unpublished Phd dissertation (University of North Texas, 2010)

Zabern, Conrad von, *De modo bene cantandi* (Mainz, c. 1473)

Zacconi, Lodovico, *Prattica di musica* (Venice, 1592)

Zarlino, Giuseffo, *Le istitutioni harmoniche* (Venice, 1558)

Zimmerman, Franklin B., *Henry Purcell: His Life and Times* (London, 1967)

Index

Pages that include a music example are marked by an asterisk.